MW01123015

STUDENT SOLUTIONS MANUA

MANAGERIAL ACCOUNTING

Second Edition

CECILY A. RAIBORN
LOYOLA UNIVERSITY—NEW ORLEANS

JESSE T. BARFIELD
LOYOLA UNIVERSITY—NEW ORLEANS

MICHAEL R. KINNEY
TEXAS A&M UNIVERSITY

PREPARED BY
MICHAEL P. KINNEY
TEXAS A&M UNIVERSITY

WEST PUBLISHING COMPANY
MINNEAPOLIS/ST. PAUL   NEW YORK   LOS ANGELES   SAN FRANCISCO

WEST'S COMMITMENT TO THE ENVIRONMENT

In 1906, West Publishing Company began recycling materials left over from the production of books. This began a tradition of efficient and responsible use of resources. Today, 100% of our legal bound volumes are printed on acid-free, recycled paper consisting of 50% new paper pulp and 50% paper that has undergone a de-inking process. We also use vegetable-based inks to print all of our books. West recycles nearly 27,700,000 pounds of scrap paper annually—the equivalent of 229,300 trees. Since the 1960s, West has devised ways to capture and recycle waste inks, solvents, oils, and vapors created in the printing process. We also recycle plastics of all kinds, wood, glass, corrugated cardboard, and batteries, and have eliminated the use of polystyrene book packaging. We at West are proud of the longevity and the scope of our commitment to the environment.

West pocket parts and advance sheets are printed on recyclable paper and can be collected and recycled with newspapers. Staples do not have to be removed. Bound volumes can be recycled after removing the cover.

Production, Prepress, Printing and Binding by West Publishing Company.

 TEXT IS PRINTED ON 10% POST CONSUMER RECYCLED PAPER   Printed with **Printwise** Environmentally Advanced Water Washable Ink

ISBN 0–314–06402–8

CONTENTS

Check Figures

Chapter 1
No check figures

Chapter 2
No check figures

Chapter 3

21. No check figures

23. No check figures

25. a. Total cost, 1,000
       pages, $340
    b. No check figures

27. No check figures

29. No check figures
    a. 2,000
    b. DL, $56,000
       Overhead, $10,000
    c. Late shift, $2,000
       Overtime, $8,000

31. a. $839,000
    b. $655,000
    c. $1,173,000

33. a. $1,500,000
    b. $1,900,000
    c. $1,300,000

35. $35,480

37. No check figures

39. No check figures

41. No check figures

43. a. No check figures
    b. $3,640
    c. $8.09
    d. Total cost, $3,703

45. No check figures

51. No check figures

53. a. $15,750
    b. No check figures

55. No check figures

57. No check figures

59. No check figures

61. No check figures

Chapter 4

23. No check figures

25. a. $Y = \$(300) + \$.015X$
    b. No check figures

27. a. Total costs:
       5,000 units, $12,750
       7,000 units, $18,150
       9,000 units, $20,950
    b. Unit costs
       5,000 units, $2.55
       7,000 units, $2.59
       9,000 units, $2.43

29. a. 1. variable, $4
          fixed, $1.36
       2. variable, $8
          fixed, $2.73
    b. 1. $5.36
       2. $10.73
    c. 1. $1,202.24
       2. $3,536.00
       3. variable, $176.00
          overapplied
          fixed, $107.76
          underapplied

31. a. $6
    b. DM, $2,485
       DL, $6,435
       OH, $8,580
    c. $650 overapplied

33. No check figures

35. a. No check figures
    b. No check figures
    c. RM, $150,000
       WIP, $2,042,000

37. a. $y = \$4,000 + \$4X$
    b. $y = \$7,245 + \$3.57X$
    c. No check figures

39. a. Checking, $110,000
       Savings, $105,000
       Loans, $155,000
    b. Checking, $108,000
       Savings, $104,222
       Loans, $157,778

41. No check figures

43. a. $9,350
    b. $2,300 overapplied

45. a. Indirect materials:
       fixed, $0
       variable, $5 per unit
       Indirect labor:
       fixed, $0
       variable, $7 per unit
       Handling:
       fixed, $200
       variable, $3 per unit
       Maintenance:
       fixed, $0
       variable, $1 per unit
       Utilities:
       fixed, $400
       variable, $2 per unit
       Supervision:
       fixed, $4,000
       variable, $0 per unit
       Overall, $Y = \$4,600 + \$18X$
    b. 920 units
    c. total cost, $21,160
    d. $22.60 per unit

47. a. Framing,
       $Y = \$4,200 + \$2.20X$
       Covering,
       $Y = \$3,000 + \$5.00X$
    b. Framing, $17,400
       Covering, $93,000

    c. total rate-normal,
       $18.64
       total rate-expected,
       $18.40
    d. No check figures

49. a. $15 per MH
    b. $136.80
    c. Cutting rate,
       $11.975 per MH
       Assembly rate,
       $10.80 per DLH

51. a. 1. total cost:
          Product A, $935,000
          Product B,
          $1,225,000
       2. total cost:
          Product A,
          $1,280,000
          Product B,
          $880,000
    b. No check figures

53. a. No check figures

55. a. $Y = \$63.90 + \$.429X$
    b. $Y = \$72.65 + \$.434X$
    c. part a, $389.94
       part b, $402.49
    d. No check figures
    e. No check figures

57. a. Commercial, $501,040
       Residential,
       $1,017,000
       Property, $319,960
    b. Commercial, $518,768
       Residential,
       $1,010,874
       Property, $308,358
    c. No check figures

59. No check figures

61. No check figures

63. No check figures

65. No check figures

67. No check figures

Chapter 5

21. No check figures

23. No check figures

25. No check figures

27. No check figures

29. a. Regular, $440,000
        Hand-sewn, $560,000
     b. No check figures

31. a. Market opportunities,
        $40 per hour
        Product development,
        $18,000 per product
        Process design,
        $4,800 per request
     b. No check figures
     c. $1,250,000

33. No check figures

35. No check figures

37. a. $6 per MH
     b. $92
     c. $89.25
     d. No check figures

39. a. Professional
        salaries, $30 per
        hour
        Building costs,
        $30 per square foot
        Risk management,
        $320 per patient,

     b. Surgery, $280,000
        Housing patients,
        $1,120,000
        Outpatient care,
        $270,000
     c. No check figures

41. a. Product A, $11.855
        Product B, $19.30
        Product C, $10.03
     b. 1. Product A,
           $11.696
           Product B,
           $14.908
           Product C, $11.60
        2. Conventional
           Product A, $14.04
           Product B, $17.89
           Product C, $13.92
           ABC:
           Product A, $14.23
           Product B, $23.16
           Product C, $12.04
     c. No check figures

43. a. TV trays, $400,000
        Lamp stands, $300,000
        Printer stands,
        $300,000
     b. Total overhead:
        TV trays, $225,700
        Lamp stands, $398,570
        Printer stands,
        $375,710
     c. No check figures

45. a. Jones, $950
        Hansen, $860
        Assad, $1,850
     b. Jones, $1,600
        Hansen, $1,600
        Assad, $1,600
     c. Jones, $1,330
        Hansen, $1,204
        Assad, $2,590
     d. No check figures

47. a. Standard, $19,940
        Specialty, $30,560
     b. Standard, $27.99
        Specialty, $32.72
     c. No check figures

49. No check figures

51. No check figures

53. No check figures

Chapter 6

23. a. $155
    b. No check figures

25. a. DMPV, quantity
       purchased, $22,750F
       DMPV, quantity
       used, $21,750
       DMQV, $18,000F

27. a. $199,375
    b. $13,750U
    c. $3,375U

29. a. DLRV, $2,550U
       DLEV, $2,062.50F

31. a. $410,000
    b. $429,250
    c. VOHSV, $5,250U
       VOHEV, $6,000U
    d. FOHSV, $12,000U
       FOHVV, $4,000F

33. No check figures

35. No check figures

37. No check figures

39. DMPV, $1,950U
    DMQV, $1,100F
    DLRV, $620U
    DLEV, $2,800U

41. a. 1,200
    b. $6,212
    c. $150U
    d. 4,000
    e. $12
    f. $14,157
    g. 3
    h. 390
    i. $5,130F
    j. 2
    k 430
    l $45F

43. a. DMPV, $44,507F
       DMQV, $30,210U
       DLRV, $1,120U
       DLEV, $1,400U
       VOHSV, $2,000F
       VOHEV, $4,000F
       FOHSV, $2,300U
       FOHVV, $3,000F
    b. No check figures

45. a. $3,020
    b. $800U
    c. $100U
    d. $60F
    e. No check figure

47. No check figures

49. a. 8,400
    b. VOHSV, $860F
       VOHEV, $240U
       FOHSV, $900U
       FOHVV, $1,200F

51. a. Standard cost per 10
       gallon batch, $30.20
    b. No check figures
    c. No check figures

53. a. 1. $13,900U
       2. $8,500U
       3. $0
       4. $1,000F
    b. No check figures

55. No check figures

57. No check figures

59. No check figures

Chapter 7

25. a. 416,000
    b. 416,000
    c. 411,200

27. a. 56,000
    b. $.25

29. a. DL, 30,000
       OH, 31,500
    b. DL, $.40
       OH, $.20
    c. DL, $2,400
       OH, $1,500

31. a. $.056
    b. $84,000

33. a. $294,000
    b. $46,000
    c. $1,080,000

35. No check figures

37. a. 120,000
    b. 75,000
    c. DM, 108,500
       CC, 105,000
    d. DM, 112,500
       CC, 115,000
    e. No check figures

39. a. 36,000
    b. DM, $45,100
       CC, $87,780
    c. DM, $1.25
       CC, $3.40
    d. $88,350

41. a. 8,000,000
    b. $40,000
    c. $1,668,000

43. a. Batter, 430
       Icing, 450
       CC, 433
    b. Batter, $3.08
       Icing, $.07
       CC, $1.98
    c. Ending WIP, $49.32
       Transferred,
       $2,255.92
    d. $1,120.02

45. a. DM, 46,000
       CC, 41,800
    b. DM, $5.45
       CC, $3.50
    c. DM, 49,000; $5.12
       CC, 44,800; $3.27
    d. $25,170
    e. No check figures

47. a. Transferred In, $1.04
       Conversion, $.20
       Materials, $.30
    b. $107,800
    c. $34,800
    d. No check figures

49. a. FIFO:
       Material, 20,400
       Conversion, 20,000
       WA:
       Material, 24,000
       Conversion, 23,000
    b. Transferred - FIFO,
       $673,000
       Transferred - WA,
       $672,000
    c. No check figures

51. a. $241,000
    b. $3,706
    c. $66,000
    d. No check figures

53. a. 1. Chemicals, 25,000
          Cans, 20,000
          CC, 24,000
       2. Chemicals, 21,000
          Cans, 20,000
          CC, 23,000
    b. 1. Chemicals, $10.96
          Cans, $.35
          CC, $2.23
       2. Chemicals, $10.88
          Cans, $.35
          CC, $1.98
    c. No check figures

55. No check figures

57. No check figures

59. No check figures

Chapter 8

25. a. $8.50
    b. $11.00

27. a. $320,000
    b. $16,000F
    c. No check figures

29. a. 10,000
    b. Net income, $16,625

31. a. $420,000
    b. No check figures

33. 50,000 units
    $1,500,000

35. a. BEP, 3,000 units
       NIBT, $1,080
    b. BEP, 3,500 units
       NIBT, $3,780

37. No check figures

39. a. $192,000
    b. $204,170
    c. $500,000
    d. $400,000
    e. $420,000

41. a. 35 hours
    b. 160 hours
    c. No check figures

43. a. 300,000 compact
       600,000 standard
    b. 514,286 compact
       514,286 standard
    c. 796,875 compact
       531,250 standard

45. a. manual-MOS, $500,000
       automated-MOS,
       $100,000
    b. No check figures
    c. No check figures
    d. Manual, $9.50
       Automated, $10.30

47. a. 100 visits
       $1,000
    b. 150 visits
    c. 3.5
    d. increase $210

49. No check figures

51. No check figures

53. No check figures

55. absorption-year 1,
    $620,000
    absorption-year 4,
    $1,060,000
    variable-year 1,
    $590,000
    variable-year 4,
    $1,085,000

57. a. $96,000
    b. $81,000
    c. No check figures

59. year 1, $70,000
    year 2, $102,000
    year 3, $198,000

61. a. $18
    b. $2,250,000
    c. 125,000
    d. NI, $200,000

63. a. absorption-1996,
       $37,500
       absorption-1997,
       $22,500
       variable-1996,
       $30,000
       variable-1997,
       $30,000
    b. absorption-1996,
       ending, $7,500
       variable-1996,
       ending, $0
    c. 2,000 units
       $20,000
    d. No check figures

65. a. $4,843,125,000
       Compact, 506,250
       Standard, 843,750
       Luxury, 337,500
    b. Compact, 1,443,750
       Standard, 2,406,250
       Luxury, 962,500
    c. Compact, 2,905,660
       Standard, 2,324,528
       Luxury, 581,132
    d. No check figures

67. a. 50%
    b. BEP, $24,000
       Hens, 1,000
       Ducklings, 2,000
    c. Hens, 3,000
       Ducklings, 6,000
    d. Total, $63,000
       Hens, 1,500
       Ducklings, 7,500

69. a. units, 7,667
       $3,066,667
    b. units, 6,733
       $2,693,333
       46.75%
    c. Proposition 1,
       income effect,
       $338,400 decrease
       Proposition 2,
       income effect,
       $86,400 decrease
       Proposition 3,
       income effect,
       $407,000 increase

71. a. VPI, 1996, $33,333
       VPI, 1997, $33,333
       Tech, 1996, $71,429
       Tech, 1997, $72,429
    b. VPI, 1996, 1.5
       VPI, 1997, 1.26
       Tech, 1996, 3.5
       Tech, 1997, 2.04
    c. VPI, $166,667
       Tech, $128,572
    d. No check figures
    e. No check figures

73. a. Operating income,
       $168,730
    b. No check figures
    c. No check figures

75. No check figures

77. a. 16,364 passengers
       $2,454,657
    b. 195 flights
    c. 171 flights
    d. 20,000 passengers
       239 flights
    e. 23,077 passengers
    f. $1,052,000
    g. 1. No check figures
       2. 17 flights
       3. 13 flights
       4. No check figures

79. No check figures

81. No check figures

83. No check figures

85. No check figures

Chapter 9

25. a. Incremental revenue:
       AA, $5,000
       BB, $50,000
       CC, $75
       Incremental cost:
       AA, $7,500
       BB, $20,000
       CC, $25

27. a. $.50 per unit
       advantage to buying
    b. $.33 per unit
       advantage to making
    c. 25,000 units

29. a. 11,250 Sanders
       0 Drills
    b. $58,750

31. a. $4,000
    b. No check figures
    c. No check figures

33. a. $700,000
    b. $790,000
    c. $142

35. a. $27,500 decrease
    b. No check figures

37. No check figures

39. No check figures

41. a. No check figures
    b. $79,000
    c. $54,000 benefit of getting Masters Degree

43. a. No check figures
    b. $137,000
    c. No check figures
    d. $26,000 increase in profits

45. a. $106,000 net cost of acceptance
    b. No check figures

47. No check figures

49. No check figures

51. a. $500
    b. $562.50
    c. $764.71

53. a. Total CM, $67,250
    b. No check figures

55. No check figures

57. a. 1. $12,000
       2. $138,000
    b. No check figures
    c. No check figures

59. No check figures

61. No check figures

63. No check figures

Chapter 10

25. No check figures

27. No check figures

29. SPV, $4,300U
    SVV, $1,000F

31. SPV, $224U
    SVV, $450F
    Cost PV, $224U
    Cost VV, $145F

33. No check figures

35. No check figures

37. No check figures

39. a. Basketballs, 20,000
       Baseballs, 40,000
    b. $40,000F
    c. $160,000F
    d. No check figures

41. No check figures

43. a. 1. $28,200F
       2. $18,000U
       3. $11,500F
    b. $5,750U
    c. No check figures
    d. No check figures

45. No check figures

47. No check figures

49. No check figures

51. No check figures

Chapter 11

21. April, 9,080
    May, 10,080
    June, 11,080

23. 41,400 pounds

25. a. $622,000
     b. $550,000

27. a. $180,000
     b. $2,000
     c. $195,200
     d. No check figures
     e. No check figures

29. a. $310,714
     b. No check figures

31. CGM, $509,900

33. No check figures

35. a. January, 35,000
         February, 31,500
         March, 29,500
         Budgeted purchases,
         M, 286,500 pounds
         N, 191,000 pounds
         O, 382,000 pounds
     b. No check figures
     c. No checkfigures

37. a. 207,000 bags
     b. 191,312.5 pounds
     c. 12,587.5 pounds
     d. $322,292.50
     e. $189,508
     f. No check figures

39. a. January, 3,220
         February, 5,640
         March, 7,520
     b. Iron:
         January, 7,260 pounds
         February, 12,220
         pounds
         March, 15,280 pounds
         Stands:
         January, 1,430
         February, 6,110
         March, 7,640
     c. January, $18,492.30
         February, $30,586.22
         March, $41,761.16
     d. January, $49,146
         February, $50,912
         March, $55,886

     e. Ending cash:
         January, $24,627.70
         February, $15,481.48
         March, $15,670.32
     f. No check figures

41. a. January, $130,749
         February, $136,484
         March, 137,431
     b. January, $69,750
         February, $63,875
         March, $63,125
     c. January, $87,880
         February, $85,880
         March, $81,075

43. a. NIBT, $9,600
     b. Total assets,
         $218,600
     c. No check figures

45. a. Cash collections:
         April, $1,880
         May, $2,040
         June, $2,380
         Cash disbursements:
         April, $2,002
         May, $1,806
         June, $2,080
     b. No check figures
     c. No check figures

47. a. Cash receipts,
         $22,000
         Cash disbursements,
         $22,050
     b. Ending cash, $523
     c. No check figures

49. No check figures

51. No check figures

53. No check figures

55. No check figures

Chapter 12

19. No check figures

21. No check figures

23. No check figures

25. a. Planned,
       .088 letters per $
       Actual,
       .089 letters per $
       Company efficiency,
       .088 letters per $
    b. .98

27. No check figures

29. Rate variance, $72F
    Efficiency variance,
    $58.50U

31. No check figures

33. No check figures

35. No check figures

37. No check figures

39. No check figures

41. No check figures

43. a. $11,450 over
       original budget
    b. Effectiveness, 1.07
    c. No check figures
    d. Variable:
       Spending, $9,200U
       Efficiency, $0
       Fixed:
       Spending, $0
       Volume, $5,250 F
    e. $50 per hour

45. a. $3,080
    b. $1,800
    c. $720

    d. $5,600
    e. $22,800

47. a. $12,000
    b. $63,400
    c. $326,400
    d. No check figures

49. No check figures

51. No check figures

53. No check figures

55. No check figures

57. No check figures

59. No check figures

Chapter 13

23. No check figures

25. No check figures

27. 537

29. a. 1,538
    b. 1,293
    c. total cost, part a,
       $1,000
       total cost, part b,
       $840
    d. No check figures
    e. No check figures

31. a. 493 pounds
    b. 360 pounds
    c. 60 pounds
    d. 36 pounds
    e. 462 pounds

33. a. No check figures
    b. RIP, $5,880
       FG, $20,000

35. No check figures

37. No check figures

39. No check figures

41. No check figures

43. No check figures

45. a. 2,000 gallons
    b. 12 orders
    c. $240
    d. No check figures

47. No check figures

49. a. rice, $299.84U
       beans, $300.00F
    b. rice, $1,000F
       beans $1,500U
    c. No check figures

51. No check figures

53. a. $25,800 net after-tax
       cash savings
    b. No check figures

55. No check figures

57. No check figures

59. No check figures

61. No check figures

Chapter 14

27. a. Proposal A, 3 years
       Proposal B, 3 years
    b. No check figures

29. $27,884

31. $59,611.20

33. a. $1,130.98
    b. 3.18 years
    c. 9.5%
    d. No check figures

35. a. Investment A,
       $1,238.25
       Investment B, $979.44
    b. Investment A, 1.05
       Investment B, 1.02
    c. No check figures

37. a. 8%
    b. No check figures

39. a. $350,102.80
    b. $393,638.18
    c. No check figures
    d. No check figures

41. $15,392.20

43. a. $7,230
    b. 1.02
    c. Approximately 10.5%
    d. 6 years
    e. 13.33%

45. a. payback, 4.99 years
       ARR, 16.26%
    b. No check figures
    c. No check figures

47. No check figures

49. No check figures

51. a. $(279,868)
    b. No check figures
    c. No check figures
    d. No check figures

53. a. $4,500,000
    b. No check figures
    c. No check figures

55. a. Minimum cash
       receipts, $171,246.96
       New admissions,
       14,271
    b. 8.06 years
    c. No check figures

57. No check figures

59. a. $68,398
    b. $70,533
    c. No check figures
    d. greater than 20%

61. a. NPV, $158,243.10
       PI, 1.15
    b. 7.4 years
    c. No check figures
    d. No check figures

63. a. 5.71%
    b. No check figures

65. a. No check figures
    b. $50,052
    c. 1.09
    d. 13%
    e. 5.6 years
    f. 21.93%
    g. No check figures

67. a. No check figures
    b. $339,786
    c. $320,708
    d. No check figures

69. a. Internal financing
       NPV, $649,248
       Bank loan NPV,
       $648,818
       Lease NPV, $586,920
    b. No check figures

71. No check figures

73. No check figures

75. No check figures

77. No check figures

Chapter 15

21. No check figures

23. No check figures

25. a. PV, $1,062,500U
       VV, $550,000F
    b. No check figures
    c. No check figures

27. a. $100,000F
    b. $300,000F
    c. $125,000F
    d. $325,000U

29. a. Upper, $55
       Lower, $35.20
    b. $46
    c. $35.20
    d. No check figures

31. a. $9,000
    b. $(27,000)
    c. $1.325
    d. No check figures

33. No check figures

35. No check figures

37. No check figures

39. a. Regular, $6.50
       Regular less variable
       selling &
       distribution, $5.90
       Standard
       manufacturing cost
       plus 15%, $5.06
       Standard variable
       manufacturing cost
       plus 20%, $3.84
    b. No check figures
    c. No check figures
    d. No check figures

41. a. $370,000 under budget
    b. No check figures
    c. No check figures
    d. No check figures

43. a. $2,070U
    b. $28,440U
    c. $71,840F
    d. No check figures
    e. No check figures

45. a. $18 per unit
    b. $127 per unit
    c. Maximum, $136
       Minimum, $118

47. a. Bottle, $5,580,000
       Perfume, $11,040,000
    b. No check figures
    c. No check figures

49. a. No check figures
    b. No check figures
    c. No check figures

51. No check figures

53. No check figures

55. No check figures

57. No check figures

59. No check figures

61. No check figures

Chapter 16

25. 1, 25%
    2, 15%
    3, 10%

27. a. $212,500
    b. $850,000
    c. .5
    d. 25%
    e. No check figures

29. a. East, $8,000
       West, $10,000
    b. No check figures

31. a. $8,000,000
    b. 22.5%

33. a. $400,000
    b. $100,000

35. a. .75
    b. 2
    c. .75
    d. 1.125

37. a. Year 1, $(200,000)
       Year 2, $(100,000)
       Year 3, $(20,000)
       Year 4, $1,200,000
       Year 5, $1,200,000
    b. Year 1, $(12,000)
       Year 2, $(6,000)
       Year 3, $(1,200)
       Year 4, $72,000
       Year 5, $72,000
    c. No check figures
    d. No check figures
    e. No check figures

39. No check figures

41. No check figures

43. No check figures

45. a. Omana, ROI, 20%
       Eastside, ROI, 18%
       RiverRun, ROI, 27.5%
    b. No check figures
    c. No check figures

47. No check figures

49. No check figures

51. a. Pleasure, 12%
       Commercial, 20%
    b. No check figures
    c. No check figures
    d. No check figures

53. a. .67
    b. 2.5
    c. .65
    d. 1.09 units per hour
    e. No check figures
    f. No check figures

55. No check figures

57. No check figures

59. No check figures

61. No check figures

63. No check figures

Management Accounting in a Global Business Environment

Questions

1. Any single accounting system can optimally meet only a limited number of needs. Because financial reporting is mandated by law for many companies, most accounting systems have been constructed to satisfy the demands of external reporting. Furthermore, the time constraints on the accounting department may limit the amount of time that can be dedicated to managerial accounting issues; the time dedicated to producing external financial data may exhaust most of the capacity of the accounting department.

3. Management accounting is the provision of all internal accounting information to managers to assist them in performing the management functions of planning, controlling, evaluating and decision making. There is a subset of both management accounting and financial accounting known as cost accounting which relates the two major systems and serves both by providing product costs for financial statements along with other information for managers.

5. Relevant information satisfies three conditions: it is logically related to the decision under consideration; it is important to the decision maker; and it has a connection to or bearing on some future endeavor. These characteristics are important because they ensure that the information will be useful to the manager who receives it.

7. Goals are a qualitative expression of desired results. Objectives are quantifiable expressions of desired results. With respect to this course, your goal may be to demonstrate basic competency in the field of management accounting. Consistent with this goal, your objective may be to achieve a minimum grade of B.

9. A primary role of information is to reduce the uncertainty that otherwise exists in making decisions. Decision making causes accountants to generate information that is consumed by managers in making decisions.

11. Manufacturing firms have the capability of producing output
    in quantities that may differ significantly from the near-
    term demand for the output. The significant difference
    between a service company and a manufacturing company is
    that the manufacturing company produces a tangible output,
    and in many cases it can be produced and stored rather than
    sold. Service outputs must be consumed as they are produced
    because they are intangible.

13. Three different inventory accounts are required to track the
    costs incurred in manufacturing products. A raw materials
    inventory account is used to track materials and supplies
    acquired from outside vendors. The work in process account
    is used to account for all costs, including raw materials
    and conversion costs, of products that have been started but
    not completed. Finally, a finished goods inventory account
    is used to account for the costs of all completed products
    that have not been sold. The finished goods inventory
    account is analogous to the merchandise inventory account
    used in merchandising firms.

15. Operating in a global environment means that more decision
    and control variables must be tracked. For example, the
    global firm must track many variables in many countries,
    such as: national rules of income taxation, sets of local
    laws of commerce, production and sourcing sites, and
    currencies. In addition, the multinational firm must
    monitor markets in many countries, deal with a multitude of
    local cultures and customs, and communicate in several
    languages.
        Some of the additional information that would be very
    valuable to the global firm would be: currency exchange
    rates; national inflation rates; details of import/export
    laws; current prices for key commodities in likely sourcing
    sites; world-wide shipping costs for various modes of moving
    goods, components and materials; intelligence information on
    political issues in all relevant local markets; and current
    information on competitors' prices in all markets. These
    various types of information are important to managers in
    safeguarding the assets of their firms and in allocating the
    firm's resources to generate an optimal return on capital.

17. There are many self-serving reasons to be a nonpolluter.
    For example, a proactive strategy to reduce pollution may
    attract environmentally-conscious consumers. Further, such
    an approach may avoid subsequent regulation of operations by
    government and may avoid legal entanglements caused by
    retroactive application of new laws.

19. No. The organizational chart only depicts the formal authority structure. It does not depict all of the organizational realities such as the informal power structure, nor does it show the grapevine or informal paths of communication.

21. The controller is the chief accountant, in charge of the accounting system and the internal control system. He or she has little-or-no access to company resources. The treasurer is in charge of the company resources (e.g., bank accounts and securities), but has no access to updating or manipulating company records.

Exercises

23.
  a. 5.
  b. 9.
  c. 7.
  d. 4.
  e. 1.
  f. 3.
  g. 8.
  h. 2.
  i. 6.
  j. 10.

25.

	Conversion	Firm type
a.	H	M
b.	M	S
c.	M	S or M
d.	L	MD
e.	M	S
f.	M	S
g.	M	S
h.	M	S
i.	M	S
j.	M	M
k.	H	M
l.	L	MD
m.	M	S or M
n.	L or M	S or M
o.	H	S

27. a. RM
     b. FG
     c. RM, WIP
     d. WIP, FG
     e. RM
     f. RM, WIP
     g. WIP, FG
     h. RM
     i. RM, WIP
     j. RM, WIP

Communication Activities

29. This is an open-ended question intended to cause the student to think about the importance, interaction, and interdependence of all functioning areas of a business from the particular viewpoint of a given discipline. A large variety of answers will result which may be evaluated on the basis of completeness, accuracy, reasonableness and quality of response. Because the question is intended to cause the student to devise his/her unique answer, no general answer is provided here.

31. The purpose of this question is to get students to think about the role of laws and ethics in the conduct of business. Among the important points that should be made in the position papers include: whether the laws in the firm's home country or local foreign law should govern the actions of firms; whether ethics or law should be the standard governing actions in foreign jurisdictions; and the extent to which "being competitive" should be a criterion in choosing a course of action for a business.

33. a. If the U.S. tax system either favored or discriminated against foreign source income, incentives would arise to engage in the shifting of profits either to or from the U.S. This would result in an artificial incentive to engage in nonvalue adding activities and could result in the movement of capital and jobs off shore. The principal concerns of the U.S. regulators are the protection of governmental revenues and preserving the competitive position of U.S. firms doing business in other countries.

     b. Tax compliance costs are likely to rise. Compliance costs will rise in response to increased levels of monitoring and regulation by various governments. As firms become more international in the scope of their operations, they will encounter the cost of complying with tax rules in more countries. Also, countries are likely to increasingly compete for the tax dollars of firms operating in their jurisdiction.

35. a.   Daewoo is likely pursuing two benefits associated with moving into third-world markets. First, there is less competition to contend with in the less developed markets. Also, Daewoo is likely trying to position itself to be a major player as the third world markets expand and develop.

     b.   From the perspective of a third-world businessman this strategy is sensible. Barter is an established form of exchange in developing economies; such transactions are much more common than they are in the developed countries. Trading in such a fashion should help Daewoo gain entry into markets. From a developed country perspective, such trading may also be sensible. The principal advantage to trading is that one may be able to avoid the risks associated with dealing in a third-world currency. On the other hand, trading involves much higher transaction costs because whatever is acquired in exchange needs to ultimately be converted to cash or some required production input. This may require a series of transactions that could be avoided if cash were received in exchange for an auto.

37. a.   The basic principles of management which should be observed in the delegation of authority include:
     *   Authority delegated must be commensurate with the responsibility assigned. One cannot have the responsibility for the operation of a given function without the authority to carry out that responsibility.
     *   Authority may be delegated to a subordinate; however, a superior is never relieved of ultimate responsibility for the subordinate's action.
     *   Authority should be delegated only to a competent individual who is capable of understanding and handling the responsibility.
     *   The individual delegating authority to a subordinate must do so in a consistent manner among subordinates and without misrepresentation.
     *   The individual delegating authority should not interfere with the subordinate's use of the authority in execution of duties.
     *   The level of authority must be clearly defined so that an individual understands and accepts the authority delegated and to assure that the individual does not exceed or underutilize the authority.

b.   Actions of supervisors which frequently undermine the effectiveness of the delegation of authority are:
*   The supervisor delegates responsibility, but fails to delegate commensurate authority.
*   The supervisor delegates incomplete or partial authority and responsibility.
*   The supervisor delegates inappropriate authority and responsibility for the nature of the task.
*   The supervisor interferes with the subordinate's duties and authority once the authority has been delegated.
*   The supervisor delegates authority and then takes it back or circumvents the subordinate in a crisis.
*   The supervisor fails to effectively and clearly communicate to all members of the organization that authority has been delegated.

c.   The actions of subordinates which frequently undermine the effectiveness of the delegation of authority include:
*   The subordinate refuses to accept the authority by continually asking the supervisor for direction rather than making the decisions.
*   Subordinates become preoccupied with the fear of criticism for mistakes and, as a result, obstruct the evaluation of their work by superiors.
*   Subordinates may fail to understand the parameters of the authority given, i.e., subordinates may overstep bounds and use authority in excess of that delegated.
*   Subordinates may underutilize the authority given and be reluctant to accept new assignments that entail new duties which may represent a greater risk of failure.

(CMA adapted)

Quality and Ethics Discussion

39. There are two purposes that are central to this problem.
     The first is to cause the students to ponder what is
     encompassed by the term "quality"; the second is to relate
     the concept of quality to the information provision function
     of the accounting department.

     It may be expected that there will be significant
     variations among the students in terms of the
     characteristics that they will identify for discriminating
     in the market for legal services. The important point to
     stress is how the student's perceptions of quality should be
     important to the law firms. It should be emphasized that it
     is the consumer's perception of quality that largely
     determines the success of a legal practice, and to be
     successful, firms should try to develop performance measures
     and information regarding their achievements in perceived
     quality.

41. You should discuss the ideas of exposure to liability and
     criminal prosecution for fraud, basis for public and
     competitor criticism for deceitful advertising, and loss of
     public goodwill with the VP of marketing. You could discuss
     the possibility of changing the advertising campaign to
     provide a basis for the increased costs-- informing the
     public that the "best ingredients cost a little more."
     Then, if all else fails, you need to decide if this is the
     type of business for which you want to work.

43. a. The quote indicates that the predominant concern of
         American businesses should be the generation of
         profits. There is nothing explicit or implied in the
         statement to indicate the profits must be derived from
         that set of activities that is legal within the local
         jurisdiction. Given that the pursuit of profit is
         constrained to legal activities, Friedman's statement
         is mere a pro capitalism statement.

     b. Ethically, one might feel that the pursuit of profit
         should be constrained such that profit is not pursued
         to the detriment of human life, human happiness, the
         environment, etc. In short, ethically, one might easily
         identify several objectives that managers should hold
         in preference to maximization of profit.

c.   If one takes a long term view of a manager's job, it might be logical to argue that the profit-maximizing actions of managers are those actions that are both legal and ethical. That is: unethical and illegal actions, in the long term, are not optimal from the view of maximizing profit. Illegal actions draw fines, lawsuits, new regulations, and other costly sanctions in the long term. Unethical acts in the long run created loss of business reputation, loss of customers, and loss of market share. Hence, in the long run there may be no conflict between Friedman's statement as to managers' obligations and the legal and ethical obligations of managers.

Management Accounting in Quality-Oriented Environments

Questions

1. Total quality management (TQM) is a philosophy of organizational management and change. At the center of the philosophy is the continuous improvement of the quality of all facets of operating the organization.

    Fundamental organizational change is required to implement TQM. Most organizations are adopting TQM after relying on inspection and monitoring to control the quality of operations; and quality control was the domain of some specific group in the organization. To adopt TQM, quality must become a foremost concern of all organizational participants. The organization must move from a philosophy of inspecting for defective work to a philosophy of building quality in. This requires a commitment from the entire organization, not just the management team.

3. Some customers simply demand more from an organization than they contribute. Such customers drain the capacity of the firm to serve more profitable clients. To better serve and retain the more profitable clients, a firm must be willing to "fire" marginal customers.

5. Employee empowerment refers to the assignment of responsibility and authority to employees to manage changes in their jobs. Additional costs that will be incurred include costs of training, and costs of bad decisions made by employees.

7. Benchmarking allows a firm to compare the quality of specific processes to the quality of firms that are viewed as excelling in such processes. By benchmarking the organization that is best at performing a given process, a firm can reasonably assess its relative quality in that process and identify specific actions that can be taken to subsequently improve the quality level.

9.   From Exhibit 2-5:
     1.   Identify and describe the organization's missions and
          goals. If necessary, translate these goals into a
          consumer's perspective.
     2.   Identify and describe all significant internal
          processes of the organization.
     3.   Determine which of the processes identified in Step 2
          are most essential to achieving the mission and goals
          identified in Step 1.
     4.   For each process identified in Step 3, select an
          appropriate organization to benchmark.
     5.   Identify those practices of the benchmark organization
          that may foster an improvement in quality and that are
          adaptable to the organization's culture.
     6.   Identify critical success factors that can be used to
          gauge improvement in the quality of each process.
     7.   Measure progress in quality initiatives by monitoring
          changes in critical success factors.
     8.   Use feedback regarding success of initiatives to design
          additional quality programs.
     9.   Do not become complacent. Strive for continuous
          improvement.

11. Quality standards are established primarily to protect the
     consumer and to standardize performance criteria.
     Standardizing performance criteria tends to reduce
     transaction costs associated with contracting and provide
     some assurance as to interfaces (e.g., a bolt of a stated
     size made by one company will fit a nut of that stated size
     made by another).

13. Having a limited number of suppliers reduces transaction
     costs associated with purchasing, receiving, and storing
     goods. Reducing the number of suppliers also provides an
     opportunity for more exchange of information between the
     firm and its remaining suppliers. This information exchange
     can serve to improve the quality of all involved firms and
     reduce their combined operating costs. The firm may also
     obtain reduced prices by providing a higher volume of
     business to a limited number of suppliers.

15.   Cycle time is the amount of time elapsed from the point a customer places an order to the point the service or product is delivered to the customer. The reduction of cycle time is achieved mostly by eliminating wasted activities and performing other functions faster. Wasted activities, such as producing defective products, create costs but provide no benefit to either the firm or the customer. Eliminating these activities reduces the firm's costs. Reducing cycle time also decreases a firm's risk and investment. A reduced cycle time translates into lower inventory levels, and hence, less risk of inventory obsolescence and losses. Additionally a reduction in cycle time may translate into a competitive edge associated with bringing a product to market faster than competitors.

17.   JIT is concerned with minimizing time, space, and energy. The JIT approach to inventory and production management strives to reduce cycle time; reduce the space required to store raw materials, work in process and finished goods; and reduce organizational energy wasted on activities that add no value for the customer.

19.   Electronic data interchange allows firms to better manage their cash balances. With EDI a firm will know the exact date a cash outflow will be charged to its bank account. Similarly, when notified by its customers that funds are being transferred electronically, the firm will know exactly when its bank account will be credited with a deposit. Thus, EDI allows a firm to manage cash more efficiently. EDI also reduces transaction costs by eliminating some of the record keeping associated with paper payments. Also eliminated are some of the errors that are associated with paper transactions.
      Alternatively, a firm may lose the benefit of "float" associated with checks that have been sent to suppliers but have not yet cleared the bank.

21.   Costs of product variety include: cost of purchasing, moving, and storing additional components; additional product and process design costs; additional advertising and promotion costs; and possibly additional distribution costs.

23.   Strategic cost management, SCM, is the linking of costs and benefits of organizational activities to organizational strategies. Thus, SCM provides feedback on the extent to which the strategies have been successfully implemented and identifies areas in need of improvement.

Chapter 2
Management Accounting in Quality-Oriented Environment

Exercises

25. a. False Adoption of TQM leads to continual change and improvement in production systems.

    b. False Accounting practices need to evolve like all other business practices as technology and competitive conditions change.

    c. False A focus on quality allows a firm to constantly change in response to new customer demands including demand for new products and product features.

    d. True

    e. True

    f. True

    g. False In benchmarking, a company will adopt only the practices of the benchmark firm that are appropriate given the firm's culture and competitive environment.

    h. True

    i. False Companies would be expected to engage in the same level of long term planning after cycle times have been reduced. However, they will have more flexibility to deal with problems or other developments with a lower cycle time.

27. a. The important dimensions of the fuel include the intensity of the heat, the type and amount of emissions given off from burning the fuel, the ability of the fuel to burn in the existing facilities, and the reliability of the supply.

    b. The greatest concern would be related to the distance of the fuel from the power plant and the likelihood that weather or other transportation problems would interrupt the flow of coal to the plant.

    c. There is no single, correct answer to this question. The loss of the jobs at the Navasota Mining Company would occur in the backyard of the power plant. This would likely create political problems. It may have an affect on the morale of power plant employees as well. On the other hand, the power plant has an obligation to its customers to deliver electricity in the most economical manner possible; also, the power plant has an obligation to control pollution. The Wyoming fuel would clearly generate less pollution than the Texas fuel.

29. a. Technophobia is fear of the unknown and fear of failure. It reflects apprehension about new experiences and unpleasant memories of prior experiences. Technophobia may also reflect a lack of confidence in the performance of higher technology.

    b. A sensible approach to educating a technophobe should begin with motivation as to why the individual should learn the technology. If this is done successfully, the person will understand the benefits to be derived from using the technology. Next, substantial training in the use of the technology should be provided. This training should be paced such that each individual feels comfortable and confident after each step in the learning process. After completing initial training, additional support should be provided for problems and questions that arise in implementing and using the technology.

    c. If technophobia could not be overcome, the affected person would become less effective in performing duties of the job, and eventually the technology would prevent the person from performing critical chores. For example, if a person in the accounting department was unable to use a personal computer or computer terminal, the person would be isolated from the firm's electronic accounting records; if a production worker was unable to operate a new computerized production machine, that person would no longer be able to do certain production operations; and if a person in marketing was unable to operate the new point-of-sale computer equipment, that individual would be unable to effectively serve customers.

31. a. The biggest change to be noted is the customer focus. The first thing Mr. Lockhart did was to ask the presidents of the railroads what he could do for them. Another big change was the commitment to solve quality-related problems by redesigning components (*set up a task force of 100 engineers*). Also, Mr. Lockhart moved headquarters to the middle of the production facility. This signalled his commitment to production, his commitment to be involved in finding solutions to quality problems, and the importance of a quality product to the success of the locomotive division.

    b. Complacency is probably related to the high barriers to entry in this industry and the fact that there was only one major competitor, and that competitor had experienced substantial problems in the recent past with quality.

    c.   The prescription for GM is the same as the one used by GE: focus on customers and meet their product requirements, build quality into the product design, and focus on eliminating wasted activities and decreasing cycle time.

    d.   Product design is obviously the foundation of a quality product. A quality design obviates the need to inspect for quality problems, to deal with products that have failed in the customer applications, and to re-engineer to solve problems that have been discovered after production.

33. a.   Tony needs the following general information:

Needed	Source
1. Long-term demand for each product	1. Marketing Department estimates
2. Measures of capacity needed to meet demand	2. Engineering Department estimates
3. Available technology regarding:	
■ desired extent of automation	■ Production engineers and top management
☐ Plant layout	☐ Production engineers and top management
O Appropriate amount of storage	O Production engineers and top management

Within the context of the above, the following specific information needs to be developed for each alternative:

Needed	Source
1. Proposed location(s) and measure of materials movements	1. Production engineers
2. Throughput	2. Production engineers
3. Additional land, building, & equipment needed with costs	3. Engineering, Accounting, and Capital Asset Procurement personnel
4. Renovation of existing facilities costs	4. Engineering, Accounting, and Capital Asset Procurement personnel
5. Salvage values on assets to be replaced	5. Capital Asset Procurement personnel
6. Costs per unit	6. Cost accounting personnel
7. Operating costs	7. Cost accounting personnel

   b.   From the above, Tony can prepare a narrative summary of the
         facts, assumptions, alternatives and recommendations, and a
         summary report in financial terms of the benefits and costs
         of each alternative, backed up by a detailed presentation
         of monetary calculations for each benefit and cost item for
         each alternative.

(CMA adapted)

Ethics and Quality Discussions
35.   a.   Time-to-market is a critically important variable in the auto industry. Significant market advantages accrue to firms that are first to introduce innovations (e.g., Chrysler and the mini van). Delays in the product development schedule cause delays in bringing the product to market and reduce the likelihood that Toyota will be the first to bring this type of car to the market.

      b.   The U.S. companies could cite that: the delays were caused by their suppliers, they have a different view of what "on time" means; or they might simply suggest that they are not accustomed to rigidly meeting deadlines. U.S. companies might also mention the geographic distance between their operations and the Japanese operations as an important factor.

      c.   The U.S. firms might focus more energy on the process of component design. They would seek to eliminate wasted activities, standardize inputs and reduce the quantity of inputs, standardize design processes, and focus on reducing cycle time for product development.

Chapter 3

Cost Terminology and Cost Flows

Questions

1. Cost is used to refer to so many different concepts, an adjective must be used to identify which particular concept of cost is being discussed. For example, there are fixed costs, period costs, expired costs, future costs, and opportunity costs.

3. A predictor is an activity measure that has a statistical association with a cost; the cost changes in a consistent, observable pattern with it. Movement in the predictor variable does not, per se, have to cause the change in the cost. A cost driver is an activity measure which is believed to have a causal relationship with a cost. While it may be easier to identify predictors than cost drivers, more confidence can be placed in the latter.
   The important distinction is that it is possible to control the cost only by controlling the cause of the cost (i.e., the cost driver). A predictor variable has no role in cost control.

5. A mixed cost is one which has both a fixed and a variable component. As the activity measure changes, the total cost changes but not directly and proportionately to changes in the activity measure.

7. A direct cost can be easily traced to the cost object. An indirect cost cannot be easily traced to a cost object; instead, an indirect cost must be allocated to the cost object.

9. Direct labor cost consists of salaries and wages of individuals who are directly involved in the conversion process, including for these same individuals, efficiency bonuses; the employer's share of social security taxes; and, usually the employer-paid insurance costs, holiday and vacation pay, and pension benefits.

11. The two basic categories of quality costs are costs of conformance and costs of nonconformance. These categories are inversely related. To reduce the costs of nonconformance, conformance costs will increase. Alternatively, a reduction in conformance costs will usually result in an increase in nonconformance costs.

17

13. This statement is false. Prime cost consists of direct
     materials cost plus direct labor cost. Conversion cost is
     composed of the cost of direct labor and overhead.
     Therefore, the sum of the two would double-count the cost of
     direct labor and would not equal total product cost.

15. Periodic reporting requirements create a burden on the
     accounting system to distinguish between events to be
     recognized in the current period and those to be recognized
     in prior or subsequent periods. Most notably, this requires
     the accounting system to distinguish between unexpired costs
     (assets) and expired costs (expenses of the current period).
     It is the periodic reporting requirement that establishes
     the demand for accrual-based accounting.

17. The costs associated with unfinished work in process would
     appear on the balance sheet as an asset. Specifically, the
     costs would appear in an inventory account balance.

19. The Cost of Goods Manufactured is the cost of goods that
     were completed and available for sale during the current
     period. The Cost of Goods Sold is the cost of inventory
     sold during the period. The difference between the two
     amounts is equal to the change in the balance in finished
     goods inventory for the period.

Exercises
21. a.   9
     b.   8, 12
     c.   11
     d.   1
     e.   4
     f.   13
     g.   7
     h.   13
     i.   2, 12
     j.   10
     k.   6
     l.   5
     m.   3

23. a. OH, fixed
    b. DM, variable
    c. DM, variable
    d. DM or OH, variable
    e. DM, variable
    f. OH, mixed
    g. DM, variable
    h. OH, fixed
    i. OH, fixed
    j. DM, variable
    k. DL, variable
    l. DM, variable
    m. DM, variable
    n. DM, variable

25. Fixed: $300   Variable: $.04 per page
    a.   1. $300 + ($.04 X 1,000) = $340
          2. $300 + ($.04 X 2,000) = $380
          3. $300 + ($.04 X 4,000) = $460

    b. The total cost is increasing because there is a
        variable cost component; if all costs were fixed the
        answer would be the same in all three cases.

27. a. DL
    b. OH
    c. DM
    d. DM
    e. DM
    f. DM
    g. DM
    h. OH
    i. DM or OH
    j. OH

29. a. Total hours worked   7,000
        Total regular hours worked   (5,000)
        Overtime hours worked   2,000

    b. To direct labor:
        7,000 hours X $8 = $56,000

        To overhead:
        $66,000 - $56,000 = $10,000

    c. Shift premiums:
        Regular hours   2,500 X ($8 X .10) = $2,000
        Overtime premiums:
        2,000 hours X ($8 X .50) = $8,000

31. a.
Direct materials	$518,000
Direct labor	321,000
Total prime cost	$839,000

b.
Direct labor		$321,000
Overhead:		
Indirect materials	$102,000	
Indirect labor	129,000	
Factory utilities	103,000	334,000
Total conversion cost		$655,000

c.
Direct materials	$518,000
Direct labor	321,000
Conversion	334,000
Total cost	$1,173,000

33. a. Period costs = Gross margin − Net income
Period costs = $2,100,000 − $600,000 = $1,500,000

   b. COGS = Revenues − Gross Margin
COGS = $4,000,000 − $2,100,000 = $1,900,000

   c. $3,200,000 − $1,900,000 = $1,300,000

35. Cost of services rendered
Direct labor:		
Veterinary salaries	$22,000	
Assistant salaries	6,200	
Office salaries	1,700[a]	
Total direct labor		$29,900
Supplies		1,400[b]
Overhead:		
Utilities	$ 720	
Depreciation	2,100	
Building rental	1,360[c]	
Total overhead		$ 4,180
Cost of services rendered		$35,480

[a] $3,400 X .50 = $1,700
[b] $3,200 − $1,800 = $1,400
[c] $1,700 X .80 = $1,360

37. a.   M, MD, S
     b.   M, MD
     c.   MD
     d.   M, MD, S
     e.   M, MD, S
     f.   M
     g.   M
     h.   M, S
     i.   M, MD, S
     j.   S
     k.   M, MD, S
     l.   S

Communication Activities
39. The memos should make the following points.
     a.   Prevention costs and appraisal costs are the most
          controllable by managers. Failure costs can be
          controlled to some extent, but mostly indirectly by
          effective spending on prevention, and, in the case of
          some external failure costs, appraisal.

     b.   Managers cannot directly control spending on failure
          costs. Since failure costs are largely a function of
          effective prevention and appraisal, the prevention and
          appraisal activities are the ones that are directly
          susceptible to managerial manipulation.

     c.   The least effective quality cost expenditure is in the
          area of external failure. If quality failures are
          going to occur, it is far better to discover such
          failures internally and avoid the costs of customer
          returns, warranty expense, and loss of goodwill. Thus,
          a business would strive to reduce failure costs, and
          particularly, external failure costs.

     d.   TQM would clearly place the quality emphasis on
          prevention. TQM strives for continuous improvement in
          satisfying customer needs. This equates to reducing
          wasted activities such as producing defective products,
          dealing with customer returns, reworking defective
          components, and assessing quality. A measure of the
          success of TQM would be measured reductions in
          expenditures for appraisal and failure. Thus, the only
          quality expenditure category that is consistent with
          TQM is prevention.

41.　Graph A represents a variable cost. Production volume is indicated to be a good predictor of this cost. An example might be direct labor or direct material. Graph B indicates that the plotted cost is not related to production volume, i.e., it is a fixed cost. This cost could be depreciation of a factory building. Graphs C and D depict mixed costs; the cost varies to some extent with changes in production volume. In Graph C, the cost changes in response to production volume more so than the cost in Graph D. So, Graph C is a mixed cost that is mostly variable and Graph D is a mixed cost that is mostly fixed. The cost in Graph C could be machine maintenance and the cost in Graph D could be factory supervision costs.

43.　a.　cost of printing invitations, step fixed
preparing the theater, step fixed
postage, variable
building stage sets, fixed
printing programs, fixed
security, fixed
costumes, fixed

　　b.　Estimate of attendees = (200 X .75) + [2 X (200 X .75)]
　　　　　　　　　　= 150 + (2 X 150) = <u>450</u>

　　　Fixed and step fixed costs = $260 + $1,000 + $1,215 + $250 + [3 X ($110 + (5 X $30))]= <u>$3,505</u>
　　　Variable costs = $.30 X 450 = <u>$135</u>
　　　Total cost = $3,505 + $135 = <u>$3,640</u>

　　c.　$3,640 ÷ 450 = <u>$8.09</u>

　　d.　Estimate of attendees =(200 X .90) + [2 X (200 X .90)]
　　　　　　　　　　= 180 + 360 = <u>540</u>
　　　Fixed costs and step fixed costs = $280 + $1,016 + $1,215 + $250 + [3 X ($110 + (5 X $30))] = $3,541
　　　Total costs = $3,541 + (.30 X 540) = <u>$3,703</u>
　　　　　$3,703 ÷ 540 = <u>$6.86</u>

45.

Cost	**Type of Cost**					
	Variable	Fixed	Direct	Indirect	Period	Product
paint ($600)	X		X			X
spirits ($50)	X		X			X
brushes ($65)	X		X			X
overalls ($24)	X			X		X
ad ($10)		X			X	
assistant ($200)	X		X			X
mileage ($.25)	X			X		X
mapsco ($15)		X			X	
tolls ($6)	X			X		X
bid ($1,800)*						
phone ($3.60)		X			X	

*opportunity cost is not applicable to above classifications

47. a.   Direct materials = $16,900 + $90,000 - $21,700
                   = <u>$85,200</u>
          Direct labor = 6,800 x $9 = <u>$61,200</u>

          Prime costs = $85,200 + $61,200 = <u>$146,400</u>

     b.   Conversion = $61,200 + $109,300 = <u>$170,500</u>

     c.

Beginning bal., work in process, 10/1	$ 32,100
Manufacturing costs:	
Direct materials $ 85,200	
Direct labor 61,200	
Overhead 109,300	
Total manufacturing costs	255,700
Total costs to account for	$287,800
Ending bal., work in process, 10/31	29,600
Cost of goods manufactured	<u>$258,200</u>

     d.

Beginning bal., finished goods, 10/1	$ 25,800
Cost of goods manufactured	258,200
Cost of goods available for sale	284,000
Ending bal., finished goods, 10/31	22,600
Cost of goods sold	<u>$261,400</u>

49. a.   Overhead = $69,400 + $12,350[a] + 45,400[b] = <u>$127,150</u>
    [a] $95,000 x .13 = $12,350
    [b] $18,000 + $92,000 - $16,700 = $93,300
     $93,300 - $47,900 = $45,400

    b.

Beg. bal., work in process, 8/1		$ 24,500
Manufacturing costs:		
Direct material	$ 47,900	
Direct labor	82,650	
Overhead	127,150	
Total manufacturing costs		257,700
Total costs to account for		$282,200
Ending bal., work in process, 8/31		19,200
Cost of goods manufactured		<u>$263,000</u>

    c.

Beg. bal., finished goods, 8/1	$ 8,000
Cost of goods manufactured	263,000
Cost of goods available for sale	$271,000
Ending bal., finished goods, 8/31	9,200
Cost of goods sold	<u>$261,800</u>

51.

	Case #1	Case #2	Case #3
Sales	$9,300	19,700[k]	$112,000
Direct materials used	1,200	6,100[h]	18,200
Direct labor	2,500[a]	4,900	32,100[m]
Prime cost	3,700	11,000[i]	50,300[n]
Conversion cost	4,800	8,200	49,300
Overhead	2,300[b]	3,300[g]	17,200
Cost of goods manufactured	6,200	14,000	68,900[o]
Beg. work in process	500	900	5,600
Ending work in process	300[c]	1,200	4,200
Beginning finished goods	800[e]	1,900	7,600
Ending finished goods	1,200	3,700[l]	4,300[p]
Cost of goods sold	5,800[d]	12,200	72,200
Gross profit	3,500	7,500[j]	39,800[q]
Operating expenses	1,300[f]	3,500	18,000
Net income (loss)	2,200	4,000	21,800[r]

[a] 3,700 - 1,200 = 2,500
[b] 4,800 - 2,500 = 2,300
[c] 500 + 1,200 + 2,500 + 2,300 - 6,200 = 300
[d] 9,300 - 3,500 = 5,800
[e] 5,800 - 6,200 + 1,200 = 800
[f] 3,500 - 2,200 = 1,300
[g] 8,200 - 4,900 = 3,300
[h] 14,000 + 1,200 - 900 - 8,200 = 6,100
[i] 6,100 + 4,900 = 11,000
[j] 4,000 + 3,500 = 7,500
[k] 12,200 + 7,500 = 19,700
[l] 1,900 + 14,000 - 12,200 = 3,700
[m] 49,300 - 17,200 = 32,100
[n] 18,200 + 32,100 = 50,300
[o] 18,200 + 32,100 + 17,200 + 5,600 - 4,200 = 68,900
[p] 7,600 + 68,900 - 72,200 = 4,300
[q] 112,000 - 72,200 = 39,800
[r] 39,800 - 18,000 = 21,800

Case

53. a.

Beginning work in process		$ 5,000
Raw materials added:		
Beginning balance	$1,000	
Raw materials purchased[a]	9,000	
Ending balance	(2,500)	
Raw materials added to work in process		7,500
Direct labor added[b]		10,500
Fixed overhead		3,500
Variable overhead		5,250
Total work in process before transfers		31,750
Transferred to finished goods		16,000
Ending work in process		$15,750

[a] $8,000 - 5,500 + 6,500 = 9,000$
[b] $1,750 \times 6 = 10,500$

b. If the insurance company needs actual cost information,
then the estimated amounts of variable and fixed
overhead will not provide the necessary data. In such a
case, the controller will need to accumulate all the
actual variable and fixed overhead charges incurred
during the period from May 1-20 and assign those costs
to the goods completed and those still in process at
the time of the flood. Such costs would include
indirect materials and labor, supervisory salaries,
utilities, repairs and maintenance, rent/depreciation
charges, insurance, taxes, etc. In most instances,
however, if the estimated overhead is reflective of
actual data, such estimates would be accepted for
inventory valuation purposes. Other information that
may be needed includes estimates of the number and type
of units destroyed and whether the units have any
salvage value.

Quality and Ethics Discussion

55.   a.   For some industries, an external or internal failure
           can have disastrous consequences. This is the case
           with the medical industry. This industry needs to
           concentrate quality control in prevention. Additional
           costs will be incurred for appraisal.

      b.   Lawn fertilizer production is an industry that would
           incur quality costs in proportions similar to those
           given in the problem. This is an industry that would
           not have significant quality control problems, but
           would have concerns with environmental pollution and
           contamination.

      c.   Similar to lawn fertilizer production, rug and carpet
           manufacturers would likely incur quality costs in a
           pattern that is similar to that given in the problem.
           This industry might concentrate slightly more spending
           in the prevention and appraisal categories than the
           lawn fertilizer industry. The consumer is likely to be
           more knowledgeable about rug and carpet quality
           considerations than quality dimensions of lawn
           fertilizer.

      d.   If the reputation of used car dealers is any
           indication, many have little regard for controlling
           external failures; accordingly, the industry's
           expenditures would be concentrated in the external
           failure category. There would be virtually no internal
           failures because there is little conversion and
           virtually no subsequent quality appraisal.

57. a. Capitalizing a cost is the same as treating the cost as an unexpired cost; expensing the cost is recognizing the cost as being expired.

  b. First, note that the change in accounting treatment did not affect any actual cash flows. Therefore, the only viable explanation is that the market was unaware that Chambers had been capitalizing these costs; perhaps the industry norm is to expense these costs. When the market learned of the actual practice with regard to these costs, it realized that it had been capitalizing (capitalizing in this sense merely refers to equating an expected stream of future cash flows to their present market value--the value of the stock) a larger income stream (a proxy for future cash flows) than actually existed. Upon learning of the actual accounting practice, the market capitalized the smaller earnings stream and the share prices dropped to reflect the lower market valuation of the lower earnings stream.

  c. As long as the financial statements fully disclose methods that were used to treat various items of expense and revenue, there is really no ethical problem. If necessary, the reader of the financial statements can simply re-create the financial statements by changing methods that were used. An ethical problem arises only if there is no disclosure of the methods used to determine income, asset, and liability measures. If this is the case, accountants certainly bear an obligation to insist that management disclose the methods used if the methods are not the usual and known practices of the industry. Otherwise, the statements are misleading.

59.   a.   This would convert a continuing variable cost (more users may be added) into a one-time fixed cost. The company's future needs may expand and the one-time purchase covers this. Something like free upgrades in the future can be better negotiated with a site license.

      b.   The cost is indirect to a particular project and should be allocated in a systematic and rational manner over the economic life of the software in a fashion similar to amortizing a patent or depreciating a machine.

      c.   After explaining to the controller that you believe the potential legal and public image costs are too high to duplicate the copies, you may want to help him formulate a plan for the site license. Otherwise, you may wish to make a proposal to top management, after advising the controller of your intentions, to meet the firm's present and future software needs.

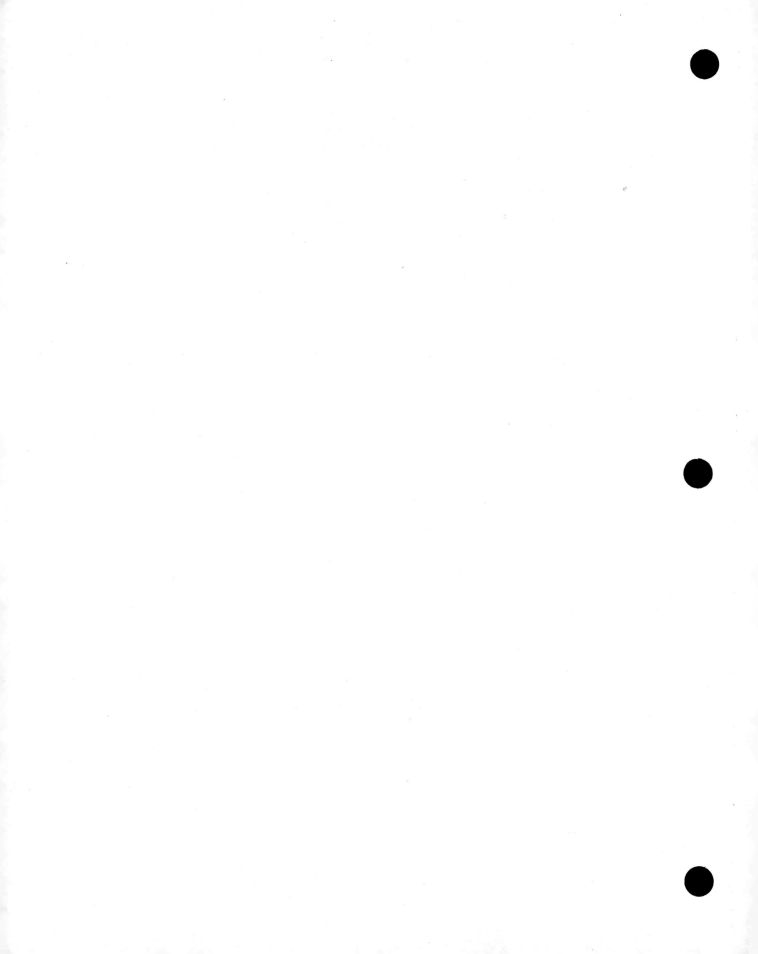

4 Including Overhead in Product and Service Costs

Questions

1. The two major types of overhead costs are production and nonproduction overhead. Production overhead is comprised of costs relating to manufacturing operations. Nonproduction overhead consists of cost incurred primarily for marketing and administration activities. As discussed in earlier chapters, production overhead has been increasing in recent years due primarily to the increased dependence of production on electronic and machine technology.

3. Job order costing is likely to be found where products are produced in discrete batches, where there is significant diversity in the types of products produced, and where the product is produced to specifications supplied by the customer. This environment is distinguished from the process costing environment in the diversity of products or services supplied to customers, the length of production runs, the unit cost of production, and the extent to which products or services are tailored to meet the needs of the individual customer.

5. Standard costing would provide the greatest cost control benefits. Standard costing requires the firm to develop standards or budgets for all three product cost pools. Such standards or budgets can then be compared to the actual costs generated for a period. Alternatively, normal costing requires only an estimate or budget for manufacturing overhead. Direct material and direct labor are assigned to production at the actual amounts.

7. For materials, the major control documents is the materials requisition form; for labor, employee time sheets are used to assign the labor costs of individual workers to individual jobs. There is no specific form that relates to overhead, but an additional important form is the job cost sheets that account for the direct material, direct labor, and overhead costs assigned to each job.

9.   Three advantages are: 1) permit assignment of overhead costs to products during a period rather than to products after it's over; 2) compensate for fluctuations in actual overhead costs that have nothing to do with activity levels; and 3) overcome costing problems caused by fluctuations in activity levels that have no impact on actual total fixed overhead costs.
They are important
  ■   to managers because they need valid and timely product costs from which to make good decisions;
  ■   to marketers because of the effect cost has on pricing decisions; and
  ■   to accountants because they need valid and timely information for financial reporting.

11.   A flexible budget is really a series of budgets with each budget representing the projected cost at different levels of activity. Costs must be separated into variable and fixed components so that it can be understood how each cost will change from one level of activity to the next.

13.   The primary criterion is that the activity measure selected to be the allocation base should be logically related to the overhead cost pool. The best allocation base would be the cost driver of the overhead cost pool.

15.   The four measures are theoretical, practical, normal, and expected capacity. Theoretical capacity assumes production can operate at 100% of potential continuously, while practical capacity takes into consideration off-days, downtime, etc., and provides a more attainable measure of output. Normal capacity is the long-run average utilization of the plant's work force and plant assets; it is customarily about 80% of practical capacity. Expected capacity is the anticipated operating level of the company during the next period. Theoretical capacity should be seldom used unless management and stakeholders expect 100% plant utilization. It will result in greater underapplication of overhead than the other measures. Practical capacity is a more realistic measure but is very difficult to attain and will usually result in underapplied overhead. Normal capacity yields a uniform product cost over time and is appealing on that basis. Expected capacity should result in a product cost which approaches actual cost. Any of the capacity levels can result in product costs approaching actual costs if under- or overapplied overhead is allocated to the accounts that contain applied overhead at the end of the year.

17. Least squares regression analysis uses all representative data points (rather than just two); and therefore, considers much more information than does the high-low method. Least squares defines a hypothetically perfect regression line which minimizes the sum of the squares of the differences of actual data points from that regression line. In contrast, the regression line defined by high-low is a simple average line extended between and through the high and low data points. Note that both methods can be used to develop a cost equation.

19. Using simple regression, the independent variable could be college credit hours. In multiple regression, the following six independent variables could be used: (1)college credit hours, (2) number of books to be purchased, (3) number of trips home, (4) number of meals eaten out, (5) number of dates or parties, and (6) number of dues payments. Multiple regression usually yields better information because more data is considered in predicting the dependent variable.

21. There are four criteria that can be used to select an allocation base. The allocation base can be 1) a measure of the benefits received by the revenue generating departments, 2) a factor that is known to be a significant cost driver in the service department, 3) a measure that is believed to provide a fair allocation of the service department cost, or 4) a measure that captures the ability of the revenue producing areas to bear the cost of the service department.

Exercises

23. a.   JOC
     b.   PC
     c.   PC
     d.   JOC
     e.   JOC
     f.   PC
     g.   JOC
     h.   PC
     i.   JOC
     j.   JOC
     k.   JOC

25. a. Maintenance expense = a + bX

$$b = \frac{\$600 - \$150}{\$60,000 - \$30,000} = \frac{\$450}{\$30,000} = \$0.015$$

a = \$600 − (\$0.015 X 60,000)
   = \$600 − \$900
   = \$(300)

Budget formula: Y = \$(300) + \$0.015X

     b. The improbable result is the negative fixed cost. Costs cannot be negative unless there is some unusual subsidy involved. The likely reasons for the negative intercept are: one of the data points used was anomalous (an outlier), there is an error in the data, or one of the observations is outside of the relevant range.

27. a.

	Record sales volume		
	5,000	7,000	9,000
Total VC	$9,250	$12,950	$15,750
VC per record	$1.85	$1.85	$1.75
Total FC	$3,500	$ 5,200	$ 5,200
FC per record	.70	.74	.58
Total cost	$12,750	$18,150	$20,950

     b.

Total cost per record	$2.55	$2.59	$2.33

29. a. 1. VOH rate = $44,000 ÷ 11,000 = $4.00
        FOH rate = $15,000 ÷ 11,000 = $1.36

     2. Products = 11,000 ÷ 2 = 5,500
        VOH rate = $44,000 ÷ 5,500 = $8.00
        FOH rate = $15,000 ÷ 5,500 = $2.73

  b. 1. OH rate = ($44,000 + $15,000) ÷ 11,000 = $5.36
      2. OH rate = $59,000 ÷ 5,500 = $10.73

  c. 1. Applied FOH = 884 x 1.36 = $1,202.24
      2. Applied VOH = 884 x 4.00 = $3,536
      3. $3,536 - $3,360 = $176 overapplied

        $1,202.24 - $1,310.00 = $(107.76) underapplied

31. a. OH rate = $60,000 ÷ 10,000 hours = $6.00 per DL hour

  b. Labor   1,430 hrs. X $4.50 per hr. = $6,435
     Applied OH   1,430 hrs. X $6.00 per hr = $8,580
     Material $17,500 - $6,435 - $8,580 = $2,485

  c. $60,000 - $59,350 = $650 overapplied

33. a. WIP: $ 27,000 $31,000 x 27/300 = $2,790
         FG: 60,000   31,000 x 60/300 = $6,200
         CGS: 213,000   31,000 x 213/300 = $22,010
         Total $300,000

     1.) Manufacturing OH   31,000
            WIP   2,790
            FG inventory   6,200
            COGS   22,010
     2.   Manufacturing OH   31,000
            COGS   31,000

  b. The allocation under part a.1. is better because it
     more nearly matches the costs that would be assigned
     under an actual costing system.

35. a.
Raw Materials	800,000	
Accounts Payable		800,000
WIP	650,000	
Raw Materials		650,000
WIP	192,000	
Accrued Wages Payable		192,000
MOH	1,200,000	
Accrued Wages Payable		400,000
Utilities Payable		300,000
Rent Payable		200,000
Accumulated Depreciation		300,000

b.
WIP	1,200,000	
MOH		1,200,000

c.
WIP: $ 650,000   Raw Materials: $800,000
      192,000   (650,000)
   1,200,000 $150,000
  $2,042,000

37. a. $\dfrac{\$16,500 - \$12,000}{2,125 - 1,000} = \dfrac{\$4,500}{1,125} = \$4.00 = b$

$\$16,500 - (\$4 \times 2,125)$
$16,500 - 8,500 = \$8,000 = a$

$y = \$8000 + \$4.00X$

b.

x	y	xy	x^2
1,000	12,000	12,000,000	1,000,000
1,250	10,900	13,625,000	1,562,500
2,000	13,300	26,600,000	4,000,000
1,500	12,100	18,150,000	2,250,000
2,125	16,500	35,062,500	4,515,625
1,750	13,000	22,750,000	3,062,500
1,800	13,700	24,660,000	3,240,000
11,425	91,500	152,847,500	19,630,625

n = 7
x = 1,632.14
y = 13,071.43

b = $\frac{152,847,500 - (7 \times 1,632.14 \times 13,071.43)}{19,630,625 - (7 \times 1,632.14 \times 1,632.14)}$
  = $\frac{\$3,506,673.68}{983,458.14}$ = \$3.57

a = \$13,071.43 - (\$3.57 × 1632.14)
  = \$7,245
Y = \$7,245 + \$3.57X

c. For multiple overhead allocation bases, the firm might consider machine hours, ageing time for the cheese, direct labor cost, pounds of material processed, pounds of raw materials processed, and ambient temperature as cost drivers. By using the additional overhead allocation bases, more homogeneous cost pools can be formed and a better statistical relationship will exist between the cost pool and the allocation base.

39. a. Checking accts:
       Administration (.40/.80) X 40,000 $ 20,000
       Personnel   (.20/.80) X 60,000   15,000
       Accounting   (.20/.80) X 60,000   15,000
       Direct costs   60,000
                                              $110,000

     Savings acct:
       Administration (.20/.80) X 40,000 $10,000
       Personnel   (.40/.80) X 60,000   30,000
       Accounting   (.20/.80) X 60,000   15,000
       Direct costs   50,000
                                             $105,000

     Loans:
       Administration (.20/.80) X 40,000 $10,000
       Personnel   (.20/.80) X 60,000   15,000
       Accounting   (.40/.80) X 60,000   30,000
                                             100,000
                                            $155,000

  b) Administration Costs ($40,000)
       Personnel   ($40,000 X .10) $ 4,000
       Accounting ($40,000 X .10)   4,000
       Checking   ($40,000 X .40)   16,000
       Savings   ($40,000 X .20)   8,000
       Loans   ($40,000 x .20)   8,000
                                       $40,000

     Personnel Costs ($60,000 + $4,000)
       Accounting ($64,000 X (.10/.90)) $ 7,111
       Checking   ($64,000 X (.20/.90))   14,222
       Savings   ($64,000 X (.40/.90))   28,444
       Loans   ($64,000 X (.20/.90))   14,222
                                          $63,999 (rounded)

     Accounting Costs ($60,000 + $4,000 + $7,111)
       Checking ($71,111 X (.20/.80)) $17,778
       Savings ($71,111 X (.20/.80))   17,778
       Loans   ($71,111 X (.40/.80))   35,556
                                         $71,112 (rounded)

  Checking = $60,000 + $16,000 + $14,222 + $17,778 = $108,000
  Savings: $50,000 + $8,000 + 28,444 + $17,778 = $104,222
  Loans: $100,000 + $8,000 + $14,222 + 35,556 = $157,778

Communication Activities

41. The memos should contain some of the following points:
 - Allowing firms to automatically recoup overhead costs provides little incentive to control such costs. With automatic reimbursement of cost, the universities are not forced to justify or budget indirect costs.

 - Perhaps the most perverse incentive associated with this research funding formula involves direct costs. Since overhead reimbursement is an automatic or preset percentage of direct costs, universities not only lack an incentive to control such costs, but actually have an incentive to inflate the costs. As the direct costs get larger, the reimbursement for overhead costs rises automatically.

 - The funding formula for research does not allow for the possibility that different research projects generate different overhead requirements. There should be a consideration of the actual cost drivers for overhead and they should be used in the funding formula rather than setting reimbursement of overhead costs based only on direct costs.

Problems

43. a.   DM $2,700
          DL   1,900
          OH   ($1,900 X 2.5)   4,750
           Total $9,350

     b.   Applied OH   ($15,600 X 2.5) $39,000
          Actual OH   (36,700)
          Overapplied OH $ 2,300

45. a.   Indirect materials:

$$\frac{\$6,000 - \$4,000}{400} = \frac{\$2,000}{400} = \$5.00 = V$$

$6,000 - (\$5 \times 1,200) = \$0 = F$

Indirect labor:

$$\frac{\$8,400 - \$5,600}{400} = \$7.00 = V$$

$8,400 - (\$7 \times 1,200) = \$0 = F$

Handling:

$$\frac{\$3,800 - \$2,600}{400} = \$3.00 = V$$

$3,800 - (\$3 \times 1,200) = \$200 = F$

Maintenance:

$$\frac{\$1,200 - \$800}{400} = \$1.00 = V$$

$1,200 - (\$1 \times 1,200) = \$0$

Utilities:

$$\frac{\$2,800 - \$2,000}{400} = \$2.00 = V$$

$2,800 - (\$2 \times 1,200) = \$400 = F$

Supervision:

$$\frac{\$4,000 - \$4,000}{400} = \$0 = V$$

$4000 = F$

a = 200 + 400 + 4000 = $4,600
b = $5 + $7 + $3 + $1 + $2 = $18
y = $4,600 + $18X

     b. $4,600 ÷ X = $5   X = 920 = expected capacity

     c.   y = 4,600 + ($18 X 920) = $21,160

     d. $4,600 ÷ 1,000 = $4.60

          $18.00 + $4.60 = $22.60

47. a.   Framing: Covering:
          a = $4,200   a = $3,000
          b = $6,600 ÷ 3,000 = $2.20   b = $45,000 ÷ 9,000 = $5.00

     b.   6,000 sofas => 6,000 MHs => 18,000 DLHs
          Framing OH: $4,200 + ($2.20 X 6,000) = $17,400
          Covering OH: $3,000 + ($5.00 X 18,000) = $93,000

     c.   Normal: $78,000 + $15,200 = $18.64 per sofa
                         5,000
          Expected: $93,000 + $17,400 = $18.40 per sofa
                         6,000

     d.   Expected capacity should be used. If normal capacity
          is used, actual gross margin will be less than 50
          percent of product cost because actual volume will be
          below the volume level used to determine the cost
          estimates, i.e., fixed overhead cost per unit will be
          above the estimated amount.

49. a. $862,200 + $432,000 = $1,294,200 = $15.00 per MH
              72,000 + 14,280   86,280

     b.   (9.00 + .12) X $15.00 = $136.80

     c.   Cutting: $862,200 ÷ 72,000 = $11.975 per MH

          Assembly: $432,000 ÷ 40,000 = $10.80 per DLH

          Total cost = ($11.975 X 9) + ($10.80 X 3)
                     = 107.78 + 32.40 = $140.18

51. a.   1.   DM cost = $360,000 ÷ 200,000 = $1.80 per lb.
               DL cost = $10
               OH rate = $1,350,000 ÷ 45,000 = $30 per DLH

               Cost assignments:
                                    Product A   Product B
               DM $135,000 $ 225,000
               DL   200,000   250,000
               OH   600,000   750,000
               Total cost $935,000 $1,225,000

               Unit Cost $93.50 $245.00

2. OH rate = $1,350,000 ÷ 50,000 = $27.00 per MH

Cost assignments:

	Product A	Product B
DM	$ 135,000	$225,000
DL	200,000	250,000
OH	945,000	405,000
Total cost	$1,280,000	$880,000
Unit Cost	$128.00	$176.00

b. The answers to parts a and b differed because the production of one product is relatively machine intensive and the production of the other is relatively labor intensive. Using direct labor hours as the overhead allocation base results in greater assignment of overhead costs to product B; using machine hours as the allocation base results in greater overhead assignment to product A.

53. a.

Raw materials	1,200,000	
Accounts Payable		1,200,000

WIP	1,065,000	
Raw Materials		1,065,000

Manufacturing Overhead	111,900	
Supplies Inventory		111,900

WIP	1,242,000	
Salaries & Wages Payable		1,242,000

Manufacturing Overhead	300,000	
Salaries & Wages Payable		300,000

Manufacturing Overhead	500,000	
Accounts Payable		500,000

WIP	911,900	
Manufacturing Overhead		911,900

b.   114J: DM: 200,000 + 212,000 $ 412,000
                 DL: 150,000 + 175,000   325,000
                 MOH: 100,000 + (1200/8000 X 911,900)   236,785
                                                    $ 973,785

       117N: DM: 1,400,000 + 158,000 $1,558,000.00
                 DL: 800,000 + 302,000   1,102,000.00
                 MOH: 600,000 +(1800/8000 X 911,900)   805,177.50
                                           $3,465,177.50

Finished Goods   973,785
  WIP   973,785

Finished Goods   3,465,177.50
  WIP   3,465,177.50

c.   Accounts Receivable   3,600,000
     Sales   3,600,000

     COGS   3,465,177.50
     Finished Goods   3,465,177.50

55. a. $\frac{450 - 150}{900 - 200} = \frac{300}{700} = \$.429 = b$

        y = a + $.429X
        $450 - ($.429 X 900) = $63.90 = a

b.

x	y	xy	x^2	
200	150	30,000	40,000	n = 8
325	220	71,500	105,625	
400	240	96,000	160,000	x = 532.5
410	245	100,450	168,100	
525	310	162,750	275,625	y = 303.75
680	395	268,600	462,400	
820	420	344,400	672,400	
900	450	405,000	810,000	
4,260	2,430	1,478,700	2,694,150	

    $b = \frac{1,478,700 - (8 \times 532.5 \times 303.75)}{2,694,150 - (8 \times 532.5 \times 532.5)} = \frac{184,725}{425,700} = \$.434$

    a = $303.75 - ($.434 X 532.5) = $72.65
    y = $72.65 + $.434X

c.   a. y = $63 + ($.429 X 760) = $389.94
      b. y = $72.65 + ($.434 X 760) = $402.49

The answers differ because the high-low method generates slightly different parameters for the cost equation relative to the parameters generated by the least squares method.

d.   The answer to part b is preferable. This answer is generated by the least squares model which is based on more information than the high-low model.

e.   One concern a manager might have is whether all of the data points are within the relevant range; another concern would be whether any of the observations represent outliers.

57. a.

	# of Employees	%	Assets Employed	%	Revenue	%
Commercial	36	20	$ 620,000	32	$ 6,760,000	40
Residential	108	60	968,750	50	8,450,000	50
P. Mgmt.	36	20	348,750	18	1,690,000	10
	180		$1,937,500		$16,900,000	

	Commercial	Residential	P. Mgmt.
Administration	$196,000	$ 588,000	$196,000
Accounting	152,640	238,500	85,860
Promotion	152,400	190,500	38,100
Total	$501,040	$1,017,000	$319,960

b.   Administration Costs   ($980,000)

	Base	Allocation
Accounting	6/192	$ 30,625
Promotion	6/192	30,625
Commercial	36/192	183,750
Residential	108/192	551,250
P. Mgmt.	36/192	183,750
		$980,000

Accounting Costs ($477,000 + $30,625)

	Base	Allocation
Promotion	$470,000/$2,407,500	$ 99,100
Commercial	$620,000/$2,407,500	130,728
Residential	$968,750/$2,407,500	204,262
P. Mgmt.	$348,750/$2,407,500	73,535
		$507,625

Promotion Costs ($381,000 + $30,625 + $99,100)

	Base	Allocation
Commercial	$6,760,000/$16,900,000	$204,290
Residential	$8,450,000/$16,900,000	255,362
P. Mgmt.	$1,690,000/$16,900,000	51,073
		$510,725

Summary of allocations:
Commercial: $183,750 + $130,728 + $204,290 = $518,768
Residential: $551,250 + $204,262 + $255,362= $1,010,874
P. Mgmt.: $183,750 + $73,535 + $51,073 = $308,358

c.   Direct method

	Commercial	Residential	P. Mgmt.
Revenue	$6,750,000	$8,450,000	$1,690,000
Direct costs	(5,245,000)	(4,589,510)	(199,200)
Service costs	(501,040)	(1,017,000)	(319,960)
Profit	$1,003,960	$2,843,490	$1,170,840

Step method

	Commercial	Residential	P. Mgmt.
Revenue	$6,750,000	$8,450,000	$1,690,000
Direct costs	(5,245,000)	(4,589,510)	(199,200)
Service costs	(518,768)	(1,010,874)	(308,358)
Profit	$ 986,232	$2,849,616	$1,182,442

The Residential Department is most profitable under both allocations.

59. a.   Empco Inc. is currently using a plant-wide overhead rate that is applied on the basis of direct labor dollars. In general, a plant-wide manufacturing overhead rate is acceptable only if a similar relationship between overhead and direct labor exists in all departments, or the company manufactures products which receive proportional services from each department. In most cases, departmental overhead rates are preferable to plant-wide overhead rates because plant-wide overhead rates do not provide:
- a framework for reviewing overhead costs on a departmental basis, identifying departmental cost overruns, or taking corrective action to improve departmental cost control;
- sufficient information about product profitability, thus increasing the difficulties associated with management decision-making.

b.   Because Empco uses a plant-wide overhead application rate on the basis of direct labor dollars, the elimination of direct labor in the Drilling Department through the introduction of robots may appear to reduce overhead cost of the Drilling Department to zero. However, this change will not reduce fixed manufacturing expenses such as depreciation, plant supervision, etc. In reality, the use of robots is likely to increase fixed expenses because of increased depreciation expense. Under Empco's current method of allocating overhead costs, these costs will be absorbed by the remaining departments.

c. 1. In order to improve the allocation of overhead costs in the Cutting and Grinding Departments, Empco should:
- establish separate overhead accounts (pools) and rates for each of these departments;
- select an application basis for each of these departments that best reflects the relationship of the departmental activity to the overhead costs incurred (e.g., direct labor hours, machine hours, etc.);
- identify, if possible, fixed and variable overhead costs and establish fixed and variable overhead rates.

2. In order to accommodate the automation of the Drilling Department in its overhead accounting system, Empco should:
- establish separate overhead accounts (pools) and rates for the Drilling Department;
- identify, if possible, fixed and variable overhead costs and establish fixed and variable overhead rates;
- apply overhead costs to the Drilling Department on the basis of robot or machine hours.

(CMA)

Ethics and Quality Discussion

61. a.   With appropriate training workers can become responsible for achieving planned levels of output and controlling the quality of their efforts. A major movement today is the decentralization of authority and responsibility. This movement pushes the decision making authority and responsibility down to the lowest levels in the organization. Decentralization creates a need for fewer levels of managers and places both the authority to act, and the responsibility for the outcome, with the person who is closest to the decision. With proper training, this person is best able to make decisions about those tasks for which he/she is directly involved and is most knowledgeable.

     b.   The traditional hostile relationship between management and workers is a real obstacle to the decentralization of authority and responsibility. This atmosphere creates mutual mistrust rather than mutual confidence in workers and managers. Furthermore, the historical precedent is for workers to work and managers to manage; there is a certain amount of discomfort in workers assuming management responsibility. It confuses the lines between workers and managers and confounds the role of the labor union in the modern organization.

63. a. Research cannot be conducted in the absence of the support provided by overhead costs. Therefore, those costs which are reasonably related to the research should be included in overhead. Frivolous costs should not.

b. There are governmental guidelines regarding allowable costs. All organizations receiving contract funds should be reminded periodically that audits of all costs for which reimbursement is requested should be expected and that administrators must act responsibly. Furthermore, the audits should be sufficiently frequent to lend credibility. Abusive behavior by recipients can backfire in that the offending institutions will have placed themselves at a competitive disadvantage with respect to potential future contracts.

c. Such allowances encourage administrators to inflate their budgets with items that would otherwise not be included and not otherwise defended except on the basis that a "third party" was bearing the cost.

d. Most taxpayers feel offended and betrayed by such extravagance.

e. A budget detailing all costs to be included should be agreed to in advance. Amendments could be made by mutual consent. The costs for which payment is requested should be presented and these costs should be subject to audit.

65. a. In accordance with the Statements on Management Accounting Number 1C (SMA 1C), "Standards of Ethical Conduct for Management Accountants," the appropriateness of Tom Savin's three alternative courses of action are listed below.

Follow Brown's directive and do nothing further. This action is inappropriate as Savin has ethical responsibilities to take further action in accordance with the following standards of ethical conduct.

- Competence: Management accountants have a responsibility to perform their professional duties in accordance with relevant laws, regulations, and technical standards.
- Integrity: Management accountants should (1) refrain from either actively or passively subverting the attainment of the organization's legitimate and ethical objectives, (2) communicate favorable as well as unfavorable information about the organization, and (3) refrain from engaging in or supporting any activity which would discredit the profession.
- Objectivity: Management accountants have a responsibility to communicate information fairly and objectively, and to disclose fully all relevant information that could reasonably be expected to influence an intended user's understanding of the reports presented.

Attempt to convince Brown to make the proper adjustments and to advise the external auditors of her actions. This action is appropriate as Savin has taken the ethical conflict to his immediate superior for resolution. Unless Savin suspects that his superior is involved, this alternative is the first step recommended by SMA 1C for the resolution of an ethical conflict.

Tell the Audit Committee of the Board of Directors about the problem and give them the appropriate accounting data. This action is not appropriate as a first step since the resolution of ethical conflicts under SMA 1C requires Savin to first discuss the matter with his immediate superior. In addition, the standard of confidentiality requires Savin to refrain from disclosing confidential information acquired in the course of his work except when authorized to do so.

b.   In accordance with SMA 1C, the next step that Tom Savin
      should take in resolving the conflict is to inform
      Brown that he is planning to discuss the conflict with
      the next higher managerial level. Savin should pursue
      discussions with successively higher levels of
      management, including the Audit Committee of the Board
      of Directors, until the matter is satisfactorily
      resolved. At the same time, Savin should "clarify
      relevant concepts by confidential discussion with an
      objective advisor to obtain an understanding of
      possible courses of action." If the ethical conflict
      still exists after exhausting all levels of internal
      review, Savin may have no course other than to resign
      from the organization.

(CMA adapted)

Chapter 5

Activity-Based Management

Questions

1. Product cost information is necessary to allow managers to accomplish two requirements: (1) financial reporting of inventories and cost of goods sold; and (2) effective and efficient conduct of the managerial functions of planning, controlling, evaluating, and decision making (e.g., pricing).

3. Value-added activities increase the worth of a product or service to the consumer. Non-value-added activities increase the time spent on a product or service but do not increase its worth. Performing any task required for production (adding materials, blending, molding, assembling, etc.) is an example of value-added activity; moving partially completed units of inventory, storing those parts, quality inspections, and allowing parts to sit and wait to be worked on are examples of non-value-added activities.

5. Non-value-added activities are attributed to the system, physical factors, and human factors. These factors, which are unique to the particular producer, can and should be changed by the producer. They add no market value or quality to the product so the consumer considers them to be non-value added.

7. A cost driver is an action or condition that directly influences and creates costs. Multiple cost drivers are used as bases for allocating costs to activity centers and to products. Cost drivers in a production activity center may include number of setups, physical layouts, and number of defects. In purchasing, cost drivers may include number of purchase orders and number of different items purchased.

9. The four levels of cost drivers are organizational, product/process, batch and unit. The traditional cost accounting system only recognizes cost drivers at the unit level.

11.   Three general steps in using activity based costing are 1)
      identify activity centers; 2)assign costs to the activity
      centers; and 3) allocate activity center costs to cost
      objects using appropriate cost drivers.

13.   Some characteristics are 1) provision of a wide variety of
      products or services; 2) differential degree of support
      services used by different products; 3) rate of growth in
      period costs; 4) extent to which common processes are used;
      5) effectiveness of current cost allocation methods, 6)
      complexity of production operations; and 7) the extent to
      which better information will translate into better
      management decisions.

15.   In ABC, control is exerted on the cause of costs which is
      the activity and its cost driver, whereas in conventional
      costing, control is focused on the cost itself. Control of
      the source of a cost is the more effective way to control
      the cost. This is analogous to treating the cause of an
      illness rather than treating the symptoms of the illness.

17.   The Pareto principle is an observation about the
      characteristics of many distributions. For example, 80
      percent of revenues are generated by 20 percent of the
      products produced; or, 80 percent of costs are generated by
      20 percent of the product components.

19.   ABC is not widely used for cost-assignments in external
      reporting. Reasons why it is not so used include: it
      wouldn't significantly affect measured income or assets, the
      ABC system is not implemented firm-wide, and ABC may not be
      fully consistent with GAAP rules or IRS rules.

Exercises
21. a. 10
     b. 9
     c. 8
     d. 2
     e. 5
     f. 7
     g. 1
     h. 6
     i. 4
     j. 3

23. a. Value added activities
         1. Taking depositions, starting process of a case.
         2. Research, increases the value of the case.
         3. Actual litigation time, also increases the value of the case.
         4. Correspondence, value added if necessary before litigation can commence, or results in desired action for the client.
         5. Contemplating litigation strategy, is value added because it adds to the value of the case being presented.

     b. Non-value-added activities
         1. Conference calls usually are done to discuss a case or explain it to the client which does not enhance its value.
         2. Travel time does not enhance the value of the case.
         3. Lunch also does not enhance the value of the case.

25. a. None of the items are value-added activities; products should be designed so that schedule changes are not needed.

     b. Number of factory schedule changes.

     c. Do a better job of planning to eliminate factory schedule changes except for those requested by a customer (in which case the customer should be charged for the cost of the change) or for critical changes necessary for significant quality improvements and cost reductions.

27. Rather than regarding the answers below as iron-clad, it may be more worthwhile to discuss the circumstances in which a cost would be classified as a specific type.
    a. O
    b. U
    c. B
    d. O
    e. P
    f. O
    g. P
    h. B
    i. P
    j. P
    k. B

29. a. Utility cost = $400,000 ÷ (85,000 + 15,000) = $4 per hour
    Inspection hours = $600,000 ÷ (5,000 + 25,000) = $20 per hour

    Regular Dictionaries
    Utility cost =$400,000 X (85,000÷100,000)= $340,000
    Inspection cost =$600,000 X (5,000÷30,000)=   100,000
    Overhead assigned to regular dictionaries = $440,000

    Hand-sewn Dictionaries
    Utility cost =$400,000 X (15,000÷100,000)= $ 60,000
    Inspection cost =$600,000 X (25,000÷30,000)=   500,000
    Overhead assigned to hand-sewn dictionaries =$560,000

    b. Resource Publishing should not stop producing the regular dictionaries. By using only machine hours, the company is currently assigning $850,000 (1,000,000 X (85,000 ÷ 100,000)) of overhead expenses to the regular dictionaries. This is excessive because it is not taking into account the amount of extra inspection needed to assure the quality of the hand-sewn dictionaries. Therefore, the profits of the regular dictionaries are understated and the profits of the hand-sewn dictionaries are overstated. The overhead allocation based on multiple cost drivers provides a better allocation of overhead costs.

31. a. Evaluation of market opportunities
$1,200,000 ÷ 30,000 = <u>$40</u> per professional hour
Product development
$3,600,000 ÷ 200 = <u>$18,000</u> per new product
Process design
$4,800,000 ÷ 1,000 = <u>$4,800</u> per engineering change
request

 b. The rates could be used in the same fashion that
standard rates and quantities are used in a standard
costing system. Additionally, the rates can be
compared to prices for similar services provided by
outside businesses.

 c. (2,000 X $40)+(25 X $18,000)+(150 X $4,800)= <u>$1,250,000</u>

33. a. It is obvious that the production process in this
company has a significant amount of non-value-added
time built into the lead time. The most likely cause of
this non-value-added time is one or more bottleneck
processes that create long wait periods when no
production is occurring and goods are simply stored or
stacked until they can pass through the process.
 A fairly simple way to determine where the
bottlenecks are is to walk through the plant and see
where materials or partially completed units are being
stacked in sight or are being brought back into the
production area from a storage location. Another
indicator of a bottleneck is where labor is waiting on
a machine to complete a process so that additional
materials can be input.
 In addition to bottlenecks, the company could be
engaging in rush orders that remove regularly scheduled
production from processing. Always trying to catch up
on backorders will create delays in processing current
orders. It is possible that if all backorders were
filled, the current orders could be processed at a much
more rapid pace. Finally, defective units caused by
rushing to complete orders will have to be reworked,
thereby causing an even longer delay in processing
time.

 b. A value chart could be developed that would identify
all of the activities associated with the production
and sale of nameplate stands. The value chart would
identify what is occurring with the nameplates during
all 21 days of the cycle time. The value chart would
identify for management the areas of operation that
need to be improved to reduce cycle time. The value
chart would also be used by management to reduce costs
by reducing or eliminating nonvalue adding activities.

Chapter 5
Activity-Based Management

35. a.   The traditional cost system, developed to value
           inventory, distorts product cost information because
           the cost system
           ■   was designed to value inventory in the aggregate
                and not relate to product cost information;
           ■   uses a common departmental or factory-wide measure
                of activity, such as direct labor hours or dollars
                (now a small portion of overall production costs)
                to distribute manufacturing overhead to products;
           ■   de-emphasizes long-term product analysis (when
                fixed costs become variable costs);
           ■   causes managers, who are aware of distortions in
                the traditional system, to make intuitive,
                imprecise adjustments to the traditional cost
                information without understanding the complete
                impact.

     b.   Outlined below are the purpose and several
           characteristics of the two noted cost systems:
           1.   Inventory valuation
                ■   Meets external reporting requirements for
                     aggregate balance sheet valuation and income
                     determination.
                ■   Provides monthly and quarterly reporting.
           2.   Activity-based costing
                ■   Differentiates costs between value-adding and
                     non-value-adding activities.
                ■   Assigns costs to products according to
                     activities involved in the production process
                     which cause these costs.

c.   1.   The benefits that management can expect from activity-based costing include the following:

- Leads to a more competitive position by evaluating activity costs, i.e., costs associated with the complexity of the transaction rather than the production volume and the cost drivers that cause the activities.
- Streamlines production processes by reducing non-value adding activities, thereby creating reduced setup times, optimal plant layout, and improved quality.
- Provides management with a more thorough understanding of product costs and product profitability for strategies and pricing decisions.
- Highlights interrelationships among activities.
- Provides feedback for opportunities for improvements in product design and production processes.
- Encourages use of non-financial measures of activity and performance.
- Provides a more appropriate means of assigning overhead to products.

2.   The steps that a company, using a traditional cost system, would take to implement activity-based costing include:

- identify activity centers and cost drivers
- assign costs to activity center cost pools using appropriate first-stage cost drivers
- assign activity center cost pools to products, services, or other cost objects using appropriate second-stage cost drivers, according to level of cost (unit, batch, products, process, and organizational levels).

(CMA adapted)

Problems

37. a.   Predetermined rate using machine hours:
          $6,000,000 ÷ 1,000,000 MHs = <u>$6</u> per MH

     b.   Cost per door:

Direct materials	$100,000
Direct labor	300,000
Applied overhead	60,000
Total cost	<u>$460,000</u>
Cost per door = $460,000 ÷ 5,000 =	<u>$92.00</u>

   c.   Predetermined rate per activity per unit of cost driver:
        Electric Power:
          $500,000 ÷ 100,000 = $5.00 per kilowatt hour
        Work Cells:
          $3,000,000 ÷ 600,000 = $5.00 per square foot
        Materials Handling:
          $1,000,000 ÷ 200,000 = $5.00 per material move
        Quality Control Inspections:
          $1,000,000 ÷ 100,000 = $10.00 per inspection
        Product Runs:
          $500,000 ÷ 50,000 = $10.00 per production run

        Cost per door:

Direct materials		$100,000
Direct labor		300,000
Applied Overhead		
Electric power ($5.00 X 1,000)	$ 5,000	
Work cells ($5.00 X 8,000)	40,000	
Materials handling ($5.00 X 100)	500	
Quality Control ($10.00 X 50)	500	
Product Runs ($10.00 X 25)	250	46,250
Total costs		<u>$446,250</u>
Divided by number of doors		5,000
Cost per door		<u>$89.25</u>

d. The activity-based costing method allocates the cost pools of manufacturing overhead to various cost drivers and then to products based on the amount or number or other bases that each product consumes in various cost drivers. Assume that Beaver Company's policy is to add 40% to manufacturing costs as gross profit to cover costs such as administrative expenses, selling expenses, financial expenses and research and development expenses, and the remainder will be a profit. In determining the selling price of the window under both methods, add 40% of total manufacturing costs:

	Present Costing System	ABC System
Unit costs	$ 92.00	$ 89.25
Plus gross profit 40%	36.80	35.70
Selling price	$128.80	$124.95

It is evident that a selling advantage results from the ABC method. As illustrated in this case, the ABC method should result in a pricing decision that makes the company more competitive in the market place. Savings in applying manufacturing overhead costs to products will enable the company to sell its products at a lower price than competitors while maintaining the same gross margin ratio.

(Copyright 1990 IMA (formerly NAA))

39. a. Professional salaries: $900,000 ÷ 30,000 = $30 per hr.
Building Costs: $450,000 ÷ 15,000 = $30 per sq. ft.
Risk management: $320,000 ÷ 1,000 = $320 per patient

b. Surgery = ($6,000 X $30) + (1,200 X $30) + (200 X $320)
= $280,000
Housing = (20,000 X $30) + (12,000 X $30)
+ (500 X $320) = $1,120,000
Outpatient Care = (4,000 X $30) + $1,800 X $30)
+ (300 X $320) = $270,000

c. Surgery: professional hours (this is an activity base that would drive many costs related to surgery and would be easy to track)
Housing patients: days in hospital (this activity base would be easy to follow and would account for use of time and space)
Outpatient care: professional hours (this would capture service provision to outpatients); or expected patient volume (this would capture those costs that are more related to capacity to provide service)

41. a. Allocation rates:
Utilities: $300,000 ÷ 60,000 = $5 per MH
Scheduling & setup: $272,000 ÷ 800 = $340 per setup
Materials handling $640,000 ÷ 1,600,000 = $0.40 per lb.

	Products		
	A	B	C
Direct costs	$ 80,000	$ 80,000	$ 90,000
Utilities	150,000	50,000	100,000
Scheduling & setup	44,200	136,000	91,800
Material handling	200,000	120,000	320,000
Total	$474,200	$386,000	$601,800
Units produced	40,000	20,000	60,000
Cost per unit	$11.855	$19.30	$10.03

b. Overhead rate: $\frac{(\$300,000 + \$272,000 + \$640,000)}{(32,000 + 18,000 + 50,000)} = \$12.12$

1.

	Products		
	A	B	C
Direct costs	$ 80,000	$ 80,000	$ 90,000
Overhead	387,840	218,160	606,000
Total	$467,840	$298,160	$696,000
Unit costs	$11.696	$14.908	$11.60

2.
Conventional
Product A: $11.696 X 1.20 = $14.04
Product B: $14.908 X 1.20 = $17.89
Product C: $11.60 X 1.20 = $13.92

ABC
Product A: $11.855 X 1.20 = $14.23
Product B: $19.30 X 1.20 = $23.16
Product C: $10.03 X 1.20 = $12.04

c.   The conventional approach to product costing used only one allocation base, direct labor hours. This allocation base was unable to fully capture the causes of overhead cost incurrence. The ABC approach developed better overhead allocation because of the superior relationship between the cost pools and the cost drivers used to allocate the overhead cost.

To the extent that there is error in determining costs, there will also be mispricing when prices are set based on costs. That is evident in this problem. Although Product A is relatively unaffected by the choice of costing system Products B and C have substantially different costs under the two systems, and, substantially different prices. The traditional costing system would result in underpricing Product B and overpricing Product C. This would affect both sales volume and company profitability.

43. a.
TV Trays:	$2 X 200,000	$ 400,000
Lamp Stands:	$15 X 20,000	300,000
Printer Stands:	$5 X 60,000	300,000
Total		$1,000,000

b. Allocation rates:
Quality control: $50,000 ÷ 140,000 = $.35714 per unit
Setups: $50,000 ÷ 500 = $100 per setup
Materials handling: $150,000 ÷ 1,000,000 = $.15 per lb.
Equipment operation: $750,000 ÷ 500,000 = $1.50 per MH

Cost allocation:

	TV Trays	Lamp Stds.	Print Stds
Quality control			
$.357 X 100,000	$ 35,700		
$.357 X 10,000		$ 3,570	
$.357 X 30,000			$ 10,710
Setups			
$100 X 100	10,000		
$100 X 200		20,000	
$100 X 200			20,000
Materials handling			
$.15 X 200,000	30,000		
$.15 X 500,000		75,000	
$.15 X 300,000			45,000
Equipment operation			
$1.50 X 100,000	150,000		
$1.50 X 200,000		300,000	
$1.50 X 200,000			300,000
Total	$225,700	$398,570	$375,710

Cost per unit:

	TV Trays	Lamp Stds.	Print Stds
DM	$2.00	$20.00	$ 2.00
DL	3.00	22.50	7.50
OH	1.13	19.93	6.26
Total	$6.13	$62.43	$15.76

c. Relative to the prices developed based on the costs of the products found using activity-based costing, costs under the traditional costing system would generate higher prices for TV Trays and lower prices for the other two products.

45. a. Send/receive goods: $6,000 ÷ 500,000 = $0.012 per lb.
Store goods: $4,000 ÷ 80,000 = $.05 per cubic foot
Move goods: $5,000 ÷ 5,000 = $1.00 per square foot
Identify goods: $2,000 ÷ 500 = $4 per package

Jones: (40,000 X $.012) + (3,000 X $.05) +
+ (300 X $1) + (5 X $4) = $950

Hansen: (40,000 X $.012) + (2,000 X $.05) +
+ (300 X $1) + (5 X $4) = $860

Assad: (40,000 X $.012) + (1,000 X $.05) +
+ (1,000 X $1) + (80 X $4) = $1,850

b. Jones: 40,000 X $.04 = $1,600
Hansen: 40,000 X $.04 = $1,600
Assad: 40,000 X $.04 = $1,600

c. Jones: $950 X 1.4 = $1,330
Hansen: $860 X 1.4 = $1,204
Assad: $1,850 X 1.4 = $2,590

d. The current pricing plan captures only one dimension of cost causality, send/receive goods. Accordingly, the prices charged for warehousing services are almost independent of the causes of the costs. As indicated in a comparison of the answers to parts b and c, an ABC-based price results in very different prices to be charged to the three customers; whereas, the existing pricing plan generates the same price for the three customers.

[Adapted from Harold P. Roth and Linda T. Sims, "Costing for Warehousing and Distribution," *Management Accounting*, (August 1991) pp. 42-45. Published by Institute of Management Accountants, Montvale, NJ.]

47. a. When product costs are calculated using ABC, the costs are assigned first to the activities causing the costs and then to the products based on the activities they consume. The following illustrates how the factory overhead costs are assigned.

Purchasing Department:
    The activity driving the purchasing department costs is the number of purchase orders. With 100 purchase orders and costs of $6,000, the cost per purchase order is $60. The final assignment of costs to products is then made based on the quantity of material used in producing each product. For example, 10,000 sq. yds. of leather were used in producing standard briefcases and 1,250 sq. yds. (0.5 X 2,500) were used in producing specialty briefcases. Using these quantities assigns 88.9 percent (10,000 ÷ 11,250) of the purchasing department costs for leather to standard briefcases and 11.1 percent (1,250 ÷ 11,250) to specialty. As shown in the following, similar calculations are used for the other materials.

	Standard		Specialty
Leather (20 X $60 X .889)	$1,067	(20 X $60 X .111)	$ 133
Fabric (30 X $60 X .80)	1,440	(30 X $60 X .20)	360
Synthetic		(50 X $60)	3,000
	$2,507		$3,493

Receiving and Inspecting Materials:
    The activity driving the cost of receiving and inspecting materials is the number of deliveries. The receiving and inspection cost per delivery is $50 ($7,500 ÷ 150). As with the purchasing department costs, the cost is then assigned to the products based on the materials used. The assignment is as follows:

	Standard		Specialty
Leather (30 X $50 X .889)	$1,333	(30 X $50 X .111)	$ 167
Fabric (40 X $50 X .80)	1,600	(40 X $50 X .20)	400
Synthetic		(80 X $50)	4,000
	$2,933		$4,567

Setting-up Production Line:
    The costs of setting-up the production line are assigned to products based on the time spent performing the activity. Since there were 50 setups for the standard product and each requires one hour, a total of 50 hours relate to standard briefcases. Similarly, the 100 setups for the specialty briefcases required two hours each for a total of 200 hours. Thus, the cost per setup hour is $40 ($10,000 ÷ 250). This results in $2,000 (50 X $40) assigned to the standard line and $8,000 (200 X $40) to the specialty line.

Inspecting Finished Goods:

The costs of inspecting the final products are assigned directly to the products based on the time spent of each product. The cost per hour is $20 ($8,000 ÷ 400). Thus, the total inspection cost for the standard briefcases is $3,000 (150 X $20) and for the specialty line, $5,000 (250 X $20).

Equipment Related Costs:

Although the equipment related costs are caused by the process rather than a specific product, they must be allocated to determine the total costs for each product. The cost per machine hour is $0.60 ($6,000 ÷ 10,000), and the cost assigned to each product is $3,000 (5,000 X $0.60).

Plant Related Costs:

Plant related costs are also allocated on the basis of machine hours. The cost is $1.30 ($13,000 ÷ 10,000) per machine hour, and the cost assigned each product is $6,500 (5,000 x $1.30).

ABC Overhead Costs Summary

When costs are assigned to products using an ABC system, the factory overhead costs for each product differ from those calculated using a direct-labor hour basis. The following summary shows the total factory overhead assigned to each product using activity-based costing:

	Standard	Specialty
Purchasing Department:		
Leather	$ 1,067	$ 133
Fabric	1,440	360
Synthetic		3,000
	$ 2,507	$ 3,493
Receiving & Inspecting Materials:		
Leather	1,333	167
Fabric	1,600	400
Synthetic		4,000
	$ 2,933	$ 4,567
Setting-up Activities	2,000	8,000
Inspecting Final Products	3,000	5,000
Machine-Related Costs	3,000	3,000
Plant-Related Costs	6,500	6,500
Total	$19,940	$30,560

b. With overhead costs assigned on the basis of activities as far as practicable, standard briefcases cost $27.99 per unit and specialty briefcases, $32.72:

	Standard		Specialty
Direct materials	$20.00		$17.50
Direct labor basis	6.00		3.00
Overhead ($19,940 ÷ 10,000)	1.99	($30,560 ÷ 2,500)	12.22
Total	$27.99		$32.72

If these ABC costs are compared with the traditional system's product costs, the standard briefcase shows a lower cost while the specialty briefcase shows a higher cost. The differences in the unit costs using the two systems are:

	Standard	Specialty
Product costs:		
Direct labor basis		
(traditional approach)	$30.49	$22.74
ABC	27.99	32.72
Total	$ 2.50	($ 9.98)
Difference as a percent of		
traditional cost	8.20%	(43.90)%

c. With ABC costing, the standard briefcase line now shows a gross profit of $2.01 ($30.00 - $27.99) per unit while the specialty line shows a loss of $0.72 ($32.00 - $32.72) per unit. Thus, CarryAll is really making a profit on the product which shows the loss using a direct-labor hour basis for allocating overhead and losing on the specialty line which appears profitable using traditional allocation procedures. The president was correct in being concerned about the profitability of the products, but the problem is with the specialty product line not with the standard line. Traditional allocation using a volume-based measure results in the high volume product subsidizing the low volume product which affects the profitability of each. When costs are traced to products based on the activity causing the costs, better costing data are available for evaluating the profitability of the various products.

[Copyright 1991 IMA (formerly NAA)]

Quality and Ethics Discussion

49. a.   Implicit in GM's actions is the concept that use of
          overtime is a cost minimizing strategy. GM must have
          determined that hiring new workers would result in less
          profit than using existing workers in overtime shifts.
          Some of the costs that might be controlled by using
          overtime would be quality costs, training costs, costs of
          firing idle workers when volume declines, workers'
          compensation insurance costs, and pension and retirement
          benefits.

     b.   On the positive side, managers can place their most
          productive and highest quality workers in the overtime
          shifts. This is an effective way to increase quality
          since only the best workers can be singled out for
          overtime work. On the negative side, if a worker does
          not want to work overtime hours, quality may suffer as
          the worker suffers from fatigue, depression, and
          indifference to the job. These behaviors could appear in
          both regular and overtime shifts.

     c.   Both managers and workers have ethical responsibilities
          with regard to overtime. It seems reasonable that
          managers should have the right to ask workers for
          overtime hours. In today's competitive environment, both
          management and workers must be committed to providing
          customers with the highest quality products and services
          they can provide. The long-term welfare of both managers
          and workers depend on this level of commitment and
          cooperation.
               However, managers must not abuse the use of overtime
          to enhance short-term profits, and they must acknowledge
          how imposed overtime affects their employees.
          Detrimental effects can be minimized if
          ■   managers ask for volunteers to work the overtime
              shifts.
          ■   a policy of imposed overtime hours applies only to a
              short-term circumstance and is not used as the
              solution to a long-term labor shortage.
          ■   management takes steps to minimize detrimental
              effects of overtime such as providing child care for
              parents with small children.

51. a.   In the modern competitive environment, to provide the
          highest quality of service to the most profitable
          customers, firms must be willing to fire unprofitable
          customers. Dropping small customers would be consistent
          with this concept. Small customers are not able to
          provide the same economy of operations that are available
          from larger customers.

    b.   There are ethical obligations in ending all business
relationships. This is particularly true for firms that
are sole suppliers of parts or materials that are
critical to their customers. At a minimum, an ethical
"firing" of a customer should
- involve an explanation as to why service is being
discontinued;
- be announced well in advance of discontinuing
services to the customer;
- be accompanied by suggestions of alternative sources
of supply;
- and, be sensitive to all negative effects that will
be suffered by the customer when service is ended.

    c.   Activity-based costing is a financial management tool.
It is not a tool for ethical management of a firm, nor is
it a tool that can expressly impound nonfinancial,
qualitative information. To the extent that factors like
customer goodwill and market reputation are involved in
decisions driven by ABC prescriptions, they will be
ignored by activity-based management. It is important to
acknowledge that these qualitative factors should not be
ignored, and in fact, may be important enough to overturn
the activity-based prescriptions.

Chapter 6

Introduction to a Standard Cost System

Questions

1. A standard costing system is a planning tool because it ties in with the organization's financial budgets. The standard costs represent an expectation about what actual costs should be. The standard costing system's contribution to organizational control involves the comparison of the actual costs incurred for a period to the standard costs. Top managers will investigate substantial deviations between actual and standard costs and take actions to bring them into alignment.

3. Target costing is a method of determining the viability of producing a new product. The analysis begins with the expected market price. Deducting a reasonable profit from the projected price provides the target cost to produce, market and distribute the new product. Managers can then compare the target cost to their expected costs. If expected costs are below the target level, the product has the potential to be a market success. Alternatively, if the target cost is below the expected cost, either methods will have to be identified to lower costs or the firm cannot produce the product and achieve the desired level of profitability.

5. Cost tables provide the information that is necessary to evaluate alternative methods of production. For example, they may contain information on material substitutes, labor alternatives or technology alternatives. By exploring combinations of alternative inputs, managers are able to identify the lowest cost approach to production and sale of new products.

7. A bill of materials provides information about the physical description of items and the quantity needed to produce one unit of product. It presents material components of a product, their specifications (including quality), and minimum quantities needed to produce a unit. It is used in a standard cost system to help in developing a standard cost card which would contain the similar quantity information (adjusted for expected waste and/or spoilage) as well as costs.

9.   Both actual and standard costs are identified in a standard costing system. It is the standard costs that flow through the product cost accounts. However, as costs are incurred the differences between actual and standard costs are captured in variance accounts. Accordingly, the variances provide a reconciliation of standard costs to actual costs.

11. Variance analysis is the process of categorizing the nature of differences (favorable and unfavorable) between standard and actual costs and seeking the reasons for the differences. Managers use the information as a means to focus their efforts. By concentrating their attention on areas where there are large differences between standard and actual costs, managers can take actions to move actual costs into alignment with the standards. This process keeps actual results consistent with planned results.

13. Computing the variance based on the quantity purchased is consistent with recognizing the variance at the earliest point in time. Since the variance is known as soon as there is agreement with the vendor on the terms of the purchase, it can be recognized at the moment the firm has made the commitment to buy the material.

15. No. Fixed overhead is generally incurred in lump-sum amounts and is only allocated to products on a per-unit basis for product costing purposes. Managers may be able to influence or control the quantity of production, and in that manner influence the fixed cost per unit, but they cannot control fixed overhead on a per-unit basis.

17. The growing use of the "conversion cost" cost pool is consistent with direct labor becoming a less significant cost in modern factories. As factories have become more automated, direct labor has been displaced by machinery. This causes direct labor costs to decline and indirect product costs to increase. In some factories it is no longer justified on a cost/benefit basis to separately track direct labor costs.

19. If standards are imposed upon workers, they will not be as willing and cooperative in attempting to meet them as the workers would be if they had participated in their development. To further enhance motivation, standards should be set at the practical level of attainability. The expected level of attainability is no challenge while the ideal level is too discouraging.

21. If the variances are insignificant, the usual practice is to close them to cost of goods sold.

Exercises

23. a.   Projected sales price $175
           Required profit   <u>(20)</u>
           Target cost   <u>$155</u>

     b.   The company has several options:
           1.   It could begin production (at a loss) and rely on
                kaizen costing techniques to lower costs in the
                future such that the product would eventually meet
                profit objectives.
           2.   The firm can work at redesigning the product and
                the production and distribution processes in an
                attempt to lower expected actual costs to the
                level of the target cost.
           3.   The company could simply elect to not produce this
                product.

25. a.   MPV: quantity purchased
           AQ X AP   AQ X SP
           45,500 X $22   45,500 X $22.50
           $1,001,000 $1,023,750
                  | |
                  | |
                  | $22,750 F |

     b.   MPV: quantity used
           AQ X AP   AQ X SP
           43,500 X $22   43,500 X $22.50
           $957,000 $978,750
                  | |
                  | |
                  | $21,750 F |

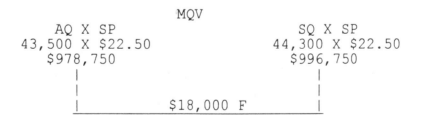

                         MQV
           AQ X SP   SQ X SP
           43,500 X $22.50   44,300 X $22.50
           $978,750 $996,750
                  | |
                  | |
                  | $18,000 F |

27. a.   27,500 X $7.25 = <u>$199,275</u>

     b.   AQ X AP   AQ X SP
           27,500 X $7.25   27,500 X $6.75
           $199,375 $185,625

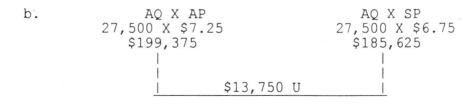

                  | |
                  | |
                  | $13,750 U |

c.
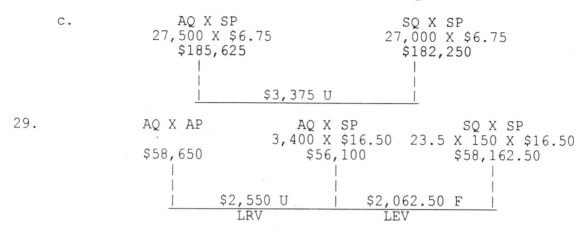

```
        AQ X SP                    SQ X SP
     27,500 X $6.75             27,000 X $6.75
        $185,625                   $182,250
           |                          |
           |                          |
           |          $3,375 U        |
```

29.

```
   AQ X AP              AQ X SP               SQ X SP
                    3,400 X $16.50     23.5 X 150 X $16.50
    $58,650             $56,100             $58,162.50
       |                   |                    |
       |                   |                    |
       |    $2,550 U       |    $2,062.50 F     |
                LRV                  LEV
```

The firm operated very near to standard cost for labor. A favorable efficiency variance was offset by an unfavorable labor rate variance. This combination may have been due to the use of a slightly higher-skilled labor mix than the standard mix.

31. a.   41,000 X .5 X ($12 + ($160,000 ÷ 20,000)) = $410,000

b. $257,250 + $172,000 = $429,250

c.
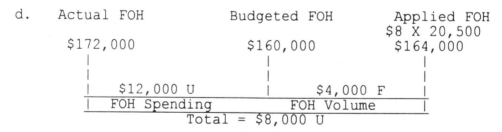

```
   Actual VOH        SP X AQ            SP X SQ
                   $12 X 21,000       $12 X 20,500
    $257,250         $252,000           $246,000
       |                |                  |
       |                |                  |
       |   $5,250 U     |    $6,000 U      |
       |  VOH Spending     VOH efficiency  |
             Total = $11,250 U
```

Note: SQ = 41,000 X .5 = 20,500

d.
```
   Actual FOH        Budgeted FOH        Applied FOH
                                        $8 X 20,500
    $172,000          $160,000           $164,000
       |                 |                  |
       |                 |                  |
       |   $12,000 U     |    $4,000 F      |
       |  FOH Spending      FOH Volume      |
             Total = $8,000 U
```

Note: SQ = 41,000 X .5 = 20,500

33. a.

Direct materials	200,000	
Accounts payable		196,300
Material price variance		3,700

b.

Work in process	184,000	
Material quantity variance	9,100	
Direct materials		193,100

c.

Work in process	96,000	
Labor rate variance	2,100	
Wages payable		94,200
Labor efficiency variance		3,900

d.

Cost of goods sold	3,600	
Material price variance	3,700	
Labor efficiency variance	3,900	
Material quantity variance		9,100
Labor rate variance		2,100

Communication Activities

35. a.   The relationship between inputs and outputs is not
          subject to precise engineering for legal work as it is
          with materials. Both the quantity and quality of the
          input is difficult to measure and specify relative to a
          desired output.

     b.   First, for routine and repetitive legal tasks,
          standards could be developed for professional hours.
          Also, standard labor rates could be developed for work
          performed by legal staff and professionals. In short,
          standard cost concepts can easily be applied to
          recurring types of legal tasks (analyzing contracts,
          reviewing loan or collateral agreements, preparing a
          promissory note, etc.). For the unusual and
          extraordinarily difficult tasks, developing standards
          would be useless and nonproductive.

     c.   A standard price arrangement could be developed such
          that, even for outside counsel, the user of legal
          services is charged a specific amount for a given,
          routine service. This would remove the incentive in
          the legal services industry to inflate hours. This
          would require the legal services industry to use the
          same retail pricing arrangement used in almost all
          other industries: a stated price for a specific
          service or product.

37. a.   The characteristics that should be present in a
          standard cost system to encourage positive employee
          motivation include:
          ■   participation in setting standards from all levels
               of the organization including purchasing,
               engineering, manufacturing and accounting;
          ■   the integration of organizational communication by
               translating the organizational goals and
               objectives into monetary terms for the employees;
          ■   support of the standard cost system by management;
               and
          ■   incorporation of standards that are perceived as
               achievable and accurate and apply to controllable
               costs.

     b.   A standard cost system should be implemented to
          positively motivate employees by
          ■   communicating the corporate objectives of a
               standard cost system;
          ■   soliciting standards from employees for which they
               will be held accountable; and
          ■   tying the individual's performance in the standard
               cost system to the individual's performance review
               and reward system.

c.   "Management by exception" is the situation where management's attention is focused only on those items that deviate significantly from the standard. The assumption is, that foregoing a thorough, detailed analysis of all items, the manager has more time to concentrate on other managerial activities.

The behavioral implications of "management by exception" include both positive and negative implications. On the positive side, this technique increases management efficiency by concentrating only on significant variances, allowing time for the manager to concentrate on other activities. On the negative side, managers tend only to focus on the negative variances rather than positive ones, limiting their employee interactions to negative reinforcement or punishment. This technique may not indicate detrimental trends at an early stage, and fragmentation of efforts can occur from dealing only with the specific problems rather than global issues.

Employee behavior could be adversely affected when "actual to budget" comparisons are used as the basis for performance evaluation. Employees may subvert the system and submit budgets that are low so (s)he can meet or exceed the budget favorably, thereby averting negative reinforcement for varying unfavorably from the budget. There may be a minimal level of motivation since exceptional performance is not rewarded. Employees may strive for mediocrity and not work up to his/her full potential.

(CMA adapted)

Chapter 6
Introduction to a Standard Cost System

Problems

39. a.

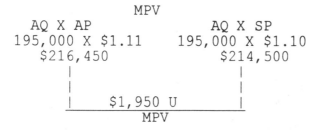

```
                        MPV
      AQ X AP              AQ X SP
  195,000 X $1.11     195,000 X $1.10
      $216,450           $214,500
         |                  |
         |                  |
         |    $1,950 U      |
         |_____|
                 MPV
```

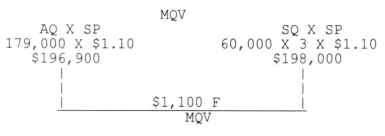

```
                    MQV
      AQ X SP                    SQ X SP
  179,000 X $1.10          60,000 X 3 X $1.10
     $196,900                  $198,000
         |                        |
         |                        |
         |       $1,100 F         |
         |_____|
                   MQV
```

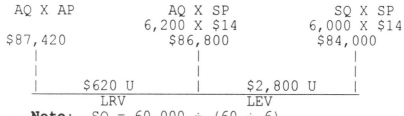

```
    AQ X AP              AQ X SP            SQ X SP
                      6,200 X $14        6,000 X $14
    $87,420             $86,800            $84,000
       |                   |                  |
       |                   |                  |
       |     $620 U        |     $2,800 U     |
       |_____|_____|
              LRV                 LEV
```

Note: SQ = 60,000 ÷ (60 ÷ 6)

41.

	Case 1	Case 2	Case 3	Case 4
Units produced	600	(d)	310	215
Standard hours per unit	2	.3	(g)	(j)
Standard hours allowed	(a)	1,200	930	(k)
Standard rate per hour	$5	(e)	$9.50	$8
Actual hours worked	1,230	1,170	(h)	450
Actual labor cost	(b)	(f)	$3,230	$3,645
Labor rate variance	$62 U	$117 U	$475 F	(l)
Labor efficiency variance	(c)	$360 F	(i)	$160 U

a. 600 X 2 = <u>1,200</u>

b. $62 U = 1,230 X (AP - $5)
    $.05 = AP - $5
    $5.05 = AP
    $5.05 X 1,230 = <u>$6,212</u>

c. $5 X (1,230 - 1,200) = <u>$150</u> U

d. 1,200 ÷ .3 = <u>4,000</u>

e. $360 F = SP X ($1,170 - 1,200)
    $360 F = SP X 30
    SP = <u>$12</u>

f.   AC = SC + variances
     AC = ($12 X 1,200) + $360 - $117
     AC = <u>$14,643</u>

g.   930 ÷ 310 = <u>3</u>

h. $475 F = AQ X (($3,230 ÷ AQ) - $9.50)
     $475 F = $3,230 - $9.50AQ
     $3,705 = $9.50 AQ
     AQ = <u>390</u>

i. $9.50 X (390 - 930) = <u>$5,130</u> F

j. $160 U = $8 X (450 - SQ)
     20 = 450 - SQ
     430 = SQ
     430 ÷ 215 = <u>2</u>

k.   <u>430</u> (see part j.)

l.   450 X ($8.10 - $8.00) = <u>$45</u> U

43. a.

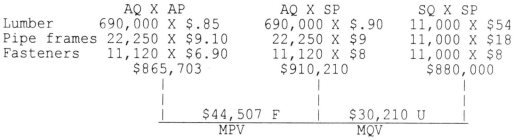

	AQ X AP	AQ X SP	SQ X SP
Lumber	690,000 X $.85	690,000 X $.90	11,000 X $54
Pipe frames	22,250 X $9.10	22,250 X $9	11,000 X $18
Fasteners	11,120 X $6.90	11,120 X $8	11,000 X $8
	$865,703	$910,210	$880,000

         $44,507 F $30,210 U
            MPV   MQV

AQ X AP	AQ X SP	SQ X SP
5,600 X $14.20	5,600 X $14	11,000 X $7
$79,520	$78,400	$77,000

         $1,120 U $1,400 U
            LRV   LEV

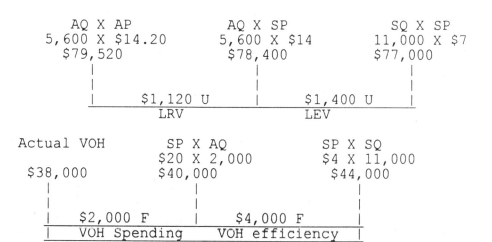

Actual VOH	SP X AQ	SP X SQ
	$20 X 2,000	$4 X 11,000
$38,000	$40,000	$44,000

         $2,000 F $4,000 F
        VOH Spending   VOH efficiency

Chapter 6
Introduction to a Standard Cost System

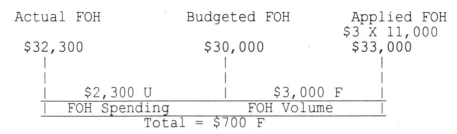

Actual FOH	Budgeted FOH	Applied FOH $3 X 11,000
$32,300	$30,000	$33,000

$2,300 U	$3,000 F
FOH Spending	FOH Volume

Total = $700 F

b. The large material price variance is mostly
    attributable to lumber ($34,500 F). Perhaps a lower
    grade of lumber was purchased. This would be
    consistent with the unfavorable material quantity
    variance which is also mostly caused by lumber ($27,000
    U).

    The direct labor rate variance is largely
    uncontrollable and would be primarily a function of
    internal labor policies. The unfavorable labor
    efficiency variance indicates more time was consumed
    than the standard allows to produce 11,000 picnic
    tables. Possibly this is due to extra time required to
    handle inferior lumber.

    The overhead variances are relatively small. The
    favorable overhead volume variance is due to the fact
    that the firm made 11,000 tables but only expected to
    make 10,000. The unfavorable fixed overhead spending
    variance may be due to any of the individual costs that
    comprise fixed overhead. To identify the actual cause
    of the cost, a line-by-line comparison of budget to
    actual costs should be conducted.

    The variable overhead spending variance could be
    due to either efficiency in using the items that
    comprise variable overhead; or alternatively, to paying
    less than standard price for those items. The
    favorable overhead efficiency variance is attributable
    to efficiency in the use of the overhead allocation
    base, machine hours (10,000 actual hours versus 11,000
    standard hours allowed). The production manager is
    likely to be given credit for this variance.

45. a. The standard cost for 8,500 units at $2.50 each is
    $21,250. Since the actual costs charged to production
    were $24,270, there is an unfavorable variance of
    $3,020.

    b. The labor rate variance is the difference between
    actual hours at actual rates and actual hours at the
    standard rate. The actual cost of $11,600 ($9,200 +
    $2,400 overtime) is compared to actual hours (2,700)
    times the standard rate ($4) or $10,800. An $800
    unfavorable variance is the result.

c. The spending variance is the difference between the actual costs ($3,100) and the budgeted costs [(($1.20 X 30,000) ÷ 12) = $3,000]. The budget variance is $100 unfavorable ($3,100 - $3,000).

d. The volume variance is attributable to the difference between actual production and the expected production volume used to estimate standard costs. The volume variance is the result of too much or too little overhead being charged to output. Expected volume is 2,500 hours (30,000 ÷ 12). Actual volume is 2,550 (8,500 X .3) hours. The volume variance is $1.20 X (2,550 - 2,500) = $60 F.

e. The unfavorable quantity variance is likely related to the purchase of inferior quality plastic which caused a number of sprinklers to be rejected upon inspection.

(CMA adapted)

47. a.
1.
Raw materials inventory	182,300	
Material price variance		5,185
Accounts payable		177,115

2.
Work in process	172,800	
Material quantity variance	2,800	
Raw materials inventory		175,600

3.
Work in process	81,000	
Labor rate variance	3,725	
Labor efficiency variance	2,600	
Wages payable		87,325

4.
Manufacturing overhead	55,910	
Various accounts		55,910

5.
Work in process	54,000	
Manufacturing overhead		54,000

6.
Variable OH efficiency variance	1,600	
Fixed OH spending variance	3,000	
Manufacturing overhead		1,910
Fixed OH volume variance		2,400
Variable OH spending variance		290

7.
Finished goods inventory	307,800	
Work in process		307,800

8.
Accounts receivable	425,000	
Sales		425,000
Cost of Goods Sold	228,000	
Finished goods inventory		228,000

b.
Cost of goods sold	5,850	
Material price variance	5,185	
Variable OH spending variance	290	
Fixed OH volume variance	2,400	
Material quantity variance		2,800
Labor rate variance		3,725
Labor efficiency variance		2,600
Variable OH efficiency variance		1,600
Fixed OH spending variance		3,000

c. Except for the material price variance, all variances would be prorated among cost of goods sold, finished goods inventory and work in process inventory based on their respective closing balances. In the case of the direct material price variance, it would be allocated to the three accounts just mentioned plus raw material inventory.

49. a.   4,200 X 2 = <u>8,400</u>

b.

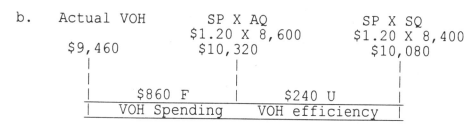

```
Actual VOH        SP X AQ              SP X SQ
                  $1.20 X 8,600        $1.20 X 8,400
   $9,460         $10,320              $10,080
      |               |                    |
      |               |                    |
      |   $860 F      |      $240 U         |
      |  VOH Spending      VOH efficiency  |
```

```
Actual FOH           Budgeted FOH        Applied FOH
                                         $3 X 8,400
   $24,900              $24,000          $25,200
      |                    |                 |
      |                    |                 |
      |     $900 U         |     $1,200 F    |
      |  FOH Spending          FOH Volume   |
```

c. The standards that would be affected include:
- labor quantity standard. This standard would likely be increased to reflect higher levels of efficiency associated with the new technology.

- labor rate standard. The labor rate standard might be increased to reflect a higher required skill to operate the higher technology.

- budgeted fixed overhead. Budgeted fixed overhead would be increased to reflect all fixed costs associated with the new technology.

- the variable overhead rate. The variable overhead rate would be adjusted to reflect the operating costs of the new machinery; it might also be adjusted to reflect lower quality appraisal costs.

- material quantity standard. The material quantity standard would likely need updating as well. This standard would be tightened to reflect less waste, scrap, and rejects. It may also need to be changed to reflect new required materials.

In addition to general managers, the vendor of the new technology would be consulted as to the operating costs of the machinery; labor experts would be consulted to develop a new labor standard; engineering specialists would be consulted to develop a new material quantity standard; and accountants would be involved to translate the information from functional experts into dollars.

51. a. Standard cost for ten-gallon batch of raspberry sherbet.

Direct material		
Raspberries (7.5 qts.* X $.80)	$6.00	
Other ingredients (10 gal. X $.45)	4.50	$10.50
Direct labor		
Sorting [(3 min. X 6 qts.)÷60) X $9.00]	$2.70	
Blending (12 min. ÷ 60) X $9.00	1.80	4.50
Packaging (40 qts.** X $.38)		15.20
Standard cost per ten-gallon batch		$30.20

* 6 quarts X (5 ÷ 4) = 7.5 quarts required to obtain 6 acceptable quarts.
** 4 quarts per gallon X 10 gallons = 40 quarts

   b. 1. In general, the purchasing manager is held responsible for unfavorable material price variances. Causes of these variances include the following.
      ▪ Failure to correctly forecast price increases.
      ▪ Purchasing nonstandard or uneconomical lots.
      ▪ Purchasing from suppliers other than those offering the most favorable terms.

      2. In general, the production manager or foreman is held responsible for unfavorable labor efficiency variances. Causes of these variances include the following.
      ▪ Poorly trained labor.
      ▪ Substandard or inefficient equipment.
      ▪ Inadequate supervision.

   c. One of the big factors affecting the quality of the raspberries is the weather. Hence, if one was able to understand exactly how weather influences the quality of the raspberry crop, and if one could forecast the seasonal weather with some accuracy, a quantity standard could be developed that would be sensitive to the influence of weather on raspberry quality. This would allow the management to evaluate the actual quantity of raspberries used against a more relevant benchmark.

(CMA)

Cases

53. a. 1.   Material price variance:
- Formula: Actual quantity X (Standard price - Actual price)
- Actual prices:
  Housing units = $44,000 ÷ 2,200 = $20 per unit
  Printed circuit boards = $75,200 ÷ 4,700 = $16 per unit
  Reading heads = $101,200 ÷ 9,200 = $11 per unit
- Variances:
  Housing units = 2,200 X ($20 - $20) = $ 0
  Printed circuit boards =
  4,700 X ($15 - $16) =   4,700 U
  Reading heads = 9,200 X ($10 - $11) =   9,200 U
  Total material price variance $13,900 U

2.   Material quantity variance:
- Formula = Standard price X (Standard quantity - Actual quantity)
- Standard quantities:
  Housing units = 2,200 X 1 =   2,200 parts
  Printed circuit boards = 2,200 X 2 = 4,400 parts
  Reading heads = 2,200 X 4 =   8,800 parts
- Variances:
  Housing units = $20 X (2,200 - 2,200) = $ 0
  Printed circuit boards
    = $15 X (4,400 - 4,700) =   4,500 U
  Reading heads = $10 X (8,800 - 9,200) =   4,000 U
  Total material quantity variance $8,500 U

3.   Variable overhead efficiency variance:
- Formula = Standard rate X (Standard hours - Actual hours)
- Standard hours allowed:
  2,200 X 4.5 hours per unit = 9,900 hours
- Variance = $2 X (9,900 - 9,900) = $ 0

4.   Variable overhead spending variance:
- Formula = (Actual hours X Standard rate) - Actual variable OH
- Variance:
  (9,900 X $2) - $18,800 = $1,000 F

5.   Reconciliation of variances:

Material price	$13,900 U
Material quantity	8,500 U
Variable overhead efficiency	0
Variable overhead spending	1,000 F
Labor rate (given)	5,660 U
Labor efficiency (given)	200 F
Total rate and efficiency variances	$26,860 U
Plus difference in cost at standard caused by operating at a level higher than budget (2,200 - 2,000) X ($139)	27,800 U
Total difference explained	$54,660 U

b.   1.   Behavioral factors that may promote friction among
          the production managers and between the production
          managers and the maintenance manager include the
          following:
          ■   The managers of the PCB and RH groups will be
              dissatisfied with the maintenance manager as
              equipment downtime has caused them to incur
              additional overtime costs.
          ■   The Assembly Group is dependent on the input
              of the other production departments. In order
              to increase production, the managers of the
              Assembly Group are likely to pressure the
              other managers. This type of pressure is
              probably the reason why the PCB and RH groups
              began rejecting parts that would normally
              have been modified and used.

     2.   An evaluation of Jack Rath's report leads to the
          conclusion that it is incomplete as he has not
          identified the real causes of the unfavorable
          results and has left management to draw its own
          conclusions. In addition, Rath has addressed only
          the labor issues and has failed to account for the
          material variances or mention the maintenance
          problems that resulted in downtime for some
          departments. The department managers are likely to
          resent the report as being unfair.

(CMA adapted)

Ethics and Quality Discussion

55. a. The partnership with Rolls Royce has favorable implications for BMW. For example, the mere fact that Rolls Royce selected BMW for its design partner reflects positively on the quality of BMW's design processes. Also, there is a favorable effect on business reputation. Other benefits that BMW receives include knowledge of Rolls Royce processes that may be internalized, an additional source of funds to maintain the firm's product design capability and the possibility of joint production of products in the future.

   b. The agreement should positively affect quality. The reason is that they will be obtaining expertise from BMW on technical design aspects. BMW undoubtedly has the resources to assemble a much more expansive engineering team. With the added business from Vickers, the continuance of a strong engineering capability at BMW will be assured. Further, Vickers will be able to concentrate the efforts of its remaining design team on the most critical design issues and leave the other design issues for BMW personnel.
   This move should improve Vickers' ability to control costs. The move will avoid some costs such as those associated with elimination of some internal departments concerned with product design. Costs should become more predictable as well. Vickers may be able to contract with BMW on a fixed cost basis for many recurring types of design services. Other contract work may be negotiated on a set fee basis.

57. a.   From a long-term cost management perspective, leaving
          China makes little sense. The potential in the Chinese
          market is enormous and the cost savings available from
          locating production facilities there are potentially
          large. It is difficult to defend Levi's move on a
          financial basis. However, it should be noted that
          currently China is not an important production site nor
          an important market; it is the future potential in
          China that is appealing.
              On a positive note, the move out of China may have
          favorably impacted Levi's reputation in the West.
          Accordingly, Levi's profits may actually rise in the
          short-term because of the favorable consumer response
          to the pull-out.
              From an ethical perspective, pulling out of China
          makes perfect sense. By discontinuing operations in
          China, Levi is signalling to the world that it has high
          regard for human rights, a concern that it places above
          the pursuit of profits. This move is likely to be
          supported by Levi's major suppliers and its work force
          as well. Still this is a rather remarkable move for a
          company that competes in an industry that is known for
          its human rights abuses, particularly its treatment of
          labor.

     b.   Most favored nation status is likely awarded to China
          because of political considerations. If China were to
          lose most favored nation status, many of the U.S. firms
          that have invested heavily in Chinese industries would
          likely incur large losses. Such firms pressure
          congress and the president to maintain the current
          trading status. Thus, the political considerations
          involve human rights on the one hand, and economic
          interests on the other. To date, the economic
          interests have prevailed in determining the U.S. trade
          policy with China.

     c.   Your reaction would depend on how you balance human
          rights issues against economic interests, and your
          perception of the magnitude of the issues. In the case
          of Levi Strauss, as opposed to certain other Western
          businesses, the current investment and dependence on
          the Chinese market was relatively trivial;
          consequently, it would be easy to support the move made
          by its management. Alternatively, one might feel
          differently as a stockholder if the Chinese market
          accounted for 35% of the firm's business.

Process Costing

Questions

1. Process costing is more likely (than job order costing) to be found in a production environment where: the products produced are homogeneous and have a low unit cost; production volume is high; and products are continuously produced (as opposed to production in small batches).

3. In this respect, process costing is very similar to job order costing. The principal document for tracking the cost of material is the material requisition form and the principal document for tracking the direct labor costs is the time sheet. For each department, the materials requisition forms identify the amount of each type of material used and the cost of each type of material. The time sheets identify the amount of labor, the hourly labor rate (for each individual), and the department that is to be charged for the labor.

5. The two methods are FIFO and weighted average. FIFO separately accounts for the costs of work performed on the beginning WIP inventory in the current period and work performed on the beginning WIP inventory in prior periods. Alternatively, the weighted average method does not distinguish between work performed on the current period's beginning inventory in prior periods from work performed on the beginning WIP inventory in the current period. This is the principal difference between the two methods and it affects the "average" unit cost.

7. The total costs are assigned to: 1) the goods that have been completed and transferred to the next down-stream department or to finished goods inventory, and 2) the goods that are not yet finished by the department and at the end of the period they are still in the departmental WIP. At the end of the period, the costs in 1) will appear in finished goods, cost of goods sold, or the WIP account of a down stream department; and the costs in 2) will appear as an asset in the departmental WIP.

9. BI + TP = EI + TO

11. No. If the products are at different stages of completion
     with regard to each cost pool, then a separate equivalent
     unit computation is necessary for each cost pool.

13. FIFO would assign a higher cost to the ending WIP. The
     logic is: under FIFO, the cost per EUP is based on only the
     current period's costs (which would, in an inflationary
     environment, be higher than the prior period's costs).
     Alternatively, weighted average would assign a cost to the
     ending WIP based on an average of the prior and current
     period's costs.

15. The firm would want to use FIFO. The reason is that FIFO
     isolates the current period's costs and activities relative
     to all other periods' costs and activities. Thus, better
     measures of cost control and activity level are generated.

17. The cost and computations resemble FIFO. The explanation is
     that standard costs rely on a period-by-period determination
     of departmental activity. This is consistent with the FIFO
     determination of equivalent units of activity.

19. Spoilage is an important cost of quality. As such it should
     be monitored so that a formal evaluation can be made of
     efforts to control spoilage costs. If costs are not
     specifically tracked, the costs of spoilage are merely
     averaged over the good units produced. In tracking spoilage
     costs, firms may want to distinguish between an expected
     amount of spoilage (normal spoilage) and unexpected spoilage
     (abnormal spoilage).

21. Suppliers contribute to quality control mostly by supplying
     nondefective, high quality materials and components.
     Additionally, suppliers may offer suggestions which
     effectively reduce the complexity of products or reduce the
     number and complexity of conversion processes so that
     quality is improved. Today, it is even possible that
     suppliers will participate in the management of material and
     component supplies and contribute regularly to research
     efforts on product and process design.

23. The journal entry would be the one that recognizes the
     transfer of goods from the most downstream department,
     Finishing, to finished goods inventory.

Exercises

25. a. Determine total units to account for:

Beginning inventory	16,000	gallons
Started this period	400,000	gallons
Total units	416,000	gallons

b. Determine equivalent units of production for materials:

Beginning inventory	16,000	gallons
Started & completed	388,000	gallons
Ending inventory	12,000	gallons
Equivalent units	416,000	gallons

c. Determine equivalent units for labor and overhead:

Beginning inventory	16,000	gallons
Started and completed	388,000	gallons
Ending inventory	7,200	gallons
Equivalent units	411,200	gallons

27. a.

	Total	DL
Beginning inventory	14,000	14,000
Started and completed	36,000	36,000
Ending inventory	10,000	6,000
EUP		56,000

b. Cost per EUP = ($2,000 + $12,000) ÷ 56,000 = $0.25

29. a.

	Total	Direct labor	Overhead
Beginning inventory	4,000	4,000	4,000
Started and completed	20,000	20,000	20,000
Ending inventory	10,000	6,000	7,500
Equivalent units		30,000	31,500

b.

Cost/EUP:	Direct labor	Overhead
Costs of beginning inventory	$ 2,000	$1,800
This period's costs	10,000	4,500
Total costs	$12,000	$6,300
Divide by EUP	30,000	31,500
Cost per EUP	$0.40	$0.20

c.

	Direct labor	Overhead
Costs transferred out:		
$0.40 * 24,000	$ 9,600	
$0.20 * 24,000		$4,800
Cost of the ending inventory:		
$0.40 * 6,000	2,400	
$0.20 * 7,500		1,500
Total costs assigned	$12,000	$6,300

31. a.
	WA
Beginning inventory	3,000,000 gals.
Started and completed	10,000,000 gals.
Units in ending inventory	1,500,000 gals.
EUP	14,500,000 gals.

Cost transferred out	$737,000
Cost of ending inventory ($0.05 * 1,500,000)	75,000
Total costs to account for	$812,000

Cost per EUP = $812,00 ÷ 14,500,000 = $.056

b. End WIP = $0.056 X 1,500,000 = $84,000

33. a.
Beginning inventory	$ 60,000
Current costs:	
DM	180,000
DL	40,000
OH	50,000
Total	330,000
Less the ending inventory	36,000
Costs transferred out	$294,000

b.
Beginning inventory	$200,000
Transferred-in costs	294,000
Current costs**	?
Total*	?
Less ending inventory	140,000
Costs transferred out	$400,000

* Total = $400,000 + $140,000 = $540,000.
** Current costs = $540,000 − ($200,000 + $294,000)
= $46,000

c. The packaging dept.:
Beginning inv.	$180,000
Costs transferred in	400,000
Current costs:	
DM	200,000
DL	400,000
OH	120,000
Total	$1,300,000
Less the ending inventory	220,000
Cost of goods manufactured	$1,080,000

Communication Activities

35. a. The variance will be due to natural irregularities in the "process." For example, some of the teeth on the bicycle gears may be worn or imperfect; some of the links on the chain may be worn or of imperfect tolerance. The effects of these irregularities would differ from trial to trial; especially, if the pedal is in a different position when each trial starts. Additionally, there may be some slippage of the tire on the ground surface that differs between the trials.

  b. The information constitutes a history of the natural variation that occurs within the process. This can be used as a statistical basis for evaluating future deviations in the process. For example, if the trials indicate that 15.1 to 16.2 revolutions of the pedals are required to move the bicycle 100 yards, managers would regard any future trial that falls outside of these bounds to be indicative of a problem in the process.

Products

37. a.   Total units to account for:
            Beginning inventory   20,000
            Units started   100,000
              Total   120,000

     b.   Total units   120,000
            Ending inventory   25,000
            Units completed   95,000
            Units in beginning WIP   (20,000)
            Units started and completed   75,000

     c.   Fifo Method: DM   CC
            Beginning inventory   16,000   10,000
            Started and completed   75,000   75,000
            Ending inventory   17,500   20,000
              EUP   108,500   105,000

     d.   Weighted average: DM   CC
            Completed and transferred   95,000   95,000
            Ending inventory   17,500   20,000
              EUP   112,500   115,000

     e.   DM   CC
            EUP FIFO   108,500   105,000
            Add EUP in Beginning WIP   4,000   10,000
            EUP weighted average   112,500   115,000

39. a.   Beginning inventory   12,000
            Units started this period   24,000
              Total units to account for   36,000

            Units to account for:
            Units in ending inventory   17,000
            Units transferred to FG inv.   19,000
              Total units accounted for   36,000

     b.   DM   CC
            Beginning inventory $ 9,500 $14,700
            Costs this period   35,600   73,080
              Total $45,100 $87,780

     c.   Beginning inventory   12,000   12,000
            Started and completed   7,000   7,000
            Ending inventory   17,000   6,800
              EUP   36,000   25,800

            Total costs $45,100 $87,780
            Divide by EUP   36,000   25,800

            Cost/EUP $1.25 $3.40

d.   Cost of finished goods:
     19,000 X ($1.25 + $3.40) = <u>$88,350</u>

Cost of ending inventory:
DM:	17,000 * $1.25 =	$21,250
Conversion:	6,800 * $3.40 =	23,120
Total		<u>$44,370</u>

41.   a. $1,600,000 ÷ $.20 = <u>8,000,000</u> pounds

b.   Cost of labor in the ending WIP=(500,000 * .40) * $0.20
                                  = <u>$40,000</u>

c. $108,000 + $1,600,000 - $40,000 = <u>$1,668,000</u>

43.   a.   Units to account for:
Beginning inventory	20
Units started	430
Total	<u>450</u>

Next, determine units accounted for:
Units transferred out	440
Units in ending inventory	10
Total	<u>450</u>

	Batter	Icing	Conversion
Beginning inventory	0	20	4
Started and completed	420	420	420
Ending inventory	10	10	9
EUP	<u>430</u>	<u>450</u>	<u>433</u>

b.
	Batter	Icing	Conversion
Total current costs	$1,324.40	$31.50	$857.34
Divide by EUP	430	450	433
Cost per EUP	$3.08	$0.07	$1.98

c. Costs to account for:
    Beginning inventory:

Batter	$60	
Conversion	32	$ 92.00

Costs this period:

Batter	$1,324.40	
Icing	31.50	
Conversion	857.34	2,213.24
Total		$2,305.24

Costs of the ending WIP inventory:

Batter	$3.08 X 10	$ 30.80
Icing	$0.07 X 10	0.70
Conversion	$1.98 X 9	17.82
Total		$ 49.32

Cost of cakes completed:

Total costs to account for	$2,305.24
Less cost assigned to the ending WIP	49.32
Cost of goods completed	$2,255.92

d. Assuming there was no beginning inventory of finished goods:

Sales:	$7.75 * 427	$3,309.25
CGS: ($2,255.92/440) X 427		2,189.23
Gross Margin		$1,120.02

45. a.

	DM	CC
Transferred out	40,000	40,000
Ending WIP	6,000	1,800
Total	46,000	41,800

b.

	DM	CC
Total costs	$250,700	$146,300
Divide by EUP	46,000	41,800
Cost per EUP	$5.45	$3.50

c.

Transferred out	40,000	40,000
Spoilage	3,000	3,000
Ending WIP	6,000	1,800
Total	49,000	44,800

Total costs	$250,700	$146,300
Divide by EUP	49,000	44,800
Cost per EUP	$5.12	$3.27
	rounded	rounded

d. 3,000 X ($5.12 + $3.27) = $25,170

e.   The method of neglect requires no assignment of cost to
spoiled units. Accordingly, the magnitude of the cost
of spoilage is never determined and managerial
attention is not focussed on spoilage.

47. a.   Total units to account for:
Beginning inventory   20,000
Started this period   80,000
   Total   100,000

Total units accounted for:
Transferred out   70,000
Ending inventory   30,000
   Total   100,000

Computation of EUP:

	Transferred in	CC	DM
Transferred out	70,000	70,000	70,000
Ending inventory	30,000	18,000	0
EUP	100,000	88,000	70,000

Costs to account for:

	Transferred in	CC	DM
Beginning WIP	$ 19,000	$ 600	$ 0
Costs this period	85,000	17,000	21,000
Total	$104,000	$17,600	$21,000
Divide by EUP	100,000	88,000	70,000
Cost/EUP	$1.04	$0.20	$0.30

b.   ($1.04 + $0.20 + $0.30) X 70,000 = $107,800

c.   Ending WIP cost:
Transferred in costs: $1.04 * 30,000 $31,200
Conversion: $0.20 * 18,000   3,600
         Total $34,800

d.   WIP-assembly   85,000
        WIP-Printing   85,000

WIP-assembly   17,000
   Wages payable & OH   17,000

WIP-assembly   21,000
   Raw materials inventory   17,000

Finished goods inventory   107,800
   WIP-assembly   107,800

Cases
49. a.   Total units to account for
          Beginning inventory   4,000
          Units started   22,000
          Total   26,000

          Total units accounted for:
          Transferred out   21,000
          Ending inventory   5,000
          Total   26,000

          EUP computation (FIFO):

	Material	**Conversion**
Beginning inventory	400	1,000
Started and completed	17,000	17,000
Ending inventory	3,000	2,000
EUP	20,400	20,000

          EUP computation (weighted average):

	Material	**Conversion**
Completed and transferred	21,000	21,000
Ending inventory	3,000	2,000
EUP	24,000	23,000

b.

Production data	Whole units	Equivalent units of production Weighted average	
		Material	Conversion
BI	4,000	3,600	3,000
Units started	22,000		
To account for	26,000		
BI completed	4,000	400	1,000
S&C	17,000	17,000	17,000
Ending WIP	5,000	3,000	2,000
Accounted for	26,000	24,000	23,000

Cost data	Total	Material	Conversion
BI cost	$113,200	$ 82,200	$ 31,000
Current costs	642,800	397,800	245,000
To acct. for	$756,000	$480,000	$276,000
Divide by EUP		24,000	23,000
Cost per EUP	$32	$20	$12

Cost assignment
Transferred out: $32 X 21,000 = $672,000
Ending inventory:
   Material $20 X 3,000 = $60,000
   Conversion $12 X 2,000   24,000   84,000
            Total costs accounted for $756,000

Production data	Whole units	Equivalent units of production FIFO	
		Material	Conversion
BI	4,000	3,600	3,000
Units started	22,000		
To account for	26,000		
BI completed	4,000	400	1,000
S&C	17,000	17,000	17,000
Ending WIP	5,000	3,000	2,000
Accounted for	26,000	20,400	20,000

Cost data	Total	Material	Conversion
BI cost	$113,200		
Current costs	642,800	$397,800	$245,000
To acct. for	$756,000		
Divide by EUP		20,400	20,000
Cost/EUP	$31.75	$19.50	$12.25

Cost assignment

```
Transferred out:
     Beginning inventory costs           $113,200
     Costs this period:
          Material   $19.50 X    400        7,800
          Conversion $12.25 X  1,000       12,250   $133,250
     Started & completed (17,000 X $31.75)           539,750
Ending inventory
          Material   $19.50 X  3,000    $ 58,500
          Conversion $12.25 X  2,000      24,500      83,000
     Total costs accounted for                      $756,000
```

c. The major difference is the way the beginning inventory
    is treated. Under FIFO, the costs and work performed
    on the beginning inventory are distinguished from the
    costs and work performed in the current period. Thus,
    for managerial control purposes, FIFO is more
    informative because it is not confounded by activities
    and costs from a prior period.

51. a. First, determine the OH cost in the Molding Dept.:
        OH = DL * .70
           = $80,000 * .70 = $56,000

```
        Beginning WIP, Molding              $ 50,000
        Add current costs:
             DM                                80,000
             DL                                80,000
             OH                                56,000
             Total                           $266,000
        Deduct ending WIP                      25,000
        Cost transferred                     $241,000
```

   b. Beg. WIP + Current costs - End WIP = Costs transferred
       $80,000 +($241,000+$40,000+DL+OH)-$50,000 = $320,000
       DL + OH = $9,000
       DL + .70DL = $9,000
       DL = $5,294 (rounded)
       OH = $3,706

   c. Again, OH = .70DL
                 = .70 * $20,000
                 = $14,000
       Beg. WIP + Current costs - End WIP = Costs transferred
       $120,000+($320,000+DM+$20,000+$14,000)-$90,000=$450,000
       DM = $66,000

d. WIP Vulcanizing   241,000
        WIP Molding   241,000

    WIP Packaging   320,000
        WIP Vulcanizing   320,000

    Finished goods   450,000
        WIP packaging   450,000

53. a. 1. The equivalent units for each cost element using
             the weighted average method:

	Direct Materials		
	Chemicals	Cans	Conversion
Units completed and transferred to Shipping	20,000	20,000	20,000
Work-in-Process at 5/31			
Chemicals (100%)	5,000		
Cans (0%)		0	
Conversion costs (80%)			4,000
Equivalent units	<u>25,000</u>	<u>20,000</u>	<u>24,000</u>

2. The equivalent units for each cost element, using
    the FIFO method:

	Direct Materials		
	Chemicals	Cans	Conversion
Transferred to Shipping from 5/1 work-in-process (4,000 @ 25%)			
Chemicals (0%)	0		
Cans (100%)		4,000	
Conversion costs (75%)			3,000
Current production transferred to Shipping (100%)	16,000	16,000	16,000
Work in process at 5/31			
Chemicals (100%)	5,000		
Cans (0%)		0	
Conversion costs (80%)			4,000
Equivalent units	<u>21,000</u>	<u>20,000</u>	<u>23,000</u>

b. 1. The cost per equivalent unit for each cost
        element, using the weighted average method, is
        presented below.

	Direct Materials		
	Chemicals	Cans	Conversion
Work-in-Process at 5/31	$ 45,600	$ 0	$ 8,125
May costs added	228,400	7,000	45,500
Total costs	$274,000	$7,000	$53,625
Divided by WA EUP	25,000	20,000	24,000
Cost per equivalent unit	$ 10.96	$ .35	$ 2.23

*   Conversion cost = Direct labor + Factory overhead

    2. The cost per equivalent unit for each cost
        element, using the FIFO method:

	Direct Materials		
	Chemicals	Cans	Conversion
May costs incurred	$228,400	$7,000	$45,500
Divided by FIFO EUP	21,000	20,000	23,000
Costs per equivalent unit	$10.88	$ .35	$ 1.98

c. The weighted average method is generally easier to use
    as the calculations are simpler. This method tends to
    obscure current period costs as the cost per equivalent
    unit includes both current costs and prior costs that
    were in the beginning inventory. This method is most
    appropriate when conversion costs, inventory levels,
    and raw material prices are stable.

    The FIFO method is based on the work done in the
    current period only. This method is most appropriate
    when conversion costs, inventory levels, or raw
    material prices fluctuate. This method should also be
    used when accuracy in current equivalent unit costs is
    important or when a standard cost system is used.

(CMA)

Ethics and Quality Discussions
55. a. A significant purpose of establishing the Saturn
Division was to develop a product and production
process that was not constrained by existing GM
practices or organizational structures. The division
was to be free standing and organized in consistency
with its objective of producing the highest quality
product using the most modern manufacturing methods.
Also, by establishing Saturn as an independent
division, GM could be certain that the Saturn line
would get all necessary funding to achieve its
objectives.

b. The integration of Saturn into the GM Small Car
Division is an important step for GM. Saturn has not
been a profitable division, but it has the potential to
provide other GM operations with a wealth of
information on methods to improve quality and
efficiency. By integrating the division back into the
company, GM is seeking to get an additional financial
return on its huge investment in Saturn by transferring
information from Saturn to other product lines in the
Small Car Division.

c. The likely impact on other products is improvement in
quality. The extent to which other product lines
benefit from the knowledge gained in the Saturn
Division will depend on how well the Small Car Division
is organized for information transfer. Also, the
division will need to have a culture that accepts
change in order to fully benefit from the information.

d. This is the risky part for GM. The danger is that
Saturn will become more like GM's other product lines
as opposed to the other product lines becoming more
like Saturn. The danger is that the Saturn line will
lose its culture of innovation and quality.
Alternatively, the culture that created the Saturn line
may be preserved and the balance of the Small Car
Division product lines may be integrated into the
culture.

57.   a.   George Wilson's considerations are determined largely
            by his position as a cost accountant, with
            responsibilities to FulRange Inc., others in the
            company, and himself. Wilson's job involves collecting,
            analyzing, and reporting operating information.
            Although not responsible for product quality, Wilson
            should exercise initiative and good judgment in
            providing management with information having potential
            adverse economic impact.
                 Wilson should determine whether the controller's
            request violates his professional or personal
            standards, or the company's code of ethics, if FulRange
            has such a code. As Wilson decided how to proceed, he
            should protect proprietary information he has and
            should not violate the chain of command by discussing
            this matter with the controller's superiors.

      b.   1.   The controller has reporting responsibilities and
                  should protect the overall company interests by
                  encouraging further study of the problem by those
                  in his department, by informing his superiors in
                  this matter, and by working with others in the
                  company to find solutions.

            2.   The quality control engineer has responsibilities
                  for product quality and should protect the overall
                  company interests by continuing to study the
                  quality of reworked rejects, informing the plant
                  manager and his staff in this matter, and working
                  with others in the company to find solutions.

            3.   The plant manager and his staff have
                  responsibilities for product quality and cost and
                  should protect the overall company interests by
                  exercising the stewardship expected of them.
                  Plant management should be sure that products meet
                  the quality standards. Absentee owners need
                  information from management, and the plant manger
                  and his staff have a responsibility to inform the
                  board of directors elected by the owners of any
                  problems that could affect the well-being of
                  FulRange.

c.   George Wilson needs to protect the interests of
     FulRange, others in the company, and himself. Wilson
     is vulnerable if he conceals the problem and it
     eventually surfaces. Wilson must take some action to
     reduce his vulnerability. One possible action that
     Wilson could take would be to obey the controller and
     prepare the advance material for the· board without
     mentioning or highlighting the probable failure of
     reworks. Because this differs from his long-standing
     practice of highlighting information with potential
     adverse economic impact, Wilson should write a report
     to the controller detailing the probable failure of
     reworks, the analysis made by himself and the quality
     control engineer, and the controller's instructions in
     this matter.

(CMA)

8 Variable Costing and Cost-Volume Profit Analysis

Questions

1. Absorption and variable costing each recognize the following as product costs: direct materials, direct labor, and variable factory overhead. Additionally, absorption costing recognizes fixed factory overhead as a product cost.

3. Variable costing classifies costs by behavior. Although absorption costing always classifies costs by function, it is possible to classify costs by function under variable costing as well.

5. Absorption costing recognizes fixed factory overhead as a product cost. Accordingly, under absorption costing, fixed overhead flows through the inventory accounts and is eventually expensed through the cost of goods sold. Alternatively, variable costing treats fixed factory overhead as a period cost and it is deducted in its entirety in the period in which it is incurred.

7. Absorption costing is required by the FASB and the SEC. The FASB and SEC are interested in the welfare of external financial statement users. These two bodies adopt the view that fixed factory overhead is a necessary expense to maintain production activity. Therefore, in the interest of the matching principle (matching a cost to its benefit), it should be treated as a product cost.

9. No. Differences between the gross margin and contribution margin are numerous and they are driven by more factors than a difference in production and sales volume. However, under the circumstance where sales and product volume are equal, net income under the two methods may be equal.

11. The relationship between net income under absorption costing and net income under variable costing is dependent on whether production volume exceeds sales volume or vice versa. If production volume exceeds sales volume, absorption costing will generate a higher net income. If sales volume exceeds production volume (inventory is drawn down), variable costing net income will exceed absorption costing net income.

13. The contribution margin fluctuates in direct proportion with sales volume, because the two elements used in its computation (selling price and variable cost) are both variable, and, thus, in total fluctuate directly with sales volume.

15. Contribution margin will decrease and breakeven point will increase.

17. Incremental analysis involves projections of cost revenues or profits from some reference point. For example, a typical reference point would be the existing sales volume or the breakeven point. Incremental analysis involves analyzing only those factors that change relative to their levels at the reference point.

19. The assumptions made in CVP analysis are linearity, no changes in inventory levels and no inflation. These assumptions all have a tendency to reduce the model's realism. As realism is reduced, so is the ability of the model to predict actual results. The quantities then, indicated by CVP analysis should be taken "as approximately correct" and not be considered as absolutes.

21. The company president should be concerned. A low margin of safety and a high degree of operating leverage means that the company is operating very close to the breakeven point. Therefore, a slight reduction in volume could possibly produce losses for the company.

23. CVP renders a short-run perspective because the assumptions which underlie CVP are true only in the short run. The implications of this are that managers should expect the results from CVP analysis to hold only temporarily and should also integrate longer run considerations into their problem-solving analyses for a balanced perspective.

Exercises

25. a.   ($400,000 + $300,000 + $150,000) ÷ 100,000 = $8.50

     b.   ($400,000 + $300,000 + $150,000 + $250,000) ÷ 100,000
          = $11.00

27. a.   ($0.12 - $0.04) X 4,000,000 = $320,000

     b. $0.08 X (4,200,000 - 4,000,000) = $16,000

     c.   Production volume variance $16,000
               Cost of goods sold $16,000

29. a.   Total CGS ($109,250 - $54,625) $54,625
          Variable product cost (9,500 X $3.50)   33,250
          Fixed production costs in CGS $21,375
          Fixed production cost per unit: $21,375÷9,500 =
          $2.25
          Total production = $22,500÷$2.25 = 10,000 units

     b.   Sales $109,250
          Cost of goods sold ($109,250 - $54,625)   54,625
          Gross margin $ 54,625
          Selling & administration costs   38,000
          Income before taxes $ 16,625

31. a.
Sales $4,000,000
Less variable CGS:
 Beginning FG $ 0
 CGM:
 (($2,000,000÷1,000,000)X1,250,000-$400,000) 2,100,000
 Goods available for sale $2,100,000
 Less ending FG   420,000   1,680,000
Product contribution margin $2,320,000
Less variable S&A expenses   1,000,000
Total contribution margin $1,320,000
Less fixed costs:
     Production $400,000
     S&A ($1,500,000 -$1,000,000)   500,000   900,000
Net income $ 420,000

     b.   Net income, variable costing $ 420,000
          Add back fixed OH inventoried under
           absorption costing:
               $400,000 X (250,000÷1,250,000)   80,000
               Net income, absorption costing $ 500,000

33. BEP in units = $400,000 ÷ ($30 - $22) = 50,000 units

Chapter 8
Absorption and Variable Costing

35. a. BEP = $16,200 ÷ ($8.00 - $2.60)
       = $16,200 ÷ $5.40 = <u>3,000</u> books

    Income before taxes = (Volume X CM) - FC
    = [(3,200 X $5.40) - $16,200] = <u>$1,080</u>

    b. BEP = $18,900 ÷ $5.40 = 3,500 books
       Income before taxes = [(4,200 X $5.40) - $18,900]
                           = <u>$3,780</u>

37. a. Income before taxes:
       Firm A: [400,000 X($16 - $11)]-$2,500,000 = <u>$(500,000)</u>
       Firm B: [400,000 X($16 - $14)]-$500,000 = <u>$300,000</u>
       In this case Firm B is preferred.

    b. Income before taxes:
       Firm A: [600,000 X($16 - $11)]-$2,500,000 = <u>$500,000</u>
       Firm B: [600,000 X($16 - $14)]-$500,000 = <u>$700,000</u>
       In this case Firm B is preferred.

    c. Income before taxes:
       Firm A: [800,000 X($16 - $11)]-$2,500,000 = <u>$1,500,000</u>
       Firm B: [800,000 X($16 - $14)]-$500,000 = <u>$1,100,000</u>
       In this case Firm A is preferred.

39. a. Units sales = ($80,000 + $40,000) ÷ $5 = <u>24,000</u> units
       24,000 X $8 = <u>$192,000</u>

    b. Income before taxes = $25,000 ÷ .6 = $41,667
       Unit sales = ($41,667 + $40,000) ÷ $4 = <u>20,417</u> units
       20,417 X ($6 + $4) = <u>$204,170</u>

    c. Income before taxes = $54,000 ÷ .6 = $90,000
       Unit sales = ($90,000 + $60,000) ÷ ($10 X .3)
                  = <u>50,000</u> units
       50,000 X $10 = <u>$500,000</u>

    d. Income before taxes = $30,000 ÷ .50 = $60,000
       Unit sales = ($60,000 + $60,000) ÷ $3 = <u>40,000</u>
       40,000 X ($3 ÷ (1 - .7) = <u>$400,000</u>

    e. Income before taxes = $40,000 ÷ .5 = $80,000
       Unit sales = ($80,000 + $25,000) ÷ (.25 X ($9 ÷ .75))
                  = <u>35,000</u> units
       35,000 X ($9 ÷ .75) = <u>$420,000</u>

41. a. BEP in hours: $2,800 ÷ ($100 - $20) = <u>35</u> hours

b. Before tax equivalent of $8,000 after-tax:
$8,000 ÷ (1 - .20) = $10,000

Required hours = ($10,000 + $2,800) ÷ $80 = <u>160</u> hours

c. Twenty-four client hours weekly will not accumulate the necessary 160 hours monthly; only 96 hours will be accumulated. Consequently, he will be 64 client hours short of achieving his income goal.

43. a.

	Compact	Standard	"Bag"
Sales	$2,000	$3,500	$9,000
Variable costs	1,800	3,000	7,800
CM	$ 200	$ 500	$1,200

BEP = $360,000,000 ÷ $1,200 = 300,000 "bags"
Compact cars = 300,000 X 1 = <u>300,000</u>
Standard cars = 300,000 X 2 = <u>600,000</u>

b.

	Compact	Standard	"Bag"
Sales	$2,000	$3,500	$5,500
Variable costs	1,800	3,000	4,800
CM	$ 200	$ 500	$ 700

BEP = $360,000,000 ÷ $700 = 514,286 "bags" (rounded)
Compact cars = 514,286 X 1 = <u>514,286</u>
Standard cars = 514,286 X 1 = <u>514,286</u>

In part a., only 900,000 total cars had to be sold to break even. In part b. a total of 1,028,572 cars must be sold to break even. The difference is caused by a shift in the sales mix requiring more of the lower (per unit) profit cars to be sold relative to the higher profit cars.

c.

	Compact	Standard	"Bag"
Sales	$2,000	$3,500	$13,000
Variable costs	1,800	3,000	11,400
CM	$ 200	$ 500	$ 1,600

BEP = $425,000,000 ÷ 1,600 = 265,625 bags
Compact cars = 265,625 X 3 = <u>796,875</u>
Standard cars = 265,625 X 2 = <u>531,250</u>

45. a.   Total cost, manual line = (100,000 X $7) + $150,000
                                   = $850,000
           Total cost, automated line = (100,000 X $3) + $630,000
                                      = $930,000
           The manual line would be most cost effective.

           Manual line, BEP = $150,000 ÷ $3 = 50,000 units
           Automated line, BEP = $630,000 ÷ $7 = 90,000 units

           MOS, manual line = (100,000 - 50,000) X $10 = $500,000
           MOS, automated line =(100,000 - 90,000)X $10 = $100,000

     b.   Total cost, manual line = (120,000 X $7) + $150,000
                                   = $990,000
           Total cost, automated line = (120,000 X $3) + $630,000
                                      = $990,000
           One would be indifferent between the two lines

     c.   Total cost, manual line = (150,000 X $7) + $150,000
                                   = $1,200,000
           Total cost, automated line = (150,000 X $3) + $630,000
                                      = $1,080,000
           Yes, now the automated line would be preferred.

     d.   Income before taxes = $60,000 ÷ (1 - .4) = $100,000

           Manual line:
           Total sales =($7 X 100,000) + $150,000 + $100,000
                       = $950,000
           Unit sales price = $950,000 ÷ 100,000 = $9.50

           Automated line:
           Total sales = ($3 X 100,000) + $630,000) + $100,000
                       = $1,030,000
           Unit sales price = $10.30

47. a.   FC = $400 + $50 + $25 + $25 + $100 + $150 = $750
           CM = $10 - ($2 + $.50) = $7.50
           BEP = $750 ÷ $7.50 = <u>100</u> visits; 100 X $10 = <u>$1,000</u>

     b.   Sales - .25Sales - $750 = .25Sales
           .5Sales = $750
           Sales = $1,500
           $1,500 ÷ $10 = <u>150</u> visits

     c.   Sales   (140 X $10) $1,400
           VC (140 X $2.5)   350
           CM $1,050
           FC   750
           Income before taxes $ 300

           DOL = $1,050 ÷ $300 = <u>3.5</u>

     d. $300 X .20 X 3.5 = <u>$210</u> increase

           Proof:
           Sales   (140 X $10) X 1.20 $1,680
           VC (140 X $2.5) X 1.20   420
           CM $1,260
           FC   750
           Income before taxes $ 510

49. a.

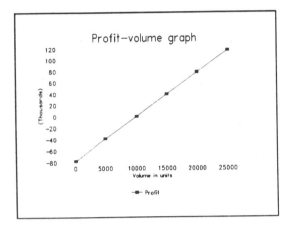

b.

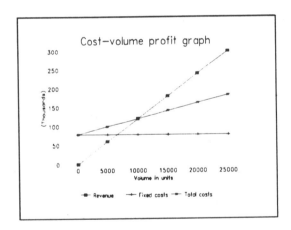

Communication Activities

51. a.   Assuming that a similar amount of total revenue is required to operate each boat, and based on per passenger revenue alone, it would appear that the *Player* is pursuing a strategy of low volume, high price. The *Queen of New Orleans* is pursuing a strategy of high volume, low price. The *Star* is pursuing a strategy of moderate volume and moderate price.

b.   Significant costs would include:

depreciation on the boat	fixed
bar drinks and food	variable
operating costs of the boat	fixed (mostly)
wages of dealers	variable
machine maintenance and repair	mixed
gaming taxes	variable
docking fees for the boat	fixed

c.   The more costs are fixed, the more the cost structure favors high volume. The more the cost structure is comprised of variable costs, the more viable is a strategy of low volume, high price. However, it is not clear that the cost structure of this industry would automatically make one strategy superior to another. The costs listed appear to be balanced between fixed and variable costs.

Chapter 8
Absorption and Variable Costing

53. a. For a large auto maker, setting the sales mix so that breakeven analysis could be conducted would be relatively difficult. Another difficulty would be distinguishing between variable and fixed costs. Some costs are difficult to classify. Another problem is that in the real world neither revenue nor costs are likely to be strictly a linear function of sales volume. Accordingly, knowledge or assumptions about the nature of nonlinearities in the cost and revenue structures would be required. Another big variable would be "where" units would be sold. Domestic sales relative to international sales may have entirely different consequences for costs and revenues. Further, the president would be required to make assumptions about short-term pricing behavior; this may be extraordinarily difficult because it might require knowledge of competitors' actions. Much short-term pricing may simply be reactive based on actions of other automakers.

    Another point is that the president may think of breakeven as more of a long-run concept that relates more to individual product lines (rather than the entire company at a specific point in time) in a life-cycle concept. This would be logical because of the huge up-front costs associated with launching a new vehicle.

  b. The congressional investigator may have been basing his statement on the fact that knowing the breakeven point is crucial management information. Because this president indicated he had no exact notion about the breakeven point, the congressional investigator may have concluded that the president was an ineffective manager. However, it is likely that the investigator possesses little knowledge about the complexity of the automotive industry. If he understood some of the complicating factors mentioned in a, he would likely have a different opinion of the president.

Problems

55. **Absorption costing**

	Year 1	Year 2	Year 3	Year 4
Sales	$3,300,000	$4,510,000	$4,620,000	$4,950,000
CGS				
BI	0	456,000	380,000	380,000
CGM	2,736,000	3,040,000	3,192,000	3,040,000
Available	$2,736,000	$3,496,000	$3,572,000	$3,420,000
EI	456,000	380,000	380,000	0
	$2,280,000	$3,116,000	$3,192,000	$3,420,000
VV	20,000	0	(10,000)	0
CGS adj.	$2,300,000	$3,116,000	$3,182,000	$3,420,000
GM	$1,000,000	$1,394,000	$1,438,000	$1,530,000
Op Exp.	380,000	446,000	452,000	470,000
NIBT	$ 620,000	$ 948,000	$ 986,000	$1,060,000

Variable costing

	Year 1	Year 2	Year 3	Year 4
Sales	$3,300,000	$4,510,000	$4,620,000	$4,950,000
CGS				
BI	0	426,000	355,000	355,000
CGM	2,556,000	2,840,000	2,982,000	2,840,000
Available	$2,556,000	$3,266,000	$3,337,000	$3,195,000
EI	426,000	355,000	355,000	0
	$2,130,000	$2,911,000	$2,982,000	$3,195,000
Product CM	$1,170,000	$1,599,000	$1,638,000	$1,755,000
Var. Sell.	180,000	246,000	252,000	270,000
Total CM	$ 990,000	$1,353,000	$1,386,000	$1,485,000
FC	400,000	400,000	400,000	400,000
NIBT	$ 590,000	$ 953,000	$ 986,000	$1,085,000

57. a.   Sales ($40 x 7,000) $280,000

        CGS:

Beg FG	$ 0	
CGM: $50,000 + ($12 X 10,000)	170,000	
Goods available	$170,000	
Less ending inventory	51,000	119,000
Gross margin		$161,000
Less period costs: $30,000 + ($5 X 7,000)		65,000
Income before taxes		$ 96,000

        b.

Sales		$280,000
Variable CGS ($12 X 7,000)		84,000
Product contribution margin		$196,000
Variable period costs ($5 X 7,000)		35,000
Total contribution margin		$161,000
Less fixed costs:		
Production	$50,000	
Period	30,000	80,000
Income before taxes		$ 81,000

  c.   Income before taxes, absorption $96,000
        Less OH in inventory ($3,000 X $5)   15,000
        Income before taxes, variable $81,000

59. Year 1:
    Fixed OH rate = $50,000 ÷ 5,000 = $10 per unit
    OH put in inventory = $10 X (5,000 - 4,000) = $10,000
    VC income = $80,000 - $10,000 = $70,000

    Year 2:
    Fixed OH rate = $54,000 ÷ 6,000 = $9
    OH in units placed in inventory = 2,000 X $9 = $18,000
    OH in units taken from inventory = 1,000 X $10 = 10,000
    Net addition to inventory $ 8,000
    VC income = $110,000 - $8,000 = $102,000

    Year 3:
    Fixed overhead rate = $70,000 ÷ 7,000 = $10
    OH in units placed in inventory = $10 X 2,000 = $20,000
    OH in units taken from inventory = $9 X 2,000 = 18,000
    Net addition to inventory $ 2,000
    VC income = $200,000 - $2,000 = $198,000

61. a.   Sales price = product CM + DM + DL + Variable OH
             = $8 + $3 + $5 + $2
             = $18

    b.   Total contribution margin = $200,000+$200,000+$350,000
                            = $750,000

        Unit total contribution margin = $18-($3+$5+$2+$2)= $6
        Units sold = $750,000 ÷ $6 = 125,000 units

        Total sales = $18 X 125,000 = $2,250,000

    c.   Units sold = 125,000

    d.   Sales   (125,000 X $18) $2,250,000
        Variable CGS ($10 X 125,000)   1,250,000
        Product contribution margin $1,000,000
        Variable S&A expenses ($2 X 125,000)   250,000
        Total contribution margin $ 750,000
        Less fixed expenses:
            Factory overhead $200,000
            S&A   350,000   550,000
        Net income $ 200,000

63. a.

Absorption costing	1996	1997
Sales ($10 X 5,000)	$50,000	$50,000
CGS		
BI	$ 0	$ 7,500
CGM	22,500	7,500
Goods available	$22,500	$15,000
Ending inventory	7,500	0
	$15,000	$15,000
Volume variance	(7,500)	7,500
Adjusted CGS	$ 7,500	$22,500
Gross margin	$42,500	$27,500
Selling and administration	5,000	5,000
Income before taxes	$37,500	$22,500
Variable costing	1996	1997
Sales ($10 X 5,000)	$50,000	$50,000
VCGS		
BI	$ 0	$ 0
CGM	0	0
Goods available	$ 0	$ 0
Ending inventory	0	0
	$ 0	$ 0
Product Contribution margin	$50,000	$50,000
Other variable costs	0	0
Total Contribution margin	$50,000	$50,000
Fixed costs	20,000	20,000
Income before taxes	$30,000	$30,000

b.
Absorption costing	1996	1997
Beginning inventory	$ 0	$ 7,500
Ending inventory	7,500	0

Variable costing: all inventories = $0

c. BEP = ($15,000 + $5,000) ÷ $10 = 2,000 units; $20,000

d. The cost structures are completely opposite. The Cowboy Log Company has an entirely variable cost. There is virtually no risk with this cost structure because if volume is low or nonexistent, costs will be correspondingly small; hence, no losses can occur. Alternatively, the Weird Company has only fixed costs. This is a more risky cost structure because if volume falls, no costs will fall proportionately. All costs will be incurred regardless of volume. This is a desirable cost structure if one is expecting to operate at a high volume. The advantage of the cost structure is that the marginal cost is $0. Consequently, once fixed costs are covered, all revenue flows directly to the bottom line. Alternatively, an all variable cost structure is favored in economically difficult times. Even if volumes get very low, the company is assured of operating in the black.

65. a.
	Compact	Standard	Luxury	"Bag"
Sales	$2,200	$3,700	$6,000	$ 37,100
Variable costs	1,900	3,000	5,000	30,700
CM	$ 300	$ 700	$1,000	$ 6,400

BEP = $1,080,000,000 ÷ $6,400 = 168,750 "bags"
Compact cars = 168,750 X 3 = 506,250
Standard cars = 168,750 X 5 = 843,750
Luxury cars = 168,750 X 2 = 337,500

b. Unit volume (bags)
    = (($1,000,000,000 ÷ .5) + $1,080,000,000) ÷ $6,400
    = 481,250 bags
Compact cars = 481,250 X 3 = 1,443,750
Standard cars = 481,250 X 5 = 2,406,250
Luxury cars = 481,250 X 2 = 962,500

c.
	Compact	Standard	Luxury	"Bag"
Sales	$2,200	$3,700	$6,000	$ 31,800
Variable costs	1,900	3,000	5,000	26,500
CM	$ 300	$ 700	$1,000	$ 5,300

Unit volume (bags)
    = (($1,000,000,000 ÷ .5) + $1,080,000,000) ÷ $5,300
    = 581,132 bags
Compact cars = 581,132 X 5 = 2,905,660
Standard cars = 581,132 X 4 = 2,324,528
Luxury cars = 581,132 X 1 = 581,132

d. On a unit-for-unit basis, luxury cars generate more
    contribution margin than the other models.
    Accordingly, as the mix shifts to more luxury cars, the
    BEP (in units) will drop and the number of cars to be
    sold to reach a specified income goal will drop.

67. a.
Total revenue per set	$24
Total variable cost per set	12
Contribution margin per set	$12

CM% for a set ($12 ÷ $24)   50%

b. BEP = $12,000 ÷ .50 = $24,000
    $24,000 ÷ $24 = 1,000 sets
    Hens = 1,000 X 1 =   1,000
    Ducklings = 1,000 X 2 = 2,000

Hens dollar sales = 1,000 X $12 =		$12,000
Ducklings dollar sales = 2,000 X $6 =		12,000
Total		$24,000

c. Revenue = ($12,000 + $24,000) ÷ .50 = $72,000
$72,000 ÷ $24 = 3,000 sets
Hens = 3,000 X 1 = 3,000
Ducklings = 3,000 X 2 = 6,000

d. Total revenue per set $42
Total variable cost per set   24
Contribution margin per set $18

CM% for a set ($18 ÷ $42) = .4286

Income before tax = $9,000 ÷ (1 - .40) = $15,000

Revenue = ($15,000 + $12,000) ÷ .4286 = $63,000
(rounded)

$63,000 ÷ $42 = 1,500 sets
Hens = 1,500 X 1 = 1,500
Ducklings = 1,500 X 5 = 7,500

69. a. $CM = $400 - ($90 + $100 + $20 + $30 + $10) = $150
CM% = $150 ÷ $400 = 37.5%

BEP in units   = ($660,000 + $190,000 + $300,000) ÷ $150
= $1,150,000 ÷ $150 = 7,667
BEP in dollars = $1,150,000 ÷ .375
= $3,066,667

b. MOS = 14,400 - 7,667 = 6,733 units
MOS = $5,760,000 - $3,066,667 = $2,693,333
MOS = 6,733 ÷ 14,400 = 46.75%

c. First compute base-case profits
(CM - FC) = ($14,400 X $150) - $1,150,000 = $1,010,000

1. New price = $400 - $40 = $360; New $CM = $110
New volume = 1.15 X 14,400 = 16,560
New total CM = 16,560 X $110 = $1,821,600
Less fixed costs   1,150,000
New profit $ 671,600
This is less than the original profit so the
president should reject this alternative.

BEP = $1,150,000 ÷ .3056 = $3,763,089

2. New VC = $250 + $30 = $280; New $CM = $120
New volume = 1.20 X 14,400 = 17,280
New total CM = 17,280 X $120 = $2,073,600
Less fixed costs   1,150,000
New profit $ 923,600
This is less than the original profit so the
president should reject this alternative.
BEP = $1,150,000 ÷ .30 = $3,833,333

3.   CM per unit remains unchanged at $150
      New volume = 1.20 X 14,400 =17,280
      New total CM = 17,280 X $150 = $2,592,000
      Less fixed costs   1,175,000
      New profit $1,417,000
      This new profit exceeds the original profit of
      $1,010,000 by $407,000 and this proposal should be
      accepted assuming that the assessments are
      reasonable and other considerations such as
      capacity constraints are not violated.
      BEP = $1,175,000 ÷ .375 = $3,133,333

71. a.

	VPI		Tech	
	1996	1997	1996	1997
Profit before taxes	$20,000	$ 38,000	$20,000	$48,000
Tax expenses	8,000	15,200	8,000	19,200
Fixed costs	10,000	10,000	50,000	50,000
Variable costs	70,000	112,000	30,000	42,000
Total CM	30,000	48,000	70,000	98,000
CM ratio	.30	.30	.70	.70

BEP = Fixed costs ÷ CM ratio
VPI-breakeven = $10,000 ÷ .300 = $33,333
Tech-breakeven = $50,000 ÷ .70 = $71,429

b.   CM $30,000 $ 48,000 $70,000 $98,000
     Divide by PBT $20,000 $ 38,000 $20,000 $48,000

     DOL =   1.5   1.26   3.5   2.04

c.   Desired profit after-tax = $200,000 X .12= $24,000
     Profit before tax = $24,000 ÷ .60 = $40,000
     VPI: (Sales X .30) - $10,000 = $40,000
              Sales X .30 = $50,000
              Sales = $166,667

     Tech: (Sales X .70) - $50,000 = $40,000
              Sales X .70 = $90,000
              Sales = $128,572

d.   VPI's cost structure consists of a greater proportion
     of variable costs and a smaller proportion of fixed
     costs than Tech. In a slow market, or at low volume
     levels, this cost structure will generate larger
     profits or smaller losses than Tech's cost structure.
     Proof of this is found in comparing the two firm's
     breakeven points. Alternatively, Tech's cost structure
     is favored when volume turns up because less of each
     dollar goes to cover variable costs. The value of this
     cost structure is demonstrated in the answers to part
     c. Thus, the cost structure of VPI is less risky; but
     the cost structure of Tech offers more upside
     potential.

e.   The following graphs are based on profit before taxes.

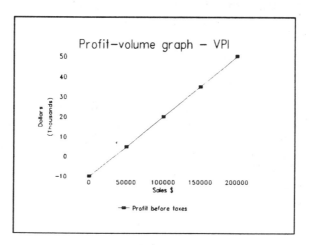

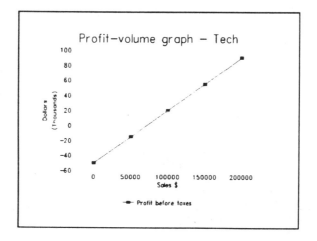

Chapter 8
Absorption and Variable Costing

Cases

73. a.

Daniels Tool & Die Corporation
Income Statement (Variable)
For the Year Ended December 31, 1997

Sales		$1,015,000
Variable Cost of Goods Sold		
Finished goods, 1/1/97	$ 16,950	
Work in process, 1/1/97	46,400	
Manufacturing costs incurred	650,600	
Total costs available	$713,950	
Work in process, 12/31/97	(61,900)	
Finished goods, 12/31/97	(13,180)	638,870
Product Contribution Margin		$ 376,130
Variable Selling Expenses		50,750
Contribution Margin		$ 325,380
Fixed Expenses		
Factory overhead	$ 37,400	
Selling	44,250	
Administrative	75,000	156,650
Operating Income		$ 168,730

Supporting calculations

Variable finished goods inventory at 1/1/97:	
Absorption finished goods inventory	$18,000
Less fixed overhead (1,050 hours X $1)	1,050
Variable finished goods inventory	$16,950

Variable work in process inventory at 1/1/97:	
Absorption work in process inventory	$48,000
Less fixed overhead (1,600 hours X $1)	1,600
Variable work in process	$46,400

Variable manufacturing costs incurred during 1997:	
Direct materials	$370,000
Direct labor (23,000 hours X $6)	138,000
Variable overhead (23,000 hours X $6.20)	142,600
Variable manufacturing costs	$650,600

The direct labor rate is ($150,000 ÷ 25,000)	$6.00

The variable overhead rate is ($155,000 ÷ 25,000)	$6.20
Variable work in process inventory at 12/31/97:	
Absorption work in process inventory	$64,000
Less fixed overhead (2,100 hours X $1)	2,100
Variable work in process inventory	$61,900

Variable finished goods inventory at 12/31/97:	
Absorption finished goods inventory	$14,000
Less fixed overhead (820 hours X $1)	820
Variable finished goods inventory	$13,180

Variable selling expenses:
   Sales of $1,015,000 X 5% $50,750

Fixed selling expenses:
   Total selling expenses $95,000
   Less variable selling expenses   50,750
   Fixed selling expenses $44,250

   b. The difference in the operating income of $270 is
       caused by the different treatment of fixed
       manufacturing overhead. Under absorption costing,
       fixed overhead costs are assigned to inventory and are
       not expensed until the goods are sold. Under variable
       costing, these costs are treated as expenses in the
       period incurred. Since the direct labor hours in the
       work in process and finished goods inventories had a
       net increase of 270 hours, the absorption costing
       operating profit is higher because the fixed factory
       overhead associated with the increased labor hours in
       inventory is not expensed when absorption costing is
       used.

	1/1/97 Inventories	12/31/97 Inventories	Differences
Work in process	1,600	2,100	500
Finished goods	1,050	820	(230)
Total	2,650	2,920	270

The increase in hours (270) times the fixed overhead
rate ($1 per hour) equals the difference in operating
incomes ($270).

c.   The advantages of using variable costing follow.
   ■   The fixed manufacturing costs are reported at incurred values, not at absorbed values, which increases the likelihood of better control over fixed costs.
   ■   Profits are directly influenced by changes in sales volume and not by changes in inventory levels.
   ■   Contribution margin by product line, territory, department, or division is emphasized and more readily ascertainable.

   The disadvantages of using variable costing follow.
   ■   Variable costing is not acceptable for tax reporting, for SEC reporting, nor for external financial reporting; therefore, companies need to adjust variable costing amounts for these purposes.
   ■   Costs other than variable costs(i.e., fixed costs and total production costs) may be ignored when making decisions, especially long-term decisions.
   ■   With the advancement of factory technology and the movement toward a fully automated factory, the fixed factory overhead may be a significant portion of the production costs. To ignore these significant costs in inventory valuation may not be acceptable.

(CMA adapted)

75. a.   Because Sun Company uses absorption costing, the net income is influenced by both sales volume and production volume. Sales volume was increased in the 11/30/96 forecast and, at standard gross profit rates, this would increase earnings before taxes by $5,600. However, during this same period, production volume was below the 1/1/96 forecast causing an unplanned volume variance of $6,000. The volume variance and the increased selling expenses (due to the 10% increase in sales) overshadowed the added profits from sales as shown below:

Increased sales		$26,800
Increased cost of sales at standard		21,200
Increased gross margin at standard		$ 5,600
Less:		
Volume variance	$6,000	
Increased selling expenses	1,340	7,340
Decrease in earnings		$ 1,740

b. The basic cause of the lower forecast of profits is low production. If raw materials can be obtained, and if it is reasonable in light of expected future sales, Sun Company could schedule heavy production which would reduce the volume variance.

c. Sun Company could adopt variable costing. Under variable costing fixed manufacturing costs would be treated as period costs and would not be assigned to production. Consequently, earnings would not be affected by production volume but only by sales volume. Statements prepared on a variable costing basis are illustrated below.

Sun Company
Forecasts of Operating Results

	Forecasts as of 1/1/96	11/30/96
Sales	$268,000	$294,800
Variable costs		
Manufacturing	$182,000	$200,200
Selling expenses	13,400	14,740
Total variable costs	$195,400	$214,940
Contribution margin	$ 72,600	$ 79,860
Fixed costs		
Manufacturing	$ 30,000	$ 30,000
Administrative	26,800	26,800
Total fixed costs	$ 56,800	$ 56,800
Earnings before taxes	$ 15,800	$ 23,060

d. Variable costing would not be acceptable for financial reporting purposes because generally accepted accounting principles require the allocation of some fixed manufacturing costs to inventory.

(CMA adapted)

77. a. CM = $150 - $40 = $110 or 73.33%
BEP = FC ÷ CM = $1,800,000 ÷ $110 = 16,364 passengers
BEP = FC ÷ CM% = $1,800,000 ÷ .7333 = $2,454,657 revenues

b. 120 X .70 = 84 seats per plane filled
16,364 ÷ 84 = 195 flights (rounded)

c. CM = $200 - $40 = $160
120 X .55 = 66 filled seats
BEP = FC ÷ CM = $1,800,000 ÷ $160 = 11,250 passengers
11,250 ÷ 66 = 171 flights (rounded)

d. CM = $150 - $60 = $90
BEP = FC ÷ CM = $1,800,000 ÷ $90 = 20,000 passengers
20,000 ÷ 84 = 239 flights (rounded)

Chapter 8
Absorption and Variable Costing

e. Aftertax income = $600,000 ÷ (1 - tax rate)
    = $600,000 ÷ (1 - .4) = $600,000 ÷ .6 = $1,000,000
    $180X = $2,000,000 + $50X + $1,000,000
    $130X = $3,000,000
    X = 23,077 passengers

f. CM for discounted fares = $120 - $40 = $80 X 12
    discounted seats = $960 each flight X 40 flights per
    day X 30 days per month = $1,152,000;
    $1,152,000 minus $100,000 additional fixed costs =
    $1,052,000 additional coverage toward pretax profits
    each month.

g. (1) New CM = $175 - $40 = $135; 120 X .60 = 72 seats;
         72 X $135 X 20 = new CM of $194,400, compared to
         $100,000 additional fixed costs. Therefore, the
         company should obtain the route.
    (2) $175X = $100,000 + $40X + $57,500
         $135X = $157,500
         X = 1,167 passengers
         1,167 ÷ 72 = 17 flights per month (rounded)
    (3) 120 X .75 = 90 seats filled
         1,167 ÷ 90 = 13 flights (rounded)
    (4)   Mountain should consider such things as:
         ■   connections to other Mountain flights that
             might be made by these passengers,
         ■   long-range potential for increased load
             factors,
         ■   increased customer goodwill in this new
             market,
         ■   increased employment opportunities for labor
             in the area, and
         ■   competition in the market.

Ethics and Quality Discussion
79.   a.   **Breakeven for a normal operating season:**
           Breakeven, high end of range:
              300,000 ÷ 5,500 = <u>54.5</u> operating days per year
           Breakeven, low end of range:
              250,000 ÷ 5,500 = <u>45.4</u> operating days per year

      b.   The yield from some fixed volume or weight of produce
           often reveals much about the quality of the produce.
           In this case, the sugar cane is only yielding about 183
           pounds of sugar per ton of sugar cane. This compares
           with a normal yield of about 208 pounds of sugar per
           ton of sugar cane.

      c.   In this sense the agricultural process of growing sugar
           cane and converting it into sugar is very similar to
           other production operations. High quality inputs to
           any production process should result in a higher yield
           ratio--more output per unit of input. In this case,
           the input quality is low (the sugar content of each
           pound of sugar cane is less than expected); thus, more
           input (in excess of a ton) is required to get the
           normal output of around 208 pounds of sugar.

81.   a.   There is nothing illegal about Klein pushing a certain
           kind of product.

      b.   Klein is responding to incentives created by the
           company. In designing the commission plan, management
           has totally ignored the relative profitability of their
           various products. By establishing an incentive scheme
           based on a straight percentage of sales they are
           encouraging the sales people to sell the highest priced
           products.

      c.   Management would probably take the view that every
           employee has a responsibility to consider the impact of
           their actions on corporate profitability. By pushing
           only high-priced items, Klein is making the company
           less profitable than it would be if a mix of products
           were sold. Management would probably suggest that
           Klein has an obligation to consider the relative
           profitability of each product as well as the affect of
           each sale on his personal compensation.

d.   Klein should take the information about relative
     profitability to management. He should show them how
     they have created incentives for him to sell only high-
     priced items which are less profitable than the low-
     priced items. He should suggest that a new
     compensation program be created, perhaps based on
     product contribution margin rather than product sales.
     This would automatically provide Klein incentive to
     sell products that generated the most corporate profit
     per unit of effort.

83. a.

	Number of children		
	20	40	60
Revenues	$ 25,000	$ 50,000	$ 75,000
Variable costs			
Supplies	(2,500)	(5,000)	(7,500)
Food	(3,750)	(7,500)	(11,250)
Fixed costs:			
Upgrade facilities	(20,000)	(20,000)	(20,000)
Equipment	(1,000)	(1,000)	(1,000)
Paraprofessionals	(8,000)	(16,000)	(24,000)
Professionals	(9,000)	(18,000)	(27,000)
Net cash flow	$(19,250)	$(17,500)	$(15,750)

b.   The difficulty with employing financial analysis of
     this type in this setting is that "a financial outcome"
     is not the primary criterion for offering the child
     care service. Consequently, by relying too much on
     financial analysis, one might be led to make decisions
     that are in conflict with the goals of creating this
     service. In this case, a strict financial view of the
     child care center would either lead the Community Club
     to abandon the project because of the substantially
     negative first year cash flow, or perhaps worse--allow
     too many children to enter the center so that it
     becomes financially viable.

         A primary ethical concern would be to balance
     financial considerations with other, more important
     objectives for establishing the child care center.

9 Relevant Costing

Questions

1. For a cost to be relevant, it must be associated with the decision; it must be important to the decision maker (for example, it must be material in amount); and its incurrence must be in the future.

3. No. To be relevant, the future variable cost must also be avoidable under one or more decision options; i.e., it must vary between decision choices.

5. At the time when Bill must make his decision as to whether he will attend the concert, the original cost of $50, paid by Jim, and the price paid by Bill, $25, both represent sunk costs. They are therefore irrelevant. The only relevant cost is the $30 opportunity cost which represents the price Ted is willing to pay for the ticket.

   Bill will incur a $30 opportunity cost. The opportunity cost represents the benefit he will sacrifice (i.e., $30 of revenue) to attend the concert.

7. All historical costs are called sunk costs. Such costs are never relevant to a decision.

9. Some of the qualitative factors would include: quality of the production processes in-house versus the quality of potential suppliers' production processes, reliability of the suppliers, whether future demand for the item in question is expected to rise or fall, the prospects for future price changes, and the number of alternative suppliers in the market.

11. This statement is probably true for most businesses. In the short run, any constraint can be binding. However, in the long run, nearly any constraint can be overcome if there is an adequate supply of capital. To the extent capital is constrained in the long run, the capital constraint may be reflected in tight supplies of other organizational inputs including technology, managerial talent and labor.

13.   The contribution margin per product unit does not take into
      account the relative quantities of inputs consumed by the
      various products. Therefore, it does not measure the amount
      of profit for each unit of the scarce resource that is
      consumed. To optimally use a scarce resource, the resource
      allocation must explicitly consider the amount of profit
      each product produces for each unit of the scarce resource
      that is consumed.

15.   Some of the items that are most likely to effect a change in
      the sales mix after they are adjusted by management include
      a change in relative sales prices of products, changes in
      commissions or incentive compensation for sales people, and
      changes in advertising efforts and promotional expenditures.

17.   The statement is true if "incremental costs" include any
      opportunity costs associated with dedication of company
      resources to this special order. For example, if a company
      were operating at full capacity and wanted to bid on a
      special order, the bid price would also have to include the
      contribution margin on the displaced product sales that
      would be made if the special order were not undertaken.

19.   The compensation structure is the primary incentive that
      management can control to direct the efforts of sales
      personnel. By manipulating the compensation structure,
      management can induce sales people to focus on certain
      product lines, certain geographical markets, or specific
      customers. This analysis is based on the assumption that
      sales personnel will act in the manner that will maximize
      their wage and commission income.

21.   Product margin measures the revenue of a product line less
      all direct and avoidable costs. The product margin is an
      excellent indicator of the change in total organizational
      profit that would occur if the product line were eliminated.
      Thus, it is a primary measure of the product's contribution
      to the organization in the "keep or eliminate decision."

23.   Linear programming is a method that is used to
      simultaneously take into account multiple organizational
      constraints while seeking to maximize organizational profit.
      Linear programming will yield a solution that maximizes
      profit while determining the optimal allocation of
      organizational resources.

Exercises

25. a.   Incremental revenue:
          Product AA: ($1.50 - $1.00) X 10,000 = <u>$5,000</u>
          Product BB: ($3.00 - $0.50) X 20,000 = <u>$50,000</u>
          Product CC: ($0.90 - $0.75) X 500 =   <u>$75</u>

          Incremental costs:
          Product AA: $.75 X 10,000 =   <u>$7,500</u>
          Product BB: $1.00 X 20,000 = <u>$20,000</u>
          Product CC: $0.10 X 500 =   <u>$50</u>

    b.   Incremental profit
          Product AA: $5,000 - $7,500 =   <u>$(2,500)</u>
          Product BB: $50,000 - $20,000 = <u>$30,000</u>
          Product CC: $75 - $50 -   <u>$25</u>

Products BB and CC should be further processed because
doing so generates incremental profits. Product AA
should not be further processed because the incremental
revenue from the additional processing will not cover
the costs of the additional processing.

27. a.

	Make	Buy
Variable costs:		
$3 X 20,000	$ 60,000	
$5 X 20,000		$100,000
Fixed costs	50,000	0
Total relevant costs	<u>$110,000</u>	<u>$100,000</u>

The firm would be $10,000 per year better off to buy
the pumps rather than make them; this is $10,000 ÷
20,000 = <u>$0.50</u> per unit.

    b.

	Make	Buy
Variable costs:		
$3 X 30,000	$ 90,000	
$5 X 30,000		$150,000
Fixed costs	50,000	0
Total relevant costs	<u>$140,000</u>	<u>$150,000</u>

The firm would be better off by $10,000 annually ($0.33 per
unit) to make the pumps.

    c.   Let X equal volume of pumps required for production.
          Cost to make: $50,000 + $3X
          Cost to buy: $ 0 + $5X

          $50,000 + $3X = $5X
          X = <u>25,000</u> units.

29. a.
	Sanders	Drills
Sales price (per unit)	$45	$28
Variable costs	30	19
CM	$15	$ 9
Divide by required machine hrs.	8	6
CM per machine hour	$1.88	$1.50

Because, the Sanders generate more CM per MH than
Drills, the company should make only Sanders:
 Total hours ÷ hours per unit = units produced
 90,000 ÷ 8 = 11,250 Sanders

   b.   ((11,250 X $15) - $110,000) = $58,750

31. a.

	Grooming	Training	Total
Revenue			
10,000 X $15	$150,000		$150,000
8,000 X $25		$200,000	200,000
Variable Costs:			
Labor:			
10,000 X 5	(50,000)		(50,000)
8,000 X 10		(80,000)	(80,000)
Materials:			
10,000 X 1	(10,000)		(10,000)
8,000 X 2		(16,000)	(16,000)
Contribution Margin	$ 90,000	$104,000	$194,000
Fixed costs	(100,000)	(90,000)	(190,000)
Net income	$(10,000)	$ 14,000	$ 4,000

   b.   CM ratios:
         Grooming: $90,000 ÷ $150,000 = .60
         Training: $104,000 ÷ $200,000 = .52

   The additional $1 should advertise Grooming services.
   For Grooming, each additional dollar of revenue
   generates $.60 of CM; for Training only $.52 of CM is
   generated from each dollar of sales.

   c.   Each billable hour of Grooming service generates $9 of
         contribution margin ($15 - $5 - $1), while an hour of
         Training services generates $13 of contribution margin
         ($25 - $10 - $2). The advertising should therefore be
         spent on the Training service.

33. a.   SP(X) = FC + VC(X) + NIBT; X = 18,000 sets
           $200 X 18,000 = $1,100,000 + ($20 + $30 + $40 + $10) X
                           18,000 + NIBT
           $3,600,000 = $1,100,000 + $1,800,000 + NIBT
           NIBT = $3,600,000 - $2,900,000 = $700,000

b. New VC = $100 - $10 + $2 = $92;
    New CM = $170 - $92 = $78 on 5,000 sets.
    Sets sold at old CM = 15,000
    ($100 X 15,000) + ($78 X 5,000) = $1,100,000 + NIBT
    $1,500,000 + $390,000 - $1,100,000 = NIBT = $790,000

    Yes, since income would increase by $90,000, it should
    accept the offer.

c. Ito Company would need to quote a selling price high enough
    to cover its variable costs of production ($92), to cover
    the current loss of $100,000 ($100 X 10,000 = $1,000,000 of
    CM minus $1,100,000 of FC), and earn the profit of $150,000.

Cost of production	$ 92
Coverage of loss ($100,000 ÷ 5,000)	20
Generation of income ($150,000 ÷ 5,000)	30
Total selling price	$142

35. a. The effect of the change on overall net income can be
        found by analyzing sales and avoidable expenses:

Sales	$250,000
Variable costs:	
Professional services	150,000
Marketing	37,500
Contribution margin	$ 62,500
Avoidable direct fixed costs	35,000
Product margin	$ 27,500

    Overall net income would decline by an amount equal to
    the Product margin, $27,500, if the After-Dinner
    segment was eliminated.

b. Some of the more important qualitative factors to be
    considered would include: the effect of the
    elimination of the After-Dinner segment on business in
    the other two segments, prospects for long-term
    increases in business volume in the After-Dinner
    segment, the effect on the company and its employees in
    closing down a segment, and what kind of alternative
    managerial actions might be successful in turning the
    segment around.

37. The objective function would be to maximize the contribution
    margin which is the sum of the contribution margins
    generated for each product. Or, maximize CM, where, CM =
    $12.50X1 + $9.00X2 + $7.30X3.

39. a.   Regardless of how you would phrase the message, you would make the point that the $300 is a sunk cost and it should not affect your friend's decision to stop gambling or to continue gambling. The amount of money "invested" does not affect the odds of winning in the future, and therefore, money that is spent is irrelevant.

     b.   No. If we assume that a payoff from a slot machine is a random event (and that no skill or learning is involved), then the odds of winning are constant for each quarter placed in the machine. Thus, the odds of winning are just as great for the 1st quarter dropped in the slot as the last quarter dropped. Irrespective of the number of quarters played, the next quarter has the same odds of winning as the first quarter.

41. a.   The relevant factors would include: the out-of-pocket costs to get a master's degree, $20,000; the starting salaries for persons with a B.A. or M.A.; the estimated time to complete the master's degree; and the years to retirement.

     b.   The real cost of getting a master's degree would include the $20,000 out-of-pocket costs as well as the opportunity cost associated with the lost wages that could be earned with the B.A. degree: $29,500 per year for two years = $59,000. Total relevant costs sum to $79,000.

     c.   The incremental benefit of the Master Degree:
          ($33,000 - $29,500) X 38 - $79,000 = $54,000

          Note some of the more important simplifying assumptions:
          ■   no discounting of cash flows is necessary.
          ■   the initial differential in wages, $3,500, will be sustained for Bobby's entire career, and
          ■   funds are available to finance pursuit of the Masters Degree.

Problems

43. a. The additional costs would have been determined by identifying the additional materials required and the conversion required. The cost of the materials added to the direct labor and manufacturing overhead costs of the required conversion activities would comprise the total costs of additional processing. The accountant would have been aided by a bill of materials and an operations flow document.

b. $150,000 - $13,000 = <u>$137,000</u>

c. The amount of joint costs allocated to any particular product line is irrelevant to whether you would produce pre-cut shirts. In a joint process, the decision to produce or not produce is made based on all relevant joint costs; however, the allocation of joint costs is irrelevant to any decisions regarding individual joint products. Once the decision to produce (any or all joint products) is made, joint costs are irrelevant to all subsequent decisions.

d. $105,000 - $39,000 - $40,000 = <u>$26,000</u> increase in profits.

45. a. Relevant costs of making:

Salaries & wages (avoidable)	$1,950,000
Office supplies	350,000
Occupancy costs	300,000
Selling and Administration	450,000
Total	<u>$3,050,000</u>

Relevant cost of buying:

Price from trucking firm	$2,500,000
Salaries and wages	150,000
Materials	100,000
Occupancy costs	300,000
Office supplies	50,000
Selling and Administration	56,000
Total	<u>$3,156,000</u>

Advantage of making: $3,156,000 - $3,050,000
= <u>$106,000</u>

b.   Some of the concerns other managers might have
      include
      ■   how the cost shifted from the Distribution
           Department will affect the evaluations of
           their departments,
      ■   how the transfer of personnel will affect
           their operations,
      ■   what the behavioral implications might be of
           shifting personnel and their
           responsibilities,
      ■   how reliable the freight company is relative
           to the Distribution department, and
      ■   whether the new arrangement creates any new
           managerial responsibilities.

47.   a.   The rationing decision should be based on a comparison
            of the contribution margin that can be generated from
            each product per unit (minute, hour, or day) of oven
            time:

	Birthday Cakes	Wedding Cakes	Sp. Occasion Cakes
Sales	$ 25	$100	$ 40
Variable Costs			
Direct materials	5	30	10
Direct labor	5	15	8
Variable overhead	2	5	4
Variable selling	3	12	5
Contribution Margin	$ 10	$ 38	$ 13
Required oven time	10 min.	80 min.	18 min.
Contribution margin per minute of oven time	$1	$0.475	$0.722

Since the birthday cakes generate the highest
contribution margin per minute of oven time, and given
the fact that demand for birthday cakes is high enough
to consume all of the oven's available time, only
birthday cakes should be produced.   This use of the
oven will maximize company profit.

b. Total available oven time in minutes = 690 X 60 =
    41,400. According to the conclusion in part a., only
    birthday cakes will be produced:
    Production in units: 41,400÷10 = 4,140 birthday cakes

Sales (4,140 X $25)		$103,500
Variable costs:		
Direct materials	(4,140 X $5)	20,700
Direct labor	(4,140 X $5)	20,700
Variable overhead	(4,140 X $2)	8,280
Variable selling	(4,140 X $3)	12,420
Contribution margin		$ 41,400
Fixed costs:		
Factory		1,200
Selling & Administrative		800
Operating income		$ 39,400

c. The marketing manager needs to be sensitive to how the
    seasons affect the demand for the company's products.
    For example, since demand is much higher during the
    holiday season, the marketing manager needs to be
    focussed on selling the mix of products that will
    maximize the firm's contribution margin.

    Alternatively, during other seasons when demand is
    slack, the marketing manager simply needs to
    concentrate on promoting all products; capacity
    constraints will not be a consideration. Since
    virtually all fixed costs are irrelevant in the short-
    term, the marketing manager should be willing to accept
    all orders that generate a positive contribution
    margin.

49. a.

		Hot Dogs	
	No Action	Strategy 1	Strategy 2
Sales	$150,000	$141,000	$165,000
Direct materials	40,000	37,600	44,000
Direct labor	15,000	14,100	16,500
Commissions	0	0	10,450
Fixed costs	45,000	45,000	45,000
Net profit	$ 50,000	$ 44,300	$ 49,050

		Burgers	
	No Action	Strategy 1	Strategy 2
Sales	$125,000	$180,000	$156,250
Direct materials	55,000	79,200	68,750
Direct labor	10,000	14,400	12,500
Commissions	0	0	7,500
Fixed costs	15,000	44,000	15,000
Net profit	$ 45,000	$ 42,400	$ 52,500
Total Profits	$ 95,000	$ 86,700	$101,550

To maximize profits, Jim should implement strategy
number 2. It would increase profits by $101,550 –
$95,000 = $6,550.

b. Jim should consider behavioral effects of both employees and customers. For customers, Jim should be confident that sales efforts of employees can shift the product mix. If Jim's assumptions are incorrect in this regard, he may add a sales commission, for example, and find that although total sales rise, the percentage of burgers sold remains as before. With regard to employees, Jim needs to make certain that the employees will find a 10% commission to be a salient incentive. Otherwise, total costs will rise but total sales may remain flat.

51. a. Selling price = incremental cost of production + commission
   SP = $.45 + .10SP
   SP = $.50
   1,000 X .50 = $500 bid price

   b. SP = $.45 + .10SP + .10SP
   SP = $.5625; 1,000 X $.5625 = $562.50 bid price

   c. SP = $.45 + ($200 ÷ 1,000) + .10SP + .05SP
   SP = $.65 + .15 SP
   SP = $.76471
   1,000 X $.76471 = $764.71 bid price

53. a.

	Shirts	Hats	Boots	Total
Revenue	$110,000	$60,000	$35,000	$205,000
Variable costs				
RM	(15,000)	(22,000)	(13,000)	(50,000)
DL	(27,000)	(10,000)	(10,000)	(47,000)
OH	(6,000)	(4,250)	(3,500)	(13,750)
S&A	(16,000)	(5,000)	(6,000)	(27,000)
CM	$ 46,000	$18,750	$ 2,500	$ 67,250
Fixed Production				(20,700)
Selling and Administration				(14,750)
Operating profit				$ 31,800

The Boots product line should be retained because it contributes $2,500 to overall profits of the company.

b. In the role of marketing manager, you might be concerned about how the elimination of one product line would affect sales of other lines. For example, although boots may not be very profitable as a product line, they may serve to draw customers into the store to purchase shirts and hats. This may indicate that some sales of other product lines are dependent on the availability of the boot line.

Cases

55. a. For May, it would appear that store 2 is more profitable. Although store 2 had lower sales than store 1, it is clear that store 1 incurred more expense. For example, store 1 spent two-thirds of the entire district advertising budget; this was 10 times more than store 2 spent. Store 1 also incurred more expense for rent and would have been allocated more district level costs because of its higher sales.

   b. Store 1 is generating the most revenue. This is given in the first bulleted statement.

   c. The incentive for store 1 is to generate as much revenue as possible, The bonus scheme for that store does not take into account any expenses. Consequently, the manager of the store can benefit from the advertising without bearing any advertising costs.

   d. Store 1 would have more incentive. Since store 2 is evaluated on net income, any expenditures for maintenance will reduce the net income that might otherwise have been recorded. Store 1 would want to spend an adequate amount for maintenance so that no machine malfunction or downtime occurs that might interfere with sales.

   e. Both bonus schemes have some problems. The bonus scheme based on sales volume is not likely to increase profits in either the short or long term because no incentive is given to the manager to be conscious of the costs that are incurred to generate revenues. The bonus based on net income is more promising. The only detrimental aspect of this performance measure is that it is short-term oriented. It encourages managers to take actions that may generate short-term profits at the expense of long-term profits. For example, a manager may forgo maintenance activities to reduce costs in the short term. However, the long term implications of this act may be higher costs resulting from broken machinery.

57. a. 1. Net income is increased by $12,000, if the
customer's offer is accepted.

Incremental revenue		$150,000
Incremental costs:		
Direct materials	$50,000	
Direct labor	80,000	
Variable overhead*	8,000	138,000
Increase in income		$ 12,000

*Variable overhead is 40% of the total overhead or
10% of DL.

   2. The minimum selling price to have no impact on net
income, $138,000, is the point at which
incremental revenue is equal to incremental costs.

   b. In periods of less than full capacity, contribution
margin pricing can be advantageous in that it will
allow a company to aggressively price toward
incremental costs while still making some contribution
to the coverage of fixed overhead. Obviously, if a
company is at full capacity and has backorders it
should give some consideration to price increases.
Price is a function of supply and demand and is
determined in the marketplace.

   c. A major pitfall to contribution margin pricing is when
all orders are priced at incremental benefit equal to
zero, fixed overhead will not be covered and
eventually the company will go out of business.
Contribution margin pricing may also create an
undesirable precedent in the market place and place a
burden on the company to produce at substantially
higher volume levels than are desirable to achieve a
given level of net income. Remember, goods should be
priced at what the market will bear to maximize the
present value of future cash flows.

(CMA adapted)

Quality and Ethics Discussion
59. a.   Some of the costs that Nissan may have considered
         include
         ■   loss of goodwill associated with firing workers,
         ■   training costs of new employees when rehiring
             becomes necessary,
         ■   quality costs that differ between experienced
             workers and new employees, and
         ■   other costs that may vary with the number of
             workers who report to work each day.

    b.   Izuzu gets the immediate benefit of experienced
         employees, lower training costs, lower quality costs,
         and less cost of supervision. Additionally, Izuzu gets
         the temporary benefit of a larger workforce without
         permanent expansion in the size of the workforce. This
         is a significant benefit because to obtain workers of
         similar quality Izuzu might normally have to offer
         lifetime employment. Another significant benefit that
         Izuzu gets is the knowledge of the Nissan workers.
         These workers may have ideas that will be helpful in
         making long-term improvements in the Izuzu operations.

    c.   The quality of operations should be enhanced for both
         companies. The Nissan workers obtain ideas on new ways
         to do their production tasks and Izuzu gets a similar
         infusion of ideas. Thus, there is an important
         information exchange that should enhance quality of
         both operations. Also, Izuzu is able to avoid hiring
         inexperienced workers, and accordingly, avoids quality
         problems associated with inexperience and lack of
         skills.

61.   a.   There are two broad ethical issues. First, what Mr.
           Lundy should do with the knowledge he has gained about
           the competitor supplier's labor practices, and second,
           what he should do with regard to sourcing keyboards.
                One can probably look at the supplier in one of
           two ways. First, by buying from the supplier, Lundy is
           essentially condoning and supporting an illegal
           practice. Furthermore, in doing so, Lundy is probably
           eliminating jobs in its own plant that will idle
           deserving and "legal" workers. Also, in taking such an
           action, Lundy may be encouraging its competitors to
           adopt similar strategies thereby negating any short-
           term gains that will accrue to Lundy in dealing with
           the supplier.
                On the other hand, one could argue (weakly) that
           by buying from the supplier, jobs are created for
           people who might otherwise have no job and literally
           face starvation. Therefore, Lundy may view itself as
           the savior of an impoverished group of people.

      b.   The advantage is a short-term financial gain and a
           short-term improvement in competitive position. The
           disadvantages are several. First, by discontinuing in-
           house production, Lundy will develop mistrust between
           the managers and workers who will fear layoffs and
           other displacements. Second, Lundy will be
           encouraging other firms in the industry to take similar
           actions which will further fire the demand for illegal
           workers. Third, quality control may suffer and the
           risk of an interruption in the supply of keyboards
           would rise. Such risks would stem from plant shut
           downs imposed by labor authorities or other legal
           actions against the supplier's operations.

      c.   First, discard the notion that ignorance of the
           supplier's hiring practices somehow makes Mr. Lundy
           less accountable for dealing with the supplier. Mr.
           Lundy is aware of the hiring practices of the supplier
           and he must deal with the issue.
                Mr. Lundy should either continue to produce the
           keyboards in-house or find a supplier who has reputable
           labor practices and offers a quality product at a
           competitive price. A consideration of all the facts
           leads a reasonable person to conclude that it would be
           unethical to buy from the unscrupulous supplier.
           Furthermore, Mr. Lundy should go to the authorities and
           report the supplier's hiring practices.

Chapter 10 — Managerial Aspects of Budgeting

Questions

1. Budgeting has significant advantages in improving communications, motivation, coordination and teamwork. One of the greatest advantages is that it allows management to visualize the future state of affairs in time to make adjustments in action in order to effect more desirable results. It is a major tool in planning and controlling. The more complex and diversified the company, and the greater the degree of competitive intensity it faces, the more important budgeting is for it.

3. Strategic planning involves setting long-range (5-10 years) goals and the strategies and policies needed to achieve those goals. It includes integrating values of key internal and external variables into the process to attempt to influence the firm's own destiny rather than constantly having to react to those forces. Tactical planning should be made within the context of strategic planning. While most tactical plans are primarily in the form of specific objectives and are short-term (12-18 months), some are longer term and address repetitive operations. An example of the latter is a corporate policy statement.

5. Key variables, or critical success factors, are those factors that are most important to the organization's ability to achieve its goals. There are internal key success factors that are susceptible to managerial control (product quality, customer satisfaction) and external key variables that are beyond managerial control (foreign exchange rates, political stability in China).

7. In general government regulations exist to protect the people and the environment, and provide a climate for fair business competition. Typically, regulations exist that prescribe practices with respect to labor, product safety, appropriate conduct in foreign business transactions, and fair trade. Exhibit 10-6 lists some of the most important regulations that exist for U.S. businesses.

9. This is because the stage of the life cycle may have a significant effect on the product's costs, sales and pricing strategies.

11. Most organizations use participatory budgeting for the following reasons: because inputs and judgments from all levels of the organization can be considered; because the budget becomes a more intimate part of the working lives of operating personnel since they had a say in its development; and because it is a more effective means of engendering a spirit of coordinated teamwork in accomplishing goals and objectives. Disadvantages are that the approach is more time consuming and that dysfunctional behavior on the part of either top managers (e.g., making undiscussed major changes) or subordinates (e.g., empire building) can undermine the process.

13. This comment refers to the fact that good budgeting requires that responsible persons act with goodwill, good faith, and a spirit of cooperation and teamwork. When this happens, one finds a minimum of budgetary game playing in the process.

15. | **Sections of budget manual** | **Reasons for the section** |
    |---|---|
    | a. Statement of purposes & desired results | a. To communicate as a first step of coordination |
    | b. Budgetary activities to be performed | b. To designate who and what is responsible |
    | c. Calendar of budgetary activities | c. To indicate time table and provide coordination of efforts |
    | d. Sample forms preparation | d. To provide for consistency |
    | e. Original, revised & approved | e. To reflect revision of process and to serve as a control document |

17. The sales price variance measures the difference between actual and budgeted total revenues that is attributable to a difference in unit sales price. The sales volume variance captures the difference between actual and total budgeted sales that is attributable to a difference in unit volume. Together, the two variances explain the difference between total actual revenues and total budgeted revenues.

19. No. Some factors that affect outcomes are beyond managerial control. A manager should be evaluated only on the controllable aspects of performance.

21. A budget must be believed to be achievable by employees.
     Achievability favorably affects the effort and attitude of
     employees as they strive to reach the targets established in
     budgets. A budget will serve as a device of discouragement
     to employees if they feel it is too difficult to achieve.
     One way of helping to insure achievability is to involve
     participation in developing the budget. The participants
     should include those who will be evaluated by the degree of
     achievement of the budget targets.

23. Zero-based budgeting, ZBB, is a process that considers
     priorities for activities and alternatives for achieving
     current and proposed activities in relationship to company
     objectives. Managers must annually (or periodically)
     evaluate which of the on-going activities should be
     continued, eliminated, or funded at a lower level.
     Government is, by nature, bureaucratic. Such an
     organizational setting has historically engendered a
     phenomenon known as empire building whereby bureaucrats ask
     for successively larger budget appropriations. ZBB is an
     antidote for empire building.

Exercises

25. a. 4
    b. 5
    c. 1
    d. 2
    e. 3
    f. 7
    g. 6

27. a. harvest
    b. development
    c development
    d. maturity
    e. growth
    f. maturity
    g. growth
    h. maturity
    i. development
    j. introduction

29.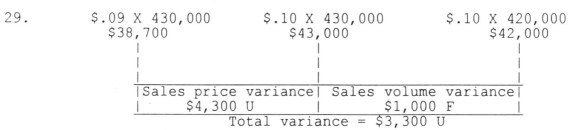

    $.09 X 430,000 $.10 X 430,000 $.10 X 420,000
      $38,700 $43,000 $42,000

    |Sales price variance| Sales volume variance|
    | $4,300 U | $1,000 F |
              Total variance = $3,300 U

The dairy sold 10,000 gallons more than budget and this
generated $1,000 of additional revenue. However, the dairy
sold its output at $.01 per gallon below the expected
selling price and this lost $4,300 of expected revenues.
These two factors are combined to explain the $3,300 revenue
shortfall.

31.

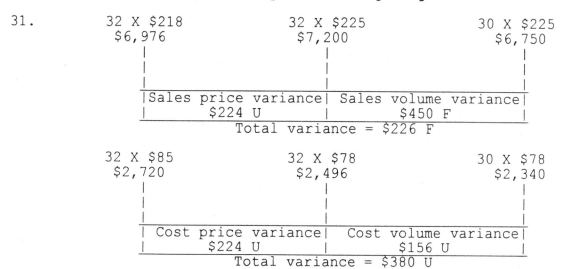

```
    32 X $218              32 X $225              30 X $225
      $6,976                 $7,200                 $6,750
         |                      |                      |
         |                      |                      |
         |                      |                      |
         |Sales price variance| Sales volume variance|
         |       $224 U       |        $450 F         |
              Total variance = $226 F

    32 X $85               32 X $78               30 X $78
      $2,720                 $2,496                 $2,340
         |                      |                      |
         |                      |                      |
         |                      |                      |
         | Cost price variance| Cost volume variance|
         |       $224 U       |        $156 U         |
              Total variance = $380 U
```

Photo Genic has a favorable volume variance. At standard
price and cost, his favorable net difference ascribed to
volume is $294 ($450 - $156). However, this advantage was
more than offset by the fact that he charged less and the
costs (cost price) he incurred were higher than expected.
The combined unfavorable price variances amount to $448
($224U + $224U). His shortfall of $154 ($4,410 - $4,256)
can be explained as follows:

Amount due to volume at standard prices	$294 F
Amount due to price difference	448 U
Net difference	$154 U

33. a.   7
     b.   5
     c.   6
     d.   8
     e.   1
     f.   2
     g.   4
     h.   3
     i.   10
     j.   9

Chapter 10
Managerial Aspects of Budgeting

Communication Activities

35. a. Long-range goals for business organizations enable an organization to develop a business philosophy which should state the direction of the organization and the limits within which the management is free to exercise discretion. The development of long-range goals are important for providing the basis for plans, enhancing efficiency of organization decision makers, and providing a basis by which alternate courses of action can be evaluated.

        Long-range goals serve as a means to orient individuals within the firm to the organization goals and provide the basis for individual goals and goal congruence. Goals also serve as standards against which long-term progress can be measured and evaluated.

  b. Long-range goals are normally set by persons at the highest level of the organization. However, input should be solicited from employees at all levels of the organization. The goals are developed by weighing various constraints, such as
- economic conditions (present and future),
- the desires of the owners and management, and
- the resources of the firm.

  c. Strategic planning is the development of a consistent set of goals, plans, resources, and measurements by which the achievement of goals can be assessed. Strategic planning recognizes that an organization functions in an environment and takes into account the interactions between the organization and its environment in everything the organization does or plans to do.

        Management control is the process by which managers ensure that resources are obtained and used in an efficient and effective manner to accomplish the organization's goals. Management control implies that performance measurements are reviewed to determine if corrective action is necessary.

        Strategic planning and management control are interrelated. Management control is carried out within the framework established by strategic planning. Management control is the process by which management evaluates the use of resources and whether the plans and long-range goals will be achieved. The purpose of management control is to encourage managers to take actions in the best interests of the organization so that the goals can be achieved.

(CMA)

37. As controller of CanadaExcel, you would interact with (and possibly direct) the efforts of an accounting staff in the Malaysian plant. Some of the more important items of information that you would need to acquire follow:

   - volume of camcorders to be assembled. This information would be acquired from existing sales and production budgets.
   - component costs. Component costs of materials acquired from within the company can be extracted from existing cost records and supplier contracts. Information on components acquired externally can be obtained from the Malaysian accounting staff and new supply contracts.
   - labor costs. Labor rate information will be supplied by the human resource or personnel staff in the Malaysian operation. Labor quantity information can be obtained from the production budget and from production personnel in Malaysia.
   - startup costs. Information on these costs including training and organizing costs can be obtained from management and the accounting staff in the Malaysian operation.

   - shipping and distribution costs. This information can be obtained from contracts with freight companies and from management in the Malaysian plant.
   - information on overhead costs. Fixed overhead relating to the plant and equipment can be obtained from vendor contracts and the construction contract relating to the new Malaysian plant. Depreciation schedules will likely be based on internal policies for depreciation methods and rates. Variable overhead information can be obtained from supplier contracts, labor contracts, engineering estimates and published rates of utility companies.
   - information on currency exchange rates. To the extent some transactions will be conducted in local currency, the controller will need the conversion rate for Canadian dollars. Such rates can be obtained from published sources such as the Wall Street Journal, and probably internally from the Treasurer's office.
   - information on support services. After obtaining estimates from Malaysian managers on the demand for support services such as accounting, engineering, personnel, and legal, estimates of the costs of these support services can be made. Existing records will provide some indication of volume/cost relationships; additional pricing information can be obtained from both the functional experts and the Malaysian managers.

150

Chapter 10
Managerial Aspects of Budgeting

In compiling the budget, the Controller would be involved in decisions such as in which currency the budget should be denoted, what accounting methods should be used to recognize budgeted activities, prescribing correct methods of accounting for fixed assets, and setting up a system of communication with the Malaysian plant in order to provide and obtain information.

Problems

39. a.   Basketballs: $800,000 ÷ $40 = <u>20,000</u> units
          Baseball Gloves: $1,200,000 ÷ $30 = <u>40,000</u> units

    b. $40 X (21,000 - 20,000) = <u>$40,000</u> F

    c.   Actual volume = 40,000 - ($240,000 ÷ $30) = 32,000
          Actual price = $1,120,000 ÷ 32,000 = $35
          Price variance = 32,000 X ($30 - $35) = <u>$160,000</u> F

    d.   Total price variance= $63,000 U + $160,000 F =$ 97,000F
          Total volume variance= $40,000 F + 240,000 U= 200,000U
          Total variance =   <u>$103,000</u>U

          Budgeted revenue exceeded actual revenue by $103,000.
          The two principal reasons that actual revenue was lower
          than budgeted revenue are (1) Basketballs were sold at
          a lower price than budgeted and (2) too few Baseball
          Gloves were sold. These negative effects were
          partially, but not completely, offset by (1) a higher
          price for Baseball Gloves and (2) a higher-than-planned
          sales volume of Basketballs.

41. a.   1.   The directive could have a significant effect on
                the care with which the budgets are prepared and
                the commitment that the division managers will
                make to achieve the budgeted results. The budget
                may have reduced significance as an operating
                plan, which will increase the uncertainty as to
                the validity of the approved budget. There also
                appears to be a decrease in the authority of the
                division managers, and there is likely to be less
                cooperation and coordination between division and
                corporate management.

          2.   The new directive would likely affect the
                preparation of future travel budgets as follows:
                the budget amount for travel expense may be
                inflated above actual needs to allow room for
                unforeseen trips, and there may be less care in
                preparation of the travel budget due to the
                division managers' decreased authority over
                travel.

    b.   The morale and motivation of the division manager and
          research staff are likely to be lowered by the
          directive because their autonomy, authority, and degree
          of participation in the budget process appear to be
          reduced.

     c.   Logically, one would have different budgeting criteria
            based on the importance of the activity to the short-
            term and long-term success of the firm. R&D is an
            activity that is integral to the firm's strategic
            initiatives; it is not a short-term activity. It is
            difficult to predict how a cut in R&D funding will
            affect the success of R&D efforts. However, for R&D to
            make its expected contributions to the firm, its
            funding should be established on a long-term basis and
            short-term funding adjustments should be avoided.

(CMA)

Cases

43. a. 1. The sales price variance should incorporate the changes for sales commissions and bad debts which amount to 5% ($46,500 ÷ $930,000; $43,750 ÷ $875,000) and 1% ($9,300 ÷ $930,000; $8,750 ÷ $875,000), respectively.

Plastic ($10.50 - $10.00) X (1 - .06)X(60,000) $28,200
Metal ($15.00 - $15.00) X (1 - .06)X(20,000)   0
   Total $28,200F

2. Sales mix variance:

Budgeted CM per unit =Budgeted CM ÷Budgeted Sales
                      = $172,500 ÷ 75,000
                      = $2.30 per unit

Actual CM per unit
   = (Actual CM - Price variance) ÷ Actual Sales
   = ($194,200 - $28,200) ÷ 80,000
   = $2.075 per unit

Summary of variances
Price
   Plastic $28,200 F
   Metal   0 $28,200 F
Mix [80,000 X ($2.30 - $2.075)]   18,000 U
Volume (5,000 units X $2.30)   11,500 F
   Total CM variance $21,700 F

b. Markley Division's expected sales   75,000 units
    Extra 10% industry increase   7,500 units
    Sales volume required to keep market share   82,500 units
    Actual sales volume   80,000 units
    Loss in market share   2,500 units
    Weighted average CM per unit $2.30
    Sales volume variance attributable
      to a reduction in market share $5,750 U

c.
Price variance
Plastic ($5.65 per unit - $5 per unit) X 60,000 $39,000 U
Metal ($6.00 per unit - $6 per unit) X 30,000   0
   Total $39,000 U

Material usage variance
Plastic (56,000 - 55,000) X $5 $5,000 U
Metal (23,000 - 22,500) X $6   3,000 U
   Total $8,000 U

Chapter 10
Managerial Aspects of Budgeting

Labor rate variance

Plastic ($6 per hour - $6.00 per hour) X 9,300		$0
Metal ($8.00 per hour - $8.00 per hour) X 5,600		0
Total		$0

Labor efficiency variance

Plastic (9,300 - 9,166.67) X $6 per hour		$800 U
Metal (5,600 - 5,625) X $8 per hour		200 F
Total		$600 U

Variable overhead spending variance

Plastic [$112,000 - (12 per hour X 9,300 hours)]		$400 U
Metal [$45,000 - ($8 per hour X 5,600 hours)]		200 U
Total		$600 U

Variable overhead efficiency variance

Plastic (9,300 - 9,166 2/3) X $12 per hour		$1,600 U
Metal (5,600 - 5,625) X $8 per hour		200 F
Total		$1,400 U

Summary of variances

Material price - plastic		$39,000 U
Material usage - plastic	$5,000 U	
- metal	3,000 U	8,000 U
Labor efficiency - plastic	$ 800 U	
- metal	200 F	600 U
Variable overhead spending - plastic	$ 400 U	
- metal	200 U	600 U
Variable overhead efficiency - plastic	$1,600 U	
- metal	200 F	1,400 U
Total variable manufacturing cost variance		$49,600 U

d. 1. The major cause of Markley Division's unfavorable profit performance is the large material price variance in the production of the plastic model - the company paid $5.65 for plastic material per chair versus the standard price of $5.00. Considering that the company is exceeding budgeted sales of plastic chairs, plus the fact that they have a lower budgeted contribution margin per unit, this excess price variance has a significant impact on company profits.

  2. The company has attempted to meet this problem by raising the price of plastic chairs. However, the price increase was only $.50. This is a relatively low increase in light of the cost change and may have contributed to the shift in sales mix to the plastic chairs.

3. Steps Markley's management might have taken to improve the division's operating income include:

- Increasing the sales price of the plastic model to fully compensate for the increase in raw material cost (i.e., at least $.65 rather than $.50).
- Attempting to improve sales mix by increased sales effort devoted to the metal model.
- Attempting to maintain market share by increased sales effort.
- Reviewing all cost control procedures to be sure they are functioning as planned.

(CMA)

Ethics and Quality Discussion

45. a.   This is a reasonable question to consider. Why should
          employers provide health care coverage to employees and
          not other kinds of services? After all, employers
          don't offer services to mow the yards of employees or
          do their grocery shopping. There are two possible
          reasons that companies provide health coverage. The
          first reason is that there are cost savings to be
          realized from purchasing health coverage as a group
          rather than as individuals. Presumably, some of those
          cost savings can be retained by the company. Secondly,
          it may be that employees, collectively, value a dollar
          of health care coverage above a dollar of cash income.
          Consequently, it is less expensive to pay a certain
          part of the labor bill by providing health care
          coverage in lieu of additional cash compensation.

     b.   Given that employer provision of health care coverage
          has become the norm in the U.S., the removal of this
          benefit may impact quality. The removal of this
          benefit will cause existing employees to question
          management's long-term commitment to them. Quality may
          suffer as the most capable employees decide to accept
          employment in firms where management has a better
          record of caring for retirees. In general, to the
          extent that quality depends on labor trusting
          management, quality may have been adversely affected by
          the removal of the retiree health benefits.

     c.   No answer provided.

     d.   The biggest consideration is whether the company has an
          ethical obligation to provide health coverage benefits
          to its retirees. Assuming the retirees accepted less
          cash compensation during their working careers in
          exchange for health care coverage during their
          retirement years, companies have a contractual, and
          ethical obligation to provide such benefits. Dropping
          the health care coverage after the retiree has provided
          (perhaps) a lifetime of labor to the company, would
          seem to violate both the letter and the spirit of the
          contract.
               Alternatively, managers have an ethical obligation
          to preserve the assets of the firm for the benefit of
          other parties. To the extent that health care costs
          have risen to levels that far exceed historical costs
          of health care, managers may need to drop or reduce
          health care coverage simply to allow the firm to
          survive. Certainly managers have ethical and
          contractual commitments to stakeholders other than
          labor.

47. a. In an unusual situation, where the top manager knows something he/she feels should not be divulged to the subordinate, such behavior may be appropriate. However, this would be most unusual, and there can be an expected cost in the form of dysfunctional behavior on the part of subordinates whose budgets were unilaterally adjusted. It is more poor human relations than poor ethics. However, one can also make the case that asking subordinates to do the unachievable is unethical.

    b. She feels that you are playing a game with her. By her building in budgetary slack, which you will counter with more rigorous budgetary targets, she will be more able to achieve the results. It does seem to be a deceptive practice to employ budgetary slack and all parties involved should attempt to build an atmosphere that encourages accurate estimation.

    c. Understanding revenues will probably have an effect on the planning of other activities because if the firm expects lower revenues, it will probably reduce planned activities in other offices of the firm. For example, lower expected revenues may make it seem infeasible to upgrade the computer graphics hardware and software of the firm.

Chapter 11

The Master Budget

Questions

1. The diversity of resources used, activities conducted, and quantities of funds provided/used generally make budgeting more important to a business than to an individual. In addition, there is no assurance of the continuity of management and, therefore, written plans are more useful than spoken plans (which may work to manage personal and family finances). The real value in writing down plans is that psychologically it is the first step to commitment to those plans.

3. It is said to be a static budget because it is based on a single level of demand. It must be static to facilitate the many time-consuming financial arrangements that must be made before beginning operations for the budget year.

5. The master budget is "driven" entirely by expected sales. Without sales, the firm would have no need to acquire resources or remain in operation.

7. The materials purchases budget is driven by the production budget and the firm's inventory policies with respect to materials. Since materials are required for production to commence, the amount of materials acquired in a particular period will reflect the production budget for that period. However, the material purchases budget will not be strictly proportional to production if the firm desires to increase or decrease its level of materials inventory.

9. Overhead must be separated into variable and fixed components so that it can be estimated. By separating overhead costs into variable and fixed cost pools, the volume dependent costs (variable) can be estimated as a function of production volume specified in the production budget, and the fixed costs can be estimated as a lump sum equal to the total of the individual costs that comprise the fixed overhead cost pool.

159

11. Managers must control cash in order to be able to pay the
     company's obligations when due. The cash budget is
     essential in control of cash in terms of: (1) cash available
     exclusive of financing; (2) cash excess/inadequacy; (3) cash
     available/needed; and (4) financing options for acquisition
     of needed cash or disposition of unneeded cash.

13. A firm's credit policies significantly affect the cash
     collection pattern. Liberal credit terms allow customers to
     pay at some point in the future without incurring
     substantial interest costs. Alternatively, a tight credit
     policy is designed to encourage credit-sale customers to pay
     early. The cash collection pattern is further influenced by
     policies regarding which customers should be granted credit.
     If risky customers are granted too much credit,
     uncollectible accounts will rise. If less risky customers
     are denied credit, total sales and cash collections will
     decline.
          A firm gives a discount for cash sales to encourage
     customers to pay cash for purchases rather than buy on
     credit. The customer can equate the cash discount to an
     interest expense incurred on credit purchases.

15. Pro forma financial statements allow management to view the
     results of their plans for the period and decide whether
     those results are acceptable. If the results are
     unacceptable, management still has time to change or adjust
     items before the start of the period. This might mean
     increasing or decreasing prices or costs or revising their
     expectations about objectives and goals.

17. When the projected cash balance on the pro forma balance
     sheet is compared with the beginning of the budget year cash
     balance, the expected change in cash for the budget year can
     be calculated. The SCF explains how this expected change in
     cash is related to the firm's operating, investing and
     financing activities.

19. The spreadsheet program allows managers to do "what if"
     analysis. This type of analysis allows the management team
     to evaluate the effects of errors in their estimates or
     possible changes in the plans. By linking the various
     budgets in the spreadsheet, a change can be made in one
     variable and its effects will automatically flow through all
     affected budgets. For example, the sales estimates could be
     changed and the impact of the sales change on all budgets
     would be shown immediately.

Exercises

21.

		April	May	June	Total
	Sales	9,000	10,000	11,000	30,000
+	Desired End.balance	800	880	960	960
=	Total needed	9,800	10,880	11,960	30,960
-	Beginning balance	720	800	880	720
=	Production	9,080	10,080	11,080	30,240

23.

		Flipper Production
	Sales	14,200
+	Desired ending balance	8,200
=	Total needed	22,400
-	Beginning balance	3,300
=	Production - pairs	19,100

		Lbs Rubber Purchases
	Production (2 X 19,100)	38,200
+	Desired ending balance	16,000
=	Total needed	54,200
-	Beginning balance	12,800
=	Purchases	41,400 pounds

25. a. $y = \$451,000 + (\$14.25 \times 12,000) = \underline{\$622,000}$

   b. Cash spent = $622,000 - $72,000 = $\underline{\$550,000}$

27. a. $194,000 - $140,000 = $54,000 portion remaining of February billings
   $54,000 ÷ .3 = $180,000 February billings

   b. $140,000 ÷ .70 = $200,000 March billings
   .01 X 200,000 = $2,000 uncollectible from March billings

   c. Collections in April:
   .29 of February billings of $180,000 = $ 52,200
   .40 of March billings of $200,000   =   80,000
   .30 of April billings of $210,000   =   63,000
       Total April collections $195,200

   d. The oral report should contain at least two methods of manipulating credit sales. Credit sales could be collected sooner if management would tighten credit policies. One method of tightening the credit policy is to simply allow fewer customers to have credit privileges. Another, less onerous possibility is to provide a larger discount for cash sales. This is a method that provides customers more incentive to pay early.

e. The two important variables would be the effect the
change in credit sales would have on sales and the
effect the change would have on cash collections and
delinquent and bad accounts. The analysis should treat
as a benefit the savings in interest costs from earlier
cash collections and fewer bad debts. The analysis
should treat as a cost the contribution margin of lost
sales resulting from the change in credit policy.

29. a.

	Units to be purchased	68,300
X	Cost per unit	X 3.80
=	Cost of purchases	$259,540
X	% payment for current month	X .40
=	Increase in accounts payable	$103,816
-	Discounts ($103,816 X .5 X .02)	(1,038)
=	Cash payments for current month	$102,778
+	Payment for May	207,936
	Cash payments for accounts payable	$310,714

b. Managers could ask creditors for additional time to pay
accounts. The other typical alternatives to raise
short-term cash are to borrow from a commercial lender
or to sell assets (e.g., factor receivables).

31.
Johnson Electrical
Pro Forma Cost of Goods Manufactured Schedule
For the Period Ending December 31, 1997

Work in process-January 1		$ 12,200
Cost of direct materials used:		
Direct materials balance-Jan. 1	$ 3,300	
Purchases of direct materials	187,700	
Total available	$191,000	
Direct materials balance-Dec. 31	6,200	
Cost of direct materials used	$184,800	
Direct labor	106,700	
Factory overhead	215,500	507,000
Total costs to be accounted for		$519,200
Work in process-Dec. 31		9,300
Cost of goods manufactured		$509,900

Communication Activities
33. a.   Rapid growth requires additional investment to support
         the firm's operating cycle. Specifically, more cash is
         consumed in producing inventory and financing
         receivables. Growth may also require additional cash
         investments in infrastructure--both people and plant
         and equipment.

    b.   Hayes could have taken several steps:
         ■   arranged with creditors for delayed payments,
         ■   rationed the higher demand with a higher sales
             price rather than trying to increase production so
             dramatically,
         ■   contract with subcontractors to finance and build
             inventory,
         ■   changed sales credit policies so that cash from
             sales is collected sooner, and
         ■   moved to JIT management of inventory to shorten
             the operating cycle and collect cash sooner.

    c.   It is a paradox that Hayes had a plan that incorporated
         intentions to expand, yet the company ended up in
         bankruptcy. Apparently, Hayes' plans either failed to
         adequately model the relationships between revenues,
         assets, expenses, and cash flows; or, the plan failed
         to capture the magnitude of the actual growth. In
         either case, the plan was ineffective because it failed
         to provide clear direction to management so that
         bankruptcy could be avoided.

    d.   Closer cooperation between marketing, production, and
         finance specialists could have resulted in an exchange
         of information that would have caused the firm to make
         different decisions. Marketing and production
         specialists could have learned from finance specialists
         about the effects of cash and capital constraints on
         decision alternatives. Ideas could have been generated
         to increase prices or take some other action to control
         demand.

Problems
35. **Production**

	January	February	March	Total
Sales	36,000	32,000	30,000	98,000
Desired ending balance	8,000	7,500	7,000	7,000
Total needed	44,000	39,500	37,000	105,000
Estimated beg. balance	9,000	8,000	7,500	9,000
Production	35,000	31,500	29,500	96,000

Purchases-Direct material M

	January	February	March	Total
Production (times 3)	105,000	94,500	88,500	288,000
Desired ending balance	6,000	5,625	5,250	5,250
Total needed	111,000	100,125	93,750	293,250
Estimated beg. balance	6,750	6,000	5,625	6,750
Purchases in pounds	104,250	94,125	88,125	286,500

Purchases-Direct material N

	January	February	March	Total
Production (times 2)	70,000	63,000	59,000	192,000
Desired ending balance	4,000	3,750	3,500	3,500
Total needed	74,000	66,750	62,500	195,500
Estimated beg. balance	4,500	4,000	3,750	4,500
Purchases in pounds	69,500	62,750	58,750	191,000

Purchases-Direct material O

	January	February	March	Total
Production (times 4)	140,000	126,000	118,000	384,000
Desired ending balance	8,000	7,500	7,000	7,000
Total needed	148,000	133,500	125,000	391,000
Estimated beg. balance	9,000	8,000	7,500	9,000
Purchases in pounds	139,000	125,500	117,500	382,000

b. The nature of the production process affects the
    efficiency of the conversion of materials into finished
    products. One of the benefits of utilizing higher
    technology is the reduction that can be achieved in
    waste, scrap, and defective products. It may be
    expected that the materials required per unit of
    finished products will drop to some extent if the new
    technology is acquired.

c. The vendor of the new technology, an in-house
    engineering department, and knowledgeable production
    managers should be able to offer valuable insights as
    to how material requirements will change with
    acquisition of the machine technology. In fact, the
    change in material requirements is likely to have been
    one of the factors that was considered in evaluating
    the purchase of the new technology.

37.   a.   **Production Budget**
           Sales   200,000
           Desired ending finished goods   12,000
           Total needed   212,000
           Beginning finished goods   5,000
           Production   207,000

           Purchases of bags:
           Production   207,000
           Desired ending balance   12,000
           Total needed   219,000
           Beginning inventory   12,000
           Purchases of bags   207,000

      b.   **Purchases of coffee beans:**
           Production (207,000 X 15/16)   194,062.50
           Desired ending balance (12,000 X 15/16)   11,250:00
           Total needed   205,312.50
           Beginning inventory   14,000.00
           Purchases of pounds of coffee beans   191,312.50

      c.   **Purchases of additional ingredients**
           Production (207,000 X 1/16)   12,937.50
           Desired ending balance (12,000 X 1/16)   750.00
           Total needed   13,687.50
           Beginning inventory   1,100.00
           Purchases of pounds of add. ingredients   12,587.50

      d.   Purchase of bags (207,000 X $.14) $ 28,980.00
           Purchase of coffee beans (191,312.50 X $1.52) 290,795.00
           Purchase of additional ingredients
                (12,587.50 X $.20)   2,517.50
           Total dollars of purchases $322,292.50

      e. $322,292.50 X .60 X (1 - .02) = $189,508 (rounded)

      f.   JIT would allow the firm to gradually reduce its
           inventories of finished goods, work in process, and raw
           materials. This would result in substantial cost
           savings and new insights into improving existing
           operations.

Chapter 11
The Master Budget

39. a. **Production Budget:**

	Jan.	Feb.	March	Total	April
Sales	6,400	5,200	7,400	19,000	8,000
Desired ending balance	1,040	1,480	1,600	1,600	1,600
Total needed	7,440	6,680	9,000	20,600	9,600
Estimated beg. balance	4,220	1,040	1,480	4,220	1,600
Production	3,220	5,640	7,520	16,380	8,000

b. **Purchases Budget**

Scrap Iron (in pounds)	Jan.	Feb.	Mar.	Total
Production (times 2)	6,440	11,280	15,040	32,760
Desired ending balance	2,820	3,760	4,000	4,000
Total needed	9,260	15,040	19,040	36,760
Beginning balance	2,000	2,820	3,760	2,000
Unit purchases (lbs.)	7,260	12,220	15,280	34,760
Unit price X units	$14,520	$24,440	$30,560	$69,520

Bookstand Bases (units)	Jan.	Feb.	Mar.	Total
Production	3,220	5,640	7,520	16,380
Desired ending balance	1,410	1,880	2,000	2,000
Total needed	4,630	7,520	9,520	18,380
Beginning balance	3,200	1,410	1,880	3,200
Unit purchases	1,430	6,110	7,640	15,180
Unit price X units	$2,574	$10,998	$13,752	$27,324
Total purchases	$17,094	$35,438	$44,312	$96,844

c.

Cash payments from:	January	February	March	Total
Dec. Accounts Payable	$ 5,800.00			$ 5,800.00
Jan.(17,094 X.75 X.99)	12,692.30			12,692.30
Jan.(17,094 X.25)		$ 4,273.50		4,273.50
Feb.(35,438 X.75 X.99)		26,312.72		26,312.72
Feb.(35,438 X.25)			$ 8,859.50	8,859.50
Mar.(44,312 X.75 X.99)			32,901.66	32,901.66
Total	$18,492.30	$30,586.22	$41,761.16	$90,839.68

d. **Cash payments for factory overhead and period expenses:**

	January	February	March	Total
Factory overhead: $24,000 + $1.30X (where X = production)	$28,186	$31,332	$33,776	$ 93,294
Period expenses: $13,600 + $.10X (where X = sales)	20,960	19,580	22,110	62,650
Total	$49,146	$50,912	$55,886	$155,944

e.

Digger Douglas
Pro Forma Cash Budget
For Three Months and First Quarter of 1998

	January	February	March	Total
Beg. cash balance	$18,320.00	$24,627.70	$ 15,481.48	$ 18,320.00
Cash collections	76,200.00	61,300.00	81,100.00	218,600.00
Total available exclusive of financing	$94,520.00	$85,927.70	$ 96,581.48	$236,920.00
Disbursements:				
Cash payments for purchases	$18,492.30	$30,586.22	$ 41,761.16	$ 90,839.68
Direct labor	2,254.00	3,948.00	5,264.00	11,466.00
Cash payments-OH & period expenses	49,146.00	50,912.00	55,886.00	155,944.00
Total disbursements	$69,892.30	$85,446.22	$102,911.16	$258,249.68
Cash excess or (inadequacy)	$24,627.70	$ 481.48	$ (6,329.68)	$(21,329.68)
Minimum cash balance desired	15,000.00	15,000.00	15,000.00	15,000.00
Cash available or (needed)	$ 9,627.70	($14,518.52)	$(21,329.68)	$(36,329.68)
Financing:				
Borrowings (repayment)	0.00	15,000.00	22,000.00	37,000.00
Interest (paid)	0.00			
Total effect of financing	0.00	$15,000.00	$ 22,000.00	$ 37,000.00
Ending cash balance	$24,627.70	$15,481.48	$ 15,670.32	$ 15,670.32

f. An inside source of information would be the purchasing department. The purchasing department would have information on credit terms for all major suppliers. The accounting clerk could confirm the credit policy by calling the vendors directly.

Chapter 11
The Master Budget

41. a.

Collections In/From		January	February	March
January				
Oct. $122,000 X .9 X .1		$ 10,980.00		
Nov. 128,000 X .9 X .4		46,080.00		
Dec. 133,000 X .9 X .1 X .99		11,850.30		
Dec. 133,000 X .9 X .4		47,880.00		
Jan. 141,000 X .1 X .99		13,959.00		
February				
Nov. 128,000 X .9 X .1			$ 11,520.00	
Dec. 133,000 X .9 X .4			47,880.00	
Jan. 141,000 X .9 X .1 X .99			12,563.10	
Jan. 141,000 X .9 X .4			50,760.00	
Feb. 139,000 X .1 X .99			13,761.00	
March				
Dec. 133,000 X .9 X .1				$ 11,970.00
Jan. 141,000 X .9 X .4				50,760.00
Feb. 139,000 X .9 X .1 X .99				12,384.90
Feb. 139,000 X .9 X .4				50,040.00
Mar. 124,000 X .1 X .99				12,276.00
Totals		$130,749.30	$136,484.10	$137,430.90

b.

Purchases	January	February	March	Total
Estimated sale (at cost)	$ 70,500	$ 69,500	$ 62,000	$202,000
+ Desired end inv. (75%)	52,125	46,500	47,625	47,625
Total needs	$122,625	$116,000	$109,625	$249,625
- Beginning inventory	52,875	52,125	46,500	52,875
= Budgeted purchases	$ 69,750	$ 63,875	$ 63,125	$196,750

c.

Cash Payments for Purchases	January	February	March
In January/From			
December	$ 41,700		
January ($69,750 X .4)	27,900		
In February/From			
January ($69,750 X .6)		$ 41,850	
February ($63,875 X .4)		25,550	
In March/From			
February ($63,875 X .6)			$ 38,325
March ($63,125 X .4)			25,250

Cash payments for S & A:

Sales			
Dec. 133,000	7,120		
Jan. 141,000	11,160	7,440	
Feb. 139,000		11,040	7,360
Mar. 124,000			10,140
Total monthly disbursements	$87,880	$85,880	$81,075

43. a.
                          Ohio Rubber Co.
                    Pro forma Income Statement
                      For February, 1998

    Sales $220,000
    Cost of Goods Sold   165,000
    Gross Margin $ 55,000
    Other expenses   (41,000)
    Net income before taxes $ 14,000

     b.
                          Ohio Rubber Co.
                    Pro forma Balanced Sheet
                       February 28, 1998

    Cash* $ 28,000
    Accounts receivable   83,600
    Inventory   47,000
    Property, plant & equipment (net)   60,000
        Total assets $218,600

    Accounts payable $180,000
    Common stock   100,000
    Retained earnings   (61,400)
        Total liabilities and owners' equity $218,600

    * Beginning cash balance $ 16,000
       Collections from prior months' sales   76,000
       Collections from current sales   132,000
       Less payments on account   (196,000)
       Ending cash balance $ 28,000

     c. This company has a negative net worth based on book
         values. Accordingly, it will be very difficult for the
         company to borrow funds needed for operating. If it can
         obtain financing, it will be required to pay
         extraordinary rates of interest and pledge specific
         assets for collateral. One thing the company could do is
         sell the accounts receivable. The cash acquired could be
         used to finance operations and reduce accounts payable.
         The firm should also examine its assets. If there are
         assets that have market values significantly above book
         values, the assets could be sold to increase income,
         reduce the negative retained earnings, and increase cash.
         However, the company must be very careful to avoid
         selling assets that are absolutely critical to its
         ability to remain a going concern. Additionally, the
         company should try to reduce the level of inventory; this
         will generate cash, increase income, and reduce the
         deficit in retained earnings.

Cases

45. a.   A Pro Forma Schedule of Cash Receipts for CrossMan
           Corporation, by month, for the second quarter of 1998, is
           presented below. (For Pro Forma Schedule purposes,
           interest expenses and/or interest income associated with
           borrowing/investing activities have not been considered.)

CrossMan Corporation
Pro Forma Schedule of Cash Receipts and Disbursements
Second Quarter 1998
(in thousands)

	April	May	June
Beginning cash balance	$ 100	$ 100	$ 100
Accounts receivable collections			
Prior month's sales (60%)	$1,080	$1,320	$1,500
Two months' prior sales (40%)	800	720	880
Total collections	$1,880	$2,040	$2,380
Cash available	$1,980	$2,140	$2,480
Disbursements			
Material purchases 1	$1,004	$1,156	$1,310
Wages (20% of current sales)	440	500	560
General & administrative 2	150	150	210
Income taxes 3	408	–	–
Total disbursements	$2,002	$1,806	$2,080
Net cash flow	$ (22)	$ 334	$ 400
Cash borrowed	122	–	–
Cash invested	–	(234)	(300)
Ending cash balance	$ 100	$ 100	$ 100

Notes

1 Material purchases:	Feb.	Mar.	April	May	June	July
Sales	$2,000	$1,800	$2,200	$2,500	$2,800	$3,000
Material cost (50%)	1,000	900	1,100	1,250	1,400	1,500
Material receipts						
Next month's costs (60%)	540	660	750	840	900	
This month's costs (40%)	400	360	440	500	560	
Total receipts	$ 940	$1,020	$1,190	$1,340	$1,460	
Material payments						
Prior month's receipts (80%)			$ 816	$ 952	$1,072	
Two months' prior receipts (20%)			188	204	238	
Total payments			$1,004	$1,156	$1,310	

2 General & Administrative expense:

Salaries (1/12 of annual)	$ 40	$ 40	$ 40
Promotion (1/12 of annual)	55	55	55
Property taxes (1/4 of annual)			60
Insurance (1/12 of annual)	30	30	30
Utilities (1/12 of annual)	25	25	25
Depreciation (non-cash item)	–	–	–
Total expense	$150	$150	$210

3 Income tax expense:

First quarter pre-tax income = Net income ÷ (1 - tax rate)
                             = $612 ÷ .6
                             = $1,020

Tax expense = .4 X $1,020
            = $408

    b.   Cash budgeting is particularly important for a rapidly expanding company such as CrossMan Corporation because as sales grow rapidly so do expenditures for product purchases. These expenditures generally precede cash receipts, often by a considerable time period, and a growing company must be prepared to finance this increasing gap between expenditures and receipts.

    c.   Yes. Monthly cash budgets ignore the timing of receipts and disbursements that occur within the month. This is a reason to prepare cash budgets for shorter time intervals.

(CMA reprinted)

Chapter 11
The Master Budget

47. a. and b.

CME, INC.
Cash Budgets
(000s omitted)

	For the year ending December 31, 1998	For month ending January 31, 1998
Cash balance, Jan. 1	$ 750	$ 750
Cash receipts:		
Program revenue	12,000	1,440(3)
Membership income	10,000(1)	0
Total cash available	$22,750	$2,190
Cash outflows:		
Seminar:		
Instruction fees	$ 8,400(2)	$ 0
Facilities	5,600	672(4)
Promotion	1,000	100(5)
Total	$15,000	$772
Salaries	960	80(6)
Benefits, staff	240	18(7)
Office lease	240	20(8)
Gen. admin.	1,500	125
Gen. promotion	600	50(9)
Research grants	3,000	500
Cap. expenditures	510	102(10)
Total	22,050	1,667
Ending cash balance	$ 700	$ 523

Supporting calculations:
(1) 100,000 members X $100 = $10,000,000
(2) $12,000,000 X 70% = $8,400,000
(3) $12,000,000 X 12% = $1,440,000
(4) $5,600,000 X 12% = $672,000
(5) $1,000,000 ÷ 10 = $100,000 (no seminar promotion in June & July)
(6) $960,000 ÷ 12 = $80,000
(7) ($240,000 − $24,000) ÷ 12 = $18,000
(8) $240,000 ÷ 12 = $20,000
(9) $600,000 ÷ 12 = $50,000
(10) $510,000 ÷ 5 = $102,000

c. The most important operating problem faced by CME, Inc. is the short-term liquidity. During the first six months, expenditures of $14.5 million are forecasted to be slightly more than double the revenue ($7.2 million). This will necessitate short-term borrowing during the second and third quarters of the year. The second most important problem is that the cash expenditures are forecasted to exceed revenue by $50,000 and this could be further compounded by interest on short-term borrowing which apparently has not been forecasted. The fees do not fully support the seminars. The total of the facility costs and the faculty costs exceed the seminar revenues.

(CMA adapted)

Ethics and Quality Discussion

49. a. The new agreement with the airline's pilots accomplishes
         two things. First, it allows Southwest Airlines to
         maintain a cost advantage over its competitors. For this
         airline a cost advantage is critical because it competes
         on the basis of price. Secondly, the airline's agreement
         with the pilots allows for the pilots to acquire common
         stock in the company. Pilot ownership of stock is
         advantageous for the company because it makes the pilots
         consider the perspective of owners in actions they take.
         Specifically, it makes them conscious of costs and makes
         them more oriented to long-term competitive issues.

     b. The stock ownership and bonus plans are likely to have
         favorable quality effects. Because the plan will force
         pilots to think like owners, both quality consciousness
         and cost consciousness should be enhanced. The stock
         ownership plan should make the pilots more long-term
         oriented in the decisions they make. Because higher
         quality frequently leads to lower costs, the pursuit of
         increased efficiency and higher profits should induce the
         pilots to be more concerned about quality.

51. a.   Comet Company does not have a legal obligation to inform
          the bank of this situation. The statements were fairly
          presented at the time they were given to the bank loan
          committee. Morally, however, Comet Company should inform
          the bank about the change in circumstances because
          company managers recognize the potential harmful
          financial implications that the customer's elimination
          would have on Comet's profitability.

     b.   The primary implication of telling the loan officer is
          that the loan will not be approved. This, in turn, could
          create enough problems that Comet will be forced out of
          business - causing harm to stockholders, creditors,
          employees, and other customer who relied on Comet's
          services. The "ripple effect" could be quite
          substantial.
               On the other hand, telling the loan officer could
          indicate Comet's willingness to work with the bank and be
          truthful in its dealings. The bank loan officer may be
          willing to renegotiate the loan terms (such as loan a
          smaller amount for the present time or adjust the
          repayment period) because of Comet's integrity in this
          matter.

     c.   The implication of not telling the loan officer is that
          Comet might get the loan and be unable to repay it. Such
          a situation could also force Comet out of business, with
          the same "ripple effect" as mentioned above.
          Additionally, depending on the size of the loan, the
          non-repayment could cause problems for the bank--ranging
          from a lower earnings-per-share for bank stockholders to
          bank failure (depending on the size of the loan and how
          many bank customers are acting in similar fashion).
               The alternative is that Comet will get the loan and
          the sales manager is correct in his/her assumption that
          the lost sales are replaced. Comet can then make the
          scheduled repayments on time and the bank is unaffected
          by the situation. (Unless the loan officer becomes aware
          of it through other means and believes Comet management
          to be less than truthful in their business dealings).

     d.   Students will have different answers for this part, based
          on what they view as the potential outcome of the
          situation, how large they believe the loan to be in
          relation to Comet's other debt and the bank total loan
          portfolio, and how accurate they believe the sales
          manager's predictions to be. Ask them to look at the
          situation from several sides (Comet's, the bank's,
          Comet's and the bank's stockholders, Comet's employees).
          Remind them that bankers are not enemies of businesses;
          the better the relationship a business has with its bank,
          the better off that business can be.

Questions

1.   Control can be exerted (a) before the activity--budgeting and standard setting; (b) during the activity--monitoring and correcting; and (c) after the activity--providing feedback.

3.   A change in volume will cause costs to change because variable costs fluctuate proportionately with volume. Inflation can cause costs to change because of increasing prices. Market forces of supply and demand can also cause costs to change. For example, in a competitive market a decrease in supply leads to an increase in price.

5.   Careful capital budgeting analysis is made before committing the firm to long-run costs such as investing in plant assets. Secondly, control of capital costs is accomplished through comparing actual with expected results during the post-investment audit.

7.   This result may be praiseworthy for some discretionary costs as long as the activities being funded are producing satisfactory outcomes, which are themselves often difficult to measure. However, other discretionary costs should be fully spent on those funded activities considered to be critical, such as preventive maintenance, safety programs and pollution abatement programs.

9.   Inputs provide the support for outputs. The relationship between inputs and outputs is a yield relationship known as efficiency. Outputs are a measure of achievement of objectives, and the relationship between outputs and objectives is called effectiveness. The set of company objectives, when accomplished, are expected to achieve company goals.

11.   A surrogate measure of output is an indirect or substitute measure. The results of discretionary cost activities are often not susceptible to direct financial measurement so non-monetary surrogate measures are often used.

13. Engineered costs are costs which bear a constant and
     observable relationship to related activities. For purposes
     of control, some discretionary costs such as quality control
     can be treated as though they were engineered costs under
     appropriate conditions.

15. A planning budget is fixed at a given level of output
     volume. Often, the actual output level will not conform to
     this planned level of output. Accordingly, costs and
     revenues will differ from the budgeted level because of
     volume differences. In evaluating the performance of
     managers who have no control over volume, it is desirable to
     have a budget that is based on the actual volume level.
     Accordingly, a flexible budget is used to evaluate the
     success of such managers and it is compiled at the actual
     level of activity.

17. Historically, costs incurred for the sake of quality are
     buried in a variety of accounts. Measuring the cost of
     quality would require a significant effort involving
     extracting costs from a variety of accounts. Even then,
     many estimates and much conjecturing would be required.
     Although quality is an easily defined concept, it is much
     more difficult to assess what portion of some costs (such as
     depreciation) were incurred for the cause of enhancing
     quality.

Exercises

19. a. 4   f. 3
    b. 6   g. 10
    c. 1   h. 8
    d. 5   i. 9
    e. 2   j. 7

21. a. Cost understanding
    b. Cost containment
    c. Cost avoidance/containment
    d. Cost reduction/avoidance
    e. Cost avoidance
    f. Cost understanding
    g. cost reduction/avoidance

23.

	(a) Discretionary-D or Committed-C	(b) Discretionary Cost Output Measure	(c) May be classified as either type
1.	C	–	no
2.	D	Increase in sales	yes
3.	D	Number of customer returns	yes
4.	C	–	no
5.	C	–	yes
6.	D	Number of inventions and innovations	yes
7.	D	Number of documents prepared	yes
8.	D	Executive turnover	yes
9.	D	Increase in sales	yes
10.	C	–	no
11.	D	Number of breakdowns	yes
12	D	Number of documents & memos prepared	yes
13.	D	Number of accidents/injuries	yes
14.	D	Level of community goodwill	yes

25. a. Secretarial Pool:
    Planned efficiency = 10,000 ÷ $114,000
                       = .088 letters per dollar
    Actual efficiency = 9,800 ÷ $109,760
                       = .089 letters per dollar

    Hospital:
    10,300 ÷ $117,260 = .088 letters per dollar

    b. Degree of effectiveness = 9,800 ÷ 10,000 = 98%

27.   a.   dollar volume of wagers
      b.   direct labor cost per drink served
      c.   average number of nights per customer served
      d.   percentage of guests served from out of state
      e.   total number of convention customers served
      f.   develop a customer evaluation form to measure quality
           based on a five point scale; use average rating for
           measure
      g.   percent of revenue from slots machine relative to total
           revenues generated

29.

Total variance = \$1,116 - (\$1,008 + \$121.50) = <u>\$13.50</u> F
Rate variance = \$1,116 - [(120 X \$9) + (8 X \$13.50)]
             = <u>\$72</u> F
Efficiency variance = \$1,188 - \$1,129.50 = <u>\$58.50</u> U
Total variance = \$72F + \$58.50 U = <u>\$13.50</u> F

31.   a.   The prevention costs would rise because that category
           would reflect the depreciation and operating costs of
           the equipment. However, both the internal and external
           failure costs would decline due to a lower level of
           defective output. Possibly, the level of appraisal
           costs would decline too.

      b.   **Engineer**-provide information on the energy consumption
           and operating costs of the machinery; and provide
           information on the technical operation of the machine
           including tolerances, production of waste and scrap,
           and likelihood of producing defective units.
           Production supervisor-provide information on the number
           and type of people required to operate the machine.
           Marketing director - provide information on the effects
           of an improvement in quality on the sales of draperies.
           Cost accountant-provide information on the costs of
           current production methods and assemble the information
           from the technical experts so that it can be presented
           to the CEO in a comprehensible manner.

      c.   There are several reasons why the company might
           rationally elect to spend \$120,000 on prevention rather
           than \$80,000 on appraisal. One reason is that the
           impact on external failure costs (50% reduction) may be
           a multi-period benefit, but only if the cost is for
           prevention rather than appraisal. Another reason is
           that there could be benefits from spending on
           prevention that are felt in the appraisal cost category
           and the internal failure category. An expenditure on
           appraisal activities is unlikely to generate such
           benefits in the other categories.

Communication Activities

33.   a.   Cost understanding and cost avoidance are demonstrated in the response. Ms. Frankel does an excellent job of relating the activities required to fill the order for the California State University system to costs incurred in her publishing company.

       b.   The regulations that must be complied with are voluminous. Because the purchaser is a unit of the State of California, it must comply with a significant number of procedural policies that exist for all state bodies. The purchasing department also has some federal regulations and some in-house policies with which it must comply.

       c.   Bureaucracies work best for high volume transactions. Centralization of authority and control through detailed policies works well to standardize procedures and standardize services. The policies are surrogates for individual authority and judgment. This arrangement does not work well in low volume, unique transactions, and the arrangement is not flexible nor sensitive to the circumstances of individual transactions. In fact, the arrangement looks ridiculous in this example. The transaction costs for purchasing this book must far exceed the price of the book. This is indicative of opportunity to cut costs. By removing many of the regulations and policies for small transactions, the State of California could save millions of tax dollars.

35. a. The proposed maintenance work order system would
         provide written documentation for all man hours and
         materials used in the maintenance department. This
         system would improve cost control by giving operating
         management (user departments) the opportunity to review
         specific maintenance charges for time and materials on
         each maintenance job charged to their department. The
         individual job cost records will provide the basis for
         feedback to the maintenance department on the quality
         and efficiency of work performed.

             By providing an estimate for each job prior to
         starting the job, the user department will have an
         opportunity to cancel unneeded work or work that
         appears to be too expensive. The maintenance
         department will be able to compare the estimates with
         estimates on similar jobs and with the actual costs
         once the job is completed in order to evaluate
         personnel performance. In addition, the estimating
         should improve scheduling of priority jobs and improve
         cost control as the estimating procedure is refined.

             The maintenance work order system will provide a
         basis for improved allocation of costs to user
         departments. If the work order system is effective and
         a buyer/seller relationship is developed between the
         user department and the maintenance department, the
         user department will insist on an efficient preventive
         maintenance program in order to minimize breakdown
         maintenance, spoilage, and lost production time.

     b. The documentation provided by the work order system
         should provide maintenance department management with
         statistics to support its request for additional
         people. If the maintenance department can develop a
         meaningful cost/benefit relationship showing a payback
         on additional personnel through reduced overtime, less
         downtime waiting for repairs, improved preventive
         maintenance, etc., rational management would authorize
         the addition of the required manpower.

(CMA)

37. a. An architectural firm would spend more on prevention
         and appraisal than firms in other industries. A
         faulty building plan could translate to loss of life
         and massive property damage. Accordingly, the
         consequences for an external failure can be severe. To
         avoid such consequences, firms are likely to invest
         heavily in training and review.

b.   Services provided by a hair salon have significantly different external risks relative to some industries such as health care or architecture. Also, the technology is very low-tech relative to technology in other industries. In general the consequences of an external failure are relatively insignificant. Thus, this type of firm would likely spend relatively less on prevention and appraisal than the other types of firms addressed in this problem.

c.   A heavy equipment manufacturer would invest heavily in product and process design. Much of the quality of the product would be determined by expenditures made before production begins. Consequently, this type of firm will spend heavily on prevention and appraisal. Even so, this type of firm will expect to have some external failures and some internal failures.

d.   In the health care profession, an external failure can mean loss of life, permanent injury, or unnecessary suffering. Further, through malpractice damages, the cost of an external failure can be extraordinarily high. For these reasons, one would expect relatively high spending for prevention and appraisal and relatively low (expected) expenditures for internal and external failure.

Problems

39. This exercise is intended to evoke student thought. Many
     different answers can be expected. The following set of
     answers is provided as an example:
     (From employer's perspective)

	Potential **Advantages**	Potential **Disadvantages**
a.	Lower cost Higher quality	Less reliable Less flexibility
b.	Lower cost Obtain experienced people	Less committed employees Less effective because employee is likely to have a full time job elsewhere
c.	Less expensive Flexibility	Less control over writers Poor quality of writing
d.	Less expensive Flexibility	Less reliable Less control Poor quality work
e.	Less expensive Flexibility	Risk of theft Poor public relations Poor service Errors
f.	School meets all classes Gives students a change Brings practical experience to classes	Inadequate classroom skills Parents' complaints
g.	Less expensive Flexibility	Lower quality credentials Lower quality delivery Not available outside of class
h.	Less expensive Flexibility	Less control over doctors Less loyalty Lower quality of services
i.	Less expensive Flexibility Quicker service Recruiting technique for full timers	Lower quality Greater obsolescence of preparer Less control Less reliability
j.	Less expensive Flexibility Less reliable	Less control Errors in work
k.	Less expensive Flexibility Recruiting technique for full timers	Lower quality Poor preparation Less control Lower reliability

41. a. This is a change intended to increase efficiency; the patient will receive the same procedure as before, but with a shorter hospital stay. This is an example of cost avoidance or cost reduction. Costs that otherwise would have been incurred for a longer hospital stay are avoided.

    b. This is a change that increases both effectiveness and efficiency; the success rate of the operation is increased and subsequent treatment for infection is avoided. This is an example of cost reduction, reducing the infection rate reduced the cost of the average treatment.

    c. This change increases the efficiency of the operation. Fewer days in the hospital are required. This change represents cost reduction because the costs associated with a longer hospital stay are avoided.

    d. This is a change that resulted in an increase in efficiency. Fewer days in the hospital are required by completing the blood work earlier. This change represents cost understanding and cost reduction. Although an increase in costs may have been incurred to get blood tests returned more quickly, this increase would be overwhelmed by the shorter hospital stay.

    e. This change may have impacted both effectiveness and efficiency. The anti-nausea drug may have increased both the rate of success of the chemotherapy while it decreased the average length of the hospital stay. This is an increase in efficiency. This change represents both cost understanding and cost avoidance/reduction. By incurring higher costs for drugs, the length of the hospital stay, and its associated costs, are reduced.

43. a.

Costs	Actual Amount	Budgeted Amount	Difference
Variable	$ 43,700	$ 32,250	$11,450
Fixed	75,250	75,250	0
Total	$118,950	$107,500	$11,450

The EDP Department exceeded its total budget; however, it was only the variable overhead that was overspent. The actual fixed overhead was exactly equal to budget.

Chapter 12
Controlling Noninventory Costs

b. Actual output ÷ planned output = 2,300 ÷ 2,150 = 1.07
       In this case, the department, provided 107% of the intended output.

c. | **Efficiency** | **Variable** | **Fixed** |
    |---|---|---|
    | Planned | 2,150 ÷ $32,250 = .067 | 2,150 ÷ $75,250 = .029 |
    | Actual | 2,300 ÷ $43,700 = .053 | 2,300 ÷ $75,250 = .031 |

Actual efficiency exceeded planned efficiency for fixed overhead; however, actual efficiency was less than planned efficiency for variable overhead.

d.

Variable overhead

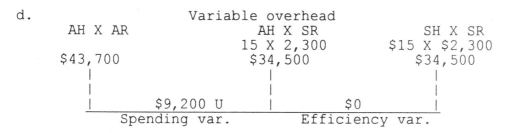

AH X AR	AH X SR 15 X 2,300	SH X SR $15 X $2,300
$43,700	$34,500	$34,500
	$9,200 U	$0
	Spending var.	Efficiency var.

Fixed overhead

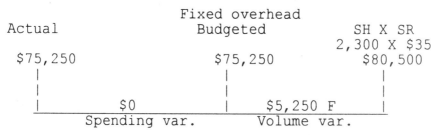

Actual	Budgeted	SH X SR 2,300 X $35
$75,250	$75,250	$80,500
	$0	$5,250 F
	Spending var.	Volume var.

e. A reasonable rate to charge would be based on planned costs per hour:

Variable	$15
Fixed	35
Total	$50

Charging user departments for their use of EDP services should cause managers to limit their use to only that which is cost beneficial to them. This, in turn, should reduce the basis which the EDP Department has been using to justify ever-increasing budget requests, thereby reducing the budget requests themselves. It would also give the EDP Department a better incentive to contain its costs.

45. a.   R = 280 X $11
          = $3,080

     b.   Z = (400 - 280) X ($25 - $10)
          = $1,800

     c.   W = 45 X $16
          = $720

     d.   F = $3,080 + $1,800 + $720
          = $5,600

     e.   T = $8,000 + $9,200 + $5,600
          = $22,800

47. a.   Z = 150 X $80 = $12,000

     b.   F = $12,000 + $5,500 + $18,200 + $9,100 +
          $13,500 + $5,100
          = $63,400

     c.   Prevention = $30,000 + $90,000 + $62,000 +
                       $38,000 + $24,000 + $19,000 +
                       $63,400
                     = $326,400

     d.   An increase in the warranty period, accompanied by no
          other changes should result in an increase in external
          failure costs. More customers will have units to
          return under the longer warranty coverage.
               This type of decision should be made by general
          management. Input to this decision should come from
          marketing (how will the increased warranty period
          affect price and competitive position), engineering
          (what is the failure rate of the product in the eighth,
          ninth, and tenth years), accounting (what are the costs
          associated with the average external failure, the costs
          of processing customer returns, value of defective
          returned units, etc.).

Cases
49. a.   The military has as its primary objective being
           prepared for war - even during peacetime. One of the
           difficulties for the military of peacetime
           administration is to keep the nation from letting down
           its guard lest it be attacked or its soldiers are
           called quickly into combat. The country cannot wait
           until war starts to begin acquiring materials and
           supplies. Part of the military's job is to stockpile
           abundant reserves so that it can withstand attempted
           attacks from foreign powers. Cost efficiency must take
           a backseat when military effectiveness is at stake.

     b.   Military preparedness is not equivalent to reckless
           waste and inefficiency. The military should stockpile
           only as much as is necessary to supply wartime needs
           for some reasonable, predetermined duration such as a
           year. This would give civilian vendors sufficient time
           to prepare to supply military needs on a continuous
           basis as long as it has needs. That way, the taxpayer
           is paying only for as much as is needed, when and if
           these items are needed. In addition, lower stockpiles
           provide for lower risk of obsolescence.

     c.   In the computer age, the military can use data base
           management systems and modern business techniques to
           plan, control, evaluate, and make decisions about
           inventory management. For example, by classifying
           inventory according to cost, turnover, and military
           significance, the administration can discriminate about
           which inventory items are worthy of extreme attention
           (e.g., perpetual records and frequent observations) and
           those items that are only worthy of minimal effort
           (e.g., annual counts and assessments).
               When the military wants to change a nonstrategic
           item such as quartz, for which it has a large supply,
           the administration should require a moratorium on the
           replacement material until existing materials have been
           phased out by use or market resale.
               Bureaucratic resistance to change is the biggest
           deterrent to implementing these ideas.

51. To: Mary Ross
    From: Barry Stein
    Subject: Explanation of November 1997 Variances

    a. The revenue mix variance resulted from a higher
        proportion of participants being eligible for
        discounts. The budgeted revenue was based on 30
        percent of the participants taking the discount; but,
        during November, 45 percent of those attending the
        courses received discounts. As a result, the weighted
        average fee dropped from $145.50 to $143.25.

    b. The most significant implication of the revenue mix
        variance is that the proportion of discount fees has
        increased by 50 percent. If the increase represents a
        trend, the implications for future profits could be
        serious as revenues per participant day will decline
        while costs are likely to remain steady or increase.

    c. The revenue timing difference was caused by early
        registrations for the December program to be held in
        Cincinnati. The early registrations resulted from the
        combined promotional mailing for both the Chicago and
        Cincinnati programs. These early registrations have
        been prematurely recognized as revenue during November.

    d. The revenue recognition in November of early
        registrations for the December courses is
        inappropriate, and, consequently, revenues during the
        month of December may be lower than expected.

    e. The primary cause of the unfavorable total expense
        variance were additional food charges, course
        materials, and instructor fees. Although these
        quantity variances are unfavorable, the increased costs
        of $10,400 are more than offset by the additional
        revenues of $40,740 with which these items are
        associated.

    f. The favorable food price variance was determined by
        multiplying the difference between the budgeted and
        actual price per participant day times the actual
        participant days. The actual price per participant day
        was determined by dividing the actual food charges by
        the total participant days ($32,000 ÷ 1,280).

g.   While the combined promotional piece had a $5,000
     unfavorable impact on November expenses, there will be
     no need for further promotion of the Cincinnati
     program. Therefore, the $20,000 budgeted for this
     purpose in December will not be expended, lowering
     planned expenses for the month.
          The promotion timing difference represents an
     incorrect matching of costs and revenue. The costs
     allocated to the Cincinnati program should be reflected
     on the December statement of operations to be matched
     against the December program.

h.   The course development variance is unfavorable to the
     November budget, but its overall impact on the company
     cannot be determined until such time as the level of
     acceptance of the new course is experienced.

(CMA)

Ethics and Quality Discussion

53. a.   There is nothing unique to civil service employment, relative to private sector employment, that makes quality either more difficult or less difficult to pursue.

     b.   The authors assume students will have little difficulty offering a variety of examples.

     c.   Hopefully, students will have examples in which their city or state government has indicated a concern for quality. Some examples that might be mentioned: higher taxes to finance better law enforcement; new fees to support community recycling; higher property taxes to support the arts in the community; or higher taxes to improve roads, schools or parks.

     d.   Examples students might offer include lower utility rates due to sales of excess water or electricity to other communities; lower garbage collection fees due to sales of recyclables; lower taxes due to downsizing governmental departments, or lower taxes due to consolidation of school districts.

     e.   It is easier in private industry to provide correct incentives to employees. Private industry is more likely to have continuity in ownership and management, and a constant objective function--maximize profits or shareholder wealth. Thus, it is relatively easy to link employee motivation to the objective function through profit sharing, bonus plans, or other types of incentives.

          In government, the objective function often changes with the political winds; there is no continuity in funding; and, it is more difficult to be customer oriented because it is more difficult to identify the customer (society, taxpayers, voters, specific user groups).

55. This problem presents a conflict between the quantity of
    service and the quality of service provided. The
    empowerment of counselors will allow counselors to make
    decisions regarding the families they serve without the
    added time involved in obtaining administrative approval.
    Similarly, establishing a set time limit for meeting with
    families and abolishing review processes will also save
    time. However, these safeguards were established originally
    to ensure that only high quality services were provided to
    the agency's clients.
         On balance, the changes outlined will allow the agency
    to be more efficient (more clients served per counselor),
    but less effective (less resolution of client problems). It
    is extremely difficult to determine whether it is more
    ethical to be effective or efficient in providing social
    services. There are ethical merits to both dimensions of
    performance. To the extent only qualified, experienced
    people are employed by the agency, one might argue that the
    changes instituted are ethically sound. Alternatively, if
    the employees are inexperienced, or marginally qualified,
    the drop in quality of services may be so profound as to be
    ethically objectionable.

57. a.   Cost understanding and cost reduction are indicated in
         the discussions of the health administrators. Cost
         understanding is indicated in the discussions linking
         the quantity of the dosage to the treatment. Cost
         reduction is indicated by the possibility of reducing
         the dosage administered to patients.

    b.   The intended consequence of using a lower dosage is to
         decrease the cost per patient treated. The unintended
         consequence may be more suffering on the part of the
         patient. If the health experts are relatively certain
         that there will be no deterioration in effectiveness of
         the drug, there are no negative ethical consequences to
         reducing the dosage. [However, the pharmaceutical
         companies may respond by doubling the price, if this
         practice becomes widespread.] In fact, for a given sum
         of money, health professionals will be able to treat
         more people. An ethical dimension arises in setting
         the dosage if a smaller dosage provides less effective
         treatment. In this case, some ethical compromise may
         involve trading off cost considerations and cost
         constraints, with effectiveness of the treatment.

    c.   The pharmaceutical company has an ethical obligation to
         not gouge the consuming public on the price of drugs.
         This includes not overstating the dosage that is
         required for effective treatment.

Chapter 13

Controlling Inventory and Production Costs

Questions

1. A items are those having the highest dollar volume; these are likely to be some of the most expensive parts and materials used in production. C items are those having the lowest dollar volume; these are likely to be parts and materials that are used in small volume or are of very low value on a per unit basis. B items are those that fall between A and C items; they have moderate dollar volume.

3. In the not-too-distant past the decision on sourcing would have been based almost exclusively on price. Although price is still a significant factor in the decision, today, companies are more likely to place weight on the ability of the supplier to deliver reliably, high quality goods. The nature of the relationship has also changed to allow for more cooperation between customer and supplier. Both the supplier and the customer realize that their mutual survival depends on jointly reducing costs and delivering greater value to the customer. To facilitate this type of communication and cooperation, firms are reducing the number of suppliers they purchase from and are attempting to purchase more standardized parts.

5. The cost of purchasing is not included because the purchase cost relates to the question "from whom to buy" rather than to the separate question "how many to buy." The latter question is the concern addressed by EOQ.

7. MRP overcomes the deficiency of ignoring relationships among inventory items by integrating interrelationships of units into the ordering process.

191

9.   Significant benefits achieved by many firms using MPR include elimination of erratic production and back orders, streamlining scheduling and receiving operations, better utilization of labor, improved utilization of space, and reduction of inventory levels.

The following problems are sometimes associated with a MRP system:

- It produces excess inventories because it is a "push" system.
- Quantity distortions may occur because the inputs to the MRP system from the bill of materials and operations flow document may be incomplete or inaccurate.
- Quantity distortions may occur because the MRP system is based on the EOQ/safety stock model. If estimates for annual usage, carrying costs, order costs and/or lead times are inaccurate, output from the MRP model will be somewhat inaccurate.
- Actual inventory may not be that shown on the accounting records.
- While the MRP system is intended to be in use at all times, some managers may not conform to this so that the system is not fully and continually implemented.

11.   JIT views inventory as a liability because it costs the company money to hold inventory. Inventory represents an investment for which there is no current demand. JIT works at streamlining operations so that carrying inventory is unnecessary.

13.   A push system is a production control system in which work centers produce inventory in excess of current needs because of lead time or economic production/order quantity requirements.

A pull system of production control is one in which parts are delivered/produced only as needed by the work center for which they are intended. Theoretically, there are no stockrooms where work centers "push" completed parts in excess of the current needs of recipient work centers.

15.   At the heart of JIT is the concept of continuous improvement to reduce costs and improve quality. Empowerment is the key to continuous improvement. It refers to providing employees the training, support and skills necessary to change their own jobs to effect improvements. Empowerment requires that employees understand how their job relates to the goals of the overall organization, and that they be involved in organizational planning and control.

17. Since JIT represents a philosophy of how to do things rather than how to produce things, many aspects of JIT can be used by non-manufacturers. The following changes needed to effectively implement JIT by non-manufacturers in relation to their purchasing techniques and employee base are:
    - Selection of a vendor should consider the following items in addition to the invoice prices:
      -having reliable delivery schedules with short lead times to allow for maintaining little or no inventory and for flexibility and speed in meeting customer needs;
      -maintaining long-term relationships with fewer vendors to improve communications, assure quality and service, obtain quantity discounts, and reduce operating costs; and
      -obtaining suppliers who are located close to the company to reduce lead times and shipping costs.
    - Small quantities should be ordered to minimize inventory carrying costs.
    - Workers are used to continually assure quality control to reduce costs and approach zero-errors.
    - The work space layout should be designed in a manner that is conducive to the flow of goods and organization of workers.
    - Employee suggestions for improving operations should be sought; these individuals often have a wealth of information that goes untapped.
    - Utilize job enrichment to improve worker flexibility and interest.

19. Because variances represent "out of control" situations, in a JIT system the situation that creates a variance must be solved "on the spot." With JIT management of inventory, quality of processes and products must be very high because poor quality translates very quickly into missed shipments and backorders. Thus, in a JIT environment, problems that create (quantity) variances are solved immediately; at period end when variances would normally be examined, the cause and solution of the variance have already been addressed. For this reason, variance analysis contributes very little to control in a JIT-managed firm. Also, price variances are not likely to occur in such firms because major inputs are acquired from suppliers under long-term pricing agreements.

21. Backflush accounting takes the production output based on a periodic inventory system and works backwards through the system with standard costs to assign production costs to inventory and cost of goods sold. Backflush accounting is quicker and easier to apply than using a perpetual system and actual costing.

Exercises
23. a. 7
     b. 5
     c. 1
     d. 2
     e. 4
     f. 9
     g. 6
     h. 8
     i. 10
     j. 3

25. a. N
     b. C
     c. C
     d. C
     e. O
     f. O
     g. C
     h. N/A
     i. O
     j. C
     k. N
     l. N/A
     m. O
     n. C
     o. N/A

27. EOQ = $\dfrac{\sqrt{(2 \times 12{,}000 \times \$6)}}{\$.50}$
         = $\sqrt{288{,}000}$
         = 537 (rounded)

29. a. EOQ = $\sqrt{((2 \times 75,000 \times \$10.25) \div \$.65)}$
        = $\sqrt{2,365,384.6}$
        = 1,538 (rounded)

   b. EOQ = $\sqrt{((2 \times 75,000 \times \$7.25) \div \$.65)}$
        = $\sqrt{1,673,076.9}$
        = 1,293 (rounded)

   c. EOQ, part a:
       ordering costs
          (75,000 ÷ 1,538) X $10.25 = $ 500 (rounded)
       carrying costs
          (1,538 ÷ 2) X $.65 =   500 (rounded)
                Total $1,000

       EOQ, part b:
       ordering costs
          (75,000 ÷ 1,293) X $7.25 = $420 (rounded)
       carrying costs
          (1,293 ÷ 2) X $.65 =   420 (rounded)
                Total $840

   d. Assuming that the company used the original EOQ (from part a.) for ordering inventory when their true costs were those presented in part b., the company's actual cost of carrying and ordering inventory would exceed $840:

       ordering costs
          (75,000 ÷ 1,538) X $7.25 = $354
       carrying costs
          (1,538 ÷ 2) X $.65 =   500
             Total costs incurred $854

       The error caused costs to be $14 higher than the cost would have been if the correct EOQ would have been used (1,293 units)

   e. An expert from the Finance or Treasury staff can provide input about the opportunity cost of capital, a major inventory carrying cost.

31. a.   EOQ = $\sqrt{(2 \times 7{,}300 \times \$8) \div \$.48}$
          = 493 pounds

     b.   Daily usage = 7,300 ÷ 365 = 20 pounds per day
          Order point = 20 X 18 = 360 pounds;
     c.   Safety stock = 20 X 3 = 60 pounds
     d.   20 X .1 X 18 = 36 pounds
     e.   for maximum usage over lead time:
                              (22 - 20) X 21 = 42
          for normal usage in extra 3 days 20 X 3 =   60
            Total safety stock   102
            Normal usage during lead time   360
            Order point   462 pounds

33. a.   RIP   186,000
              Accounts Payable   186,000

          Conversion Costs   282,000
              Various accounts   282,000

          RIP   281,880
              Conversion Costs   281,880

          Finished Goods   468,000
              RIP   468,000

          Accounts Receivable   644,000
              Sales   644,000

          Cost of Goods Sold   460,000
              Finished Goods   460,000

b.

RIP		FG	
6,000		12,000	
186,000	468,000	468,000	460,000
281,880			
5,880		20,000	

Communication Activities

35.   a.   The large customers account for a significant
           percentage of the business of small firms. This gives
           the large firms a tremendous amount of leverage in
           influencing decisions of small firms and in obtaining
           concessions on price or other considerations from the
           smaller firms.

      b.   Large firms prefer to do business with small firms for
           obvious economic reasons. Having substantial clout
           with the smaller firms, the large customer can use its
           strong bargaining position to obtain both favorable
           prices for products and other valuable concessions.
           For example, the large firm may be able to induce the
           small firm to invest in specific production equipment
           or use a particular mode of delivery to improve its
           service. Also, because of the uneven power
           relationship, the large firm can probably prod the
           small firm into making changes in product design or
           process design to improve quality.

      c.   Some empirical evidence suggests that when a large
           customer adopts JIT, many of the customer's inventory
           management problems are simply handed down to
           suppliers. For example, some evidence indicates that
           although the large customer's inventory levels may
           decline, the supplier's inventories rise in order to
           meet JIT delivery schedules. This causes the smaller
           firm to increase its investment in inventories and
           squeezes its profit margins.

      d.   A diversified set of customers reduces the risk of the
           business. With a diversified customer base, a firm is
           not at jeopardy if a customer cancels orders or decides
           to obtain its inputs elsewhere. This is the principal
           advantage of the broad customer base. The disadvantage
           may be a lack of economies of scale. If each customer
           is purchasing different products or components, the
           demand for any single product may be fairly limited.
           This is an advantage of dealing with a large customer.
           A firm can specialize in producing a narrow product
           line and achieve significant economies of scale in
           doing so. Additionally, if there is significant
           cooperation with the large customer, the exchange of
           information may lead to opportunities to jointly reduce
           costs and increase profits.

37.   a.   The two most significant problems could be the lack of
           resources to provide the necessary training and the
           lack of leverage to obtain the cooperation of
           suppliers. Substantial training is required to
           establish the culture and the employee capabilities
           needed for empowerment and continuous improvement.
           Also, experts need to be available to realign incentive
           pay systems to provide the correct motivation for the
           JIT system to be successful.
                Suppliers may not see any valid reasons to change
           their delivery systems to meet the needs of a single
           customer. It might simply be more profitable for them
           to drop the customer. JIT cannot be implemented
           without the support and cooperation of suppliers.

      b.   The culture has much to do with the potential to
           successfully implement JIT. If the culture is one that
           willingly accepts change and recognizes the need for
           change to remain competitive, the likelihood of
           successfully implementing JIT is enhanced. However, if
           the culture is characterized by mistrust between labor
           and management, focuses on individual achievements
           rather than group and team achievements, and expects
           management to be the problem solvers in the
           organization, then implementing JIT will be an
           overwhelming challenge.
                Before attempting to implement JIT, the company
           should have attempted to change the culture. In order
           to implement JIT, the company had to make too many
           changes at once for the culture to absorb.

c.   The environment and culture should have been changed
     before the company attempted to implement JIT. For
     example, some of the changes that should have been
     implemented include:

- drop the piece rate pay plan. The company should
  have adopted a new incentive system that
  encouraged both individual achievement and group
  or team achievement. Additionally, incentives
  should have been devised that encouraged both
  short-term and long-term achievement.

- an in-house training program and pool of expertise
  should have been developed. To implement JIT, the
  company needed to first train its employees to
  accept responsibility for their jobs and develop
  tools for continuous improvement.

- consult with suppliers. Either new suppliers
  needed to be found or existing suppliers needed to
  be provided time to adjust to the JIT delivery
  schedule.

- develop a better system of communication. In a
  JIT system, employees must be encouraged to make
  suggestions to decrease costs, improve quality and
  increase customer value. The organizational
  structure should support this needed
  communication.

- layout of facilities. To implement JIT, there
  must be communication between adjacent work
  stations. This may require a rearranging the work
  area.

- do a pilot implementation. Rather than fully
  implementing JIT immediately, many firms find it
  worthwhile to implement JIT in one facet of
  operations or in a single plant. This allows the
  firm a chance to learn about problems and identify
  solutions to implementing JIT. The company can
  use the knowledge and experience gained in the
  pilot implementation to better structure a
  complete implementation.

- the company should have defined exactly what
  benefits were expected from implementing JIT.
  This would allow the implementation to be more
  goal oriented and provide a basis against which
  the success of the implementation could be
  measured.

- implementation plan. The company might have
  devised an actual implementation plan which would
  have anticipated some of the problems the firm
  experienced.

39.   a.   It is important to recognize that adapting a JIT
           approach to some aspects of management doesn't mean
           that Americans have to do everything exactly the way
           the Japanese do. Demographic differences do impose
           difficulties for some companies for some aspects of
           JIT, such as extreme inventory minimization. Others
           can work around these difficulties. While cultural
           differences do exist, U.S. workers have traditionally
           had a strong work ethic involving dependability,
           concern for quality, cooperative behavior, and respect
           for authority. Facing stiffer global competition is
           expected to heighten these traditional U.S. values. In
           any event, American firms simply need to take advantage
           of any tools to help us improve performance to maintain
           or increase our competitive position.

      b.   The geography of the U.S. makes the JIT concept more
           difficult to implement than in Japan. The U.S. is
           simply a much larger country. This creates the
           possibility for a supplier and a customer to be located
           at great distances from one another For example, a
           firm may have an important supplier located a distance
           of 3,000 miles away. This makes the management of raw
           material, supply, and component inventories more
           difficult to manage on a JIT basis. However, work in
           process inventory and finished goods inventories might
           still be managed on a JIT basis with the same success
           as Japanese firms.

      c.   For companies whose vendors are at great distances, the
           required logistics of JIT may not all be susceptible to
           effective accomplishment. For companies whose
           management-employee relationships are strained, some of
           the JIT approaches may not be as effective as when
           there is a spirit of cooperation and teamwork.

      d.   The logistics problems may be addressed by discussing
           the problems with vendors with respect to long-term
           purchase commitments, variations on the focused factory
           arrangements, and vendor use of closer warehousing -
           perhaps with consignees and other creative solutions.
                The personnel difficulties can be addressed by
           leadership and incentives to get everyone on the team
           and by demonstrating that use of JIT can be a win-win
           approach to meeting competition and earning more and
           developing further.

41.   a.   Other engineering changes may be made to change the mix of material inputs, or the nature of conversion processes, to reduce costs or improve quality. Engineering changes may also be made to add product features, replace a special part with a standard part, or simplify the production process.

      b.   Shutting down the plant provides assurance that no additional flawed products will be built. Also, many employees in the plant may be working on building the necessary replacement part for the fuel tank assembly.

      c.   A product failure is either discovered internally or externally. If discovered internally, the flaw is likely to be uncovered during routine quality inspections. This, of course, is the way in which a company prefers to discover a product defect. Externally, the product flaw is discovered by customers using the products.

Chapter 13
Controlling Inventory and Production Costs

Problems

43. a.   Only the costs that would actually vary over the short run with the number of orders placed would be considered:

Cost per order for supplies	$0.90
Phone expense	4.20
Total	$5.10

   b.   Only the costs that would actually vary in the short run with the quantity of materials stored would be considered:

Insurance premium	$0.11
Obsolescence cost	.12
Total	$0.23

45. a.   EOQ = $\sqrt{((2 \times 24{,}000 \times \$10) \div \$.12)}$
         = <u>2,000</u> gallons

   b.   24,000 ÷ 2,000 = <u>12</u> orders per year

   c.
Ordering costs:	(24,000 ÷ 2,000) X $10	$120
Carrying costs:	($2,000 ÷ 2) X $0.12	120
Total costs increase to		$240

   d.   Common problems that can be encountered include:
   - the EOQ is not obtainable from the vendor; minimum lot size is larger;
   - substantial price discounts are available from purchasing a quantity larger than EOQ;
   - the EOQ model has flaws:
     - the EOQ formula ignores relationships among inventory items (2 wheels per axle);
     - the EOQ model offers no insights as to how to reduce ordering and carrying costs;
     - the EOQ model ignores fixed costs; often these are very large relative to the variable costs;
   - inadequate storage space may be available to store the EOQ;
   - the company may have insufficient cash resources to purchase the EOQ.

47. a.   D
   b.   U
   c.   T
   d.   T
   e.   T
   f.   T
   g.   D
   h.   T
   i.   T
   j.   D

49. a.   Usage variance, Rice:
            Current standard

5 X 50,000 X $.02	$ 5,000.00

            Actual

16,562 X 16 X $.02	5,299.84
Total	$ 299.84 U

            Current standard

Beans 7 X 50,000 X $.03	$10,500.00

            Actual

Beans 21,250 X 16 X $.03	10,200.00
Variance	$ 300.00 F

    b.   Rice (5 - 6) X 50,000 X $.02 $1,000 F
          Beans (7 - 6) X 50,000 X $.03 $1,500 U

    c.   The company may have made the change to respond to consumer preferences (more beans less rice translates into higher sales), because the firm wanted to change the nutrition content of the soup, or because of limited availability of rice in the required quantities and quality.

51.
  1. RIP   24,904,000

1. RIP	24,904,000	
Material Purchase Price Variance	480	
Accounts Payable		24,904,480
Accounts Payable	24,904,480	
Cash		24,904,480
2. Conversion Costs	2,918,000	
Accumulated Depreciation		321,000
Cash		103,000
Accounts Payable		2,494,000
Accounts Payable	2,494,000	
Cash		2,494,000
3. RIP (2,080,000 X $1.40)	2,912,000	
Conversion Cost Variance	6,000	
Conversion Costs		2,918,000
Conversion Costs	14,432,000	
Accumulated Depreciation		4,000,000
Cash		9,325,000
Accounts Payable		1,107,000
Accounts Payable	1,107,000	
Cash		1,107,000
RIP (10,320,000 X $1.40)	14,448,000	
Conversion Cost Variances		16,000
Conversion Costs		14,432,000

Cases

53. a.   The after-tax net cash savings realized by AgriCorp's Service Division as a result of the just-in-time inventory program is $25,800, calculated as reflected below.

After-Tax Net Cash Savings

		Cash Savings (Loss)
Funds released from inventory investment	$400,000	
Interest before tax [.09 ÷ (1 − .4)] .15		$60,000
Insurance savings ($80,000 X .60)		48,000
Warehouse rental [(8,000 sq. ft. X .75) X $2.50 per sq. ft.]		15,000
Transferred employees - no effect		−
Contribution of lost sales (3,800 units @ $10.00) (Note 1)		(38,000)
Overtime premium (7,500 units @ $5.60) (Note 2)		(42,000)
Net cash savings before tax		$43,000
Income taxes @ .40		17,200
Net cash savings after tax		$25,800

Note 1:
Calculation of unit contribution margin

Revenue ($6,160,000 ÷ 280,000 units)		$22.00
Less variable costs:		
Cost of Goods sold ($2,660,000 ÷ 280,000 units)	$9.50	
Selling and administrative expenses ($700,000 ÷ 280,000 units)	2.50	12.00
Contribution margin		$10.00

Note 2:
The incremental cost of $5.60 per unit for overtime is less than the additional $10.00 per unit contribution for the 7,500 units that would have been lost sales.

b. Factors, other than financial, that should be
    considered before a company implements a just-in-time
    inventory program include

    ▪ customer dissatisfaction. Stockouts of finished
      goods and/or spare parts could result in
      customers' downtime which may not be acceptable
      and may also be costly.

    ▪ distributor relations. Stockouts of spare parts
      and/or finished goods can impair the
      manufacturer's image with its distributors who
      represent the direct contacts with the ultimate
      (customer) user.

    ▪ supplier dissatisfaction. Placement of smaller and
      more frequent orders can result in higher material
      and delivery costs from suppliers. Additionally,
      with changes in the suppliers' production and
      procurement processes, they may choose to
      discontinue being suppliers to a just-in-time
      customer.

    ▪ competition. The marketplace will determine the
      impact of service degradation due to stockouts.
      Brand loyalty can deteriorate when service
      standards are lowered.

(CMA reprinted)

Ethics and Quality Discussion

55. a.   The examples clearly indicate the dependence of
           companies on their suppliers to control quality. For
           example, if a soda company purchases cans from an
           aluminum company that contain shards of metal, quality
           of the final product is defective despite how well the
           company's internal processes may produce soda. Faulty
           inputs lead to defective output, and it doesn't matter
           whether the faults occur in the supplier's plant or the
           customer's plant.

     b.   For many businesses it is the perception of quality
           that matters. It is also likely that the "actual"
           quality and the perceived quality sometimes diverge.
           Even though, in reality, no soda bottles may be
           contaminated with metal shards, if consumers think
           contamination exists sales will be adversely affected.
           Similarly, to the extent foreign objects in soda go
           undetected, actual poor quality may be perceived as
           high quality. However, in the long run, consumers'
           perceptions are not likely to deviate far from actual
           quality levels.

     c.   There are ethical considerations in quality control of
           food products. It is those cases where the consumer
           might not be able to detect the flaws that creates the
           ethical conflict. In those cases where quality failure
           would be obvious to the consumer, no ethical conflict
           exists because both ethics and economics mandate that
           such units be kept from consumers.
               However, with a slight imperfection in the product
           that could have negative health consequences, but not
           necessarily so, a company may perceive that it is
           economically better off not to scrap units in inventory
           or recall units that have been sold. The consequence
           of selling such units if no harm is caused the consumer
           is higher profits for the company. If consumers become
           ill the consequences are health related problems and
           costs for consumers, and possible legal actions for the
           company.

57.   a.   Unions typify the historically hostile relations
           between managers and workers. Unions were founded on
           the basis of unfair treatment of workers by owners and
           managers. Consequently, the mistrust between
           management and unions is an artifact of that historical
           context--unions oppose managers and represent workers.
           Naturally, then, unions will be suspicious of any new
           initiatives by managers that require workers to
           cooperate with managers. Unions are simply not
           structured to accommodate or facilitate cooperation.

      b.   Ethics aside, managers have an obligation to not use
           quality as an excuse to fire workers or oppose unions.
           Doing so undermines their credibility and will render
           future attempts to instill real changes ineffective.
               Ethically, managers have an obligation to not make
           workers the victims of their own quality and efficiency
           achievements. If workers use their own (private)
           knowledge as the basis for changes in the firms
           operations that improve quality and efficiency,
           managers must not exploit that knowledge; i.e., no
           manager can ask a worker to work himself out of a job.

      c.   Workers and managers are mutually dependent on the
           ability of their firms to compete in the global market
           place. Without cooperation between the two groups the
           company will not be able to adopt the strategies that
           are necessary to effectively compete. Workers have an
           obligation to utilize all of their skills and talents
           to improve the quality of their work and the output of
           the firm. This means workers are ethically obligated
           to make a good faith effort to cooperate with managers
           in devising and implementing new programs and to share
           their knowledge about the firm's products and
           processes.

Capital Asset Selection and Capital Budgeting

Questions

1. A capital asset is an asset that provides benefits to the firm for more than one year. Capital assets are primarily distinguished from other assets in that they have longer lives, and they exist only to provide the capacity for the firm to produce, distribute and market goods.

3. The screening evaluation is used only to determine if a project meets some predetermined standard (net present value >0, for example). In simply meeting this criterion, the project is not necessarily going to be funded. To be funded, a project must be evaluated based on how it compares to other projects which have also passed the screening criterion. This comparison will involve preference criteria. The preference criteria may take into account nonfinancial data: safety considerations, legal requirements, public service obligations, etc. Also, the preference criteria will need to take into account that some projects are mutually exclusive, others are mutually inclusive, and yet others are independent.

5. Independent projects exist when the acceptance of one project does not imply either acceptance or rejection of the other projects: Examples of independent projects:
   1. Computerized accounting system, new production equipment.
   2. New product line, employee safety training program.
   3. New production/operation control system, R&D for product development.

7. The purpose of discounted cash flow analysis is to account for the opportunity cost of money for transactions that occur at different points in time. There is no opportunity cost associated with accounting accruals, only cash transactions. Accordingly, discounted cash flow analysis focuses only on those transactions in which an opportunity cost (interest) exists--cash transactions.

9. A timeline is simply a graphical display of all cash flows associated with a project. The timeline shows both the amount and the timing of the cash flows. It is a helpful tool in organizing or structuring discounted cash flow analysis. Use of a timeline helps prevent oversight of certain cash flows and facilitates the netting of cash flows that occur at a common point in time.

11. The payback period is the amount of time required for cash inflows to recoup the initial cost of an investment. Usually, no allowance is made for the time value of money in computing the payback period. This is one reason it is normally used only in conjunction with other methods. Another reason is that the payback method ignores all cash flows that occur after the payback period.

13. If the NPV = 0, then the projected return on the project is equal to the discount rate. If the NPV < 0, the project's expected return is below the firm's discount rate; and if the NPV > 0, the expected return exceeds the firm's discount rate.

15. The profitability index, PI, is a measure that provides more information about relative "profitability" of two projects that are of dissimilar size. The PI relates the present value of each project to its initial cost. The net present value measure provides no indication of the actual cost of each investment.

17. Unique to the IRR, two major weaknesses are: 1) the IRR ignores the dollar magnitude of alternative projects, and 2) projects with large cash outflows in the later years of their lives may generate multiple IRRs.

19. Depreciation is a noncash expense and would normally be ignored in a discounted cash flow framework. However, depreciation becomes relevant in light of an analysis that involves income taxation. The fact that depreciation is an expense that is deductible in determining tax expense (a real cash flow) makes it a relevant consideration. Depreciation serves to reduce the cash outflow for income taxes.

21. a. yes
    b. no
    c. yes

23. The post-investment audit provides information about the reliability of the estimates that were used as a basis for justifying an investment. The post-investment feedback provides information about the judgment of the manager and information to improve the capital budgeting process. It also provides a basis for managerial control in that actual cash flows can be compared to projected cash flows.

25. The accounting rate of return is the only method which relies on accrual-based accounting information rather than cash flows. Net income is determined by both cash flows and noncash expenses and revenues. For example, depreciation is a noncash expense, and the gain recognized on the sale of an asset is a noncash revenue.

Chapter 14
Capital Asset Selection and Capital Budgeting

Exercises

27. a.   payback = $120,000 ÷ $40,000 = <u>3</u> years for both
         projects

    b.   Clearly, the projects are not equally desirable, even
         though they have the same payback. Project B's life is
         1 full year longer than project A. This indicates a
         need to use a secondary method to evaluate capital
         projects when the payback method is used.

29. Time: t0   t1   t2   t3   t4   t5
     Amount $(100,000) $50,000 $50,000 $20,000 $20,000 $20,000

Cash flow Description	time	Amount	Discount Factor	Present Value
Purchase machine	t0	$(100,000)	1.0000	$(100,000)
Cash inflow	t1	50,000	.9091	45,455
Cash inflow	t2	50,000	.8265	41,325
Cash inflow	t3	20,000	.7513	15,026
Cash inflow	t4	20,000	.6830	13,660
Cash inflow	t5	20,000	.6209	12,418
NPV				$ 27,884

31. $12,000 X 4.9676 = <u>$59,611.20</u>

33. a.

Cash flow Description	Time	Amount	Discount Factor	Present Value
Purchase machine	t0	$(7,000)	1.0000	$(7,000.00)
Cash inflows	t1-t5	2,200	3.6959	8,130.98
NPV				$ 1,130.98

    b. $7,000 ÷ $2,200 = <u>3.18</u> years

    c.   Present value of cash inflows = $7,000 + $1,447
                                        = $8,447
          $8,447 ÷ 2,200 = 3.8395, which is very close to the
          discount factor for 9.5% at 5 years.

    d.   The Treasury and Finance staff would have the most
          expertise in determining the company's cost of capital
          and managing the company's capital.

35. a.
Project A

Cash flow Description	Time	Amount	Discount Factor	Present Value
Purchase project	t0	($25,000)	1.0000	$ (25,000.00)
Cash inflows	t1-t3	3,000	2.4437	7,331.10
Cash inflow	t4	3,250	.6587	2,140.77
Cash inflow	t5	28,250	.5935	16,766.38
NPV				$ 1,238.25

Project B

Cash flow Description	Time	Amount	Discount Factor	Present Value
Purchase project	t0	($40,000)	1.0000	$ (40,000.00)
Cash inflows	t1-t3	4,800	2.4437	11,729.76
Cash inflow	t4	4,400	.6587	2,898.28
Cash inflow	t5	44,400	.5935	26,351.40
NPV				$ 979.44

   b.   Project A: ($25,000 + $1,238.25) ÷ $25,000 = 1.05
                                                       rounded

        Project B: ($40,000 + $979.44) ÷ $40,000 = 1.02
                                                     rounded

   c.   Project A is preferred because it has a higher NPV and
        generates more NPV per dollar invested; Project A would
        also have a higher internal rate of return.

37. a. $55,475 ÷ $12,000 = 4.6229 (discount factor)
          4.6229 corresponds to a discount rate of 8%

     b.   No, this is not an acceptable investment. Since the
          project has an internal rate of return of 8%, it would
          have a negative NPV if 10% was used as the discount rate.

39. a.   **Straight-line method:**
          Annual depreciation = $1,500,000 ÷ 8 = $187,500
          Tax benefit = $187,500 X .35 = $65,625
          PV = $65,625 X 5.3349 = $350,102.80 (rounded)

     b.

          Accelerated method
          $1,500,000 X .15 X .35 X .9091 = $ 71,591.63
          $1,500,000 X .22 X .35 X .8265 =   95,460.75
          $1,500,000 X .21 X .35 X .7513 =   82,830.83
          $1,500,000 X .21 X .35 X .6830 =   75,300.75
          $1,500,000 X .21 X .35 X .6209 =   68,454.22
               Total $393,638.18

c.   The company might choose the straight line method. The
     straight-line method would defer more of the depreciation
     deductions to the later years of the project's life so
     that more benefit would be obtained from the rising tax
     rates.

d.   Tax experts should be consulted. In particular, the
     company should consult with the tax department of an
     accounting firm that carefully tracks tax policy.
     Although no individual can always predict congressional
     actions to change tax laws, firms that monitor pending
     tax legislation and discussions in congressional
     committees have a better picture than others of future
     changes in tax laws.

41. $4,000 + ($300 X 37.974) = $15,392.20

43. a.

Cash flow Description	time	Amount	Discount Factor	Present Value
Purchase blender	t0	$(300,000)	1.0000	$(300,000)
Cost savings	t1-t10	50,000	6.1446	307,230
NPV				$ 7,230

b. $307,230 ÷ $300,000 = 1.02 (rounded)

c. $50,000 X discount factor = $300,000
     discount factor = 6.000 (10 year annuity)
     IRR = approximately 10.5%

d. $300,000 ÷ $50,000 = 6 years

e.   change in net income = $50,000 - ($300,000 ÷ 10)
                          = $20,000
     ARR = $20,000 ÷ ($300,000 ÷ 2) = 13.33%

45. a.   After-tax cash flow
          =(($40,000-$4,000)X.7)+[((($150,000 - $20,000) ÷ 8)X .30]
          = $25,200 + $4,875 = $30,075

Year	Amount	Cumulative
1	$30,075	$ 30,075
2	30,075	60,150
3	30,075	90,225
4	30,075	120,300
5	30,075	150,375

     payback = 4 years + ((150,000 - 120,300) ÷ 30,075)
             = 4.99 years
     After tax income
         = [$36,000 - (($150,000 - $20,000) ÷ 8)]X .7
         = $13,825
     ARR = $13,825 ÷ (($150,000 + $20,000) ÷ 2) = 16.26%

b.   Yes, quantitatively, this is an acceptable investment.
      Both the accounting rate of return and the payback
      measures exceed the investment criteria.

c.   Before purchasing the new scale, the company would want
      to evaluate the effect of the new scale on the perceived
      quality of their service, whether they have personnel
      with the skills to operate the scale, their backup plans
      if the scale fails to work correctly, and how competitors
      might respond to the installation of the computerized
      scale.

Chapter 14
Capital Asset Selection and Capital Budgeting

Communication Activities

47. Some of the factors which affect the decision of whether to delay the investment in new cleaning equipment are given below. Each factor can have two sides, i.e., delay versus no delay, depending upon the circumstances involved.
    - Unemployment, inflation rate, and business conditions in general.
      -Business outlook improving-do not delay.
      -Business outlook deteriorating-delay.
    - Unemployment, inflation rate, and business conditions all affect the climate for business and should be considered.
    - Difficulty with acquisition and installation of equipment and training of operators.
      -Great difficulty-do not delay.
      -Little difficulty-delay.
      The greater the lead time involved, the sooner the equipment should be acquired so that it is ready when needed.
    - Extent of operating efficiency improvements.
      -Great-do not delay.
      -Little-delay.
      The greater the efficiency, the less the delay because costs will be saved even though volume does not increase.
    - Inflation rate in cost of equipment.
      -Cost of equipment expected to increase drastically-do not delay.
      -Cost of equipment not expected to increase drastically-delay.
      Company wants to minimize its initial cost outlay.
    - Dependability of present equipment and likelihood of breakdown.
      -Dependability is not good-do not delay.
      -Dependability is good-delay.
    - Chance for technological advances in equipment.
      -No chance-do not delay.
      -Likely-delay.
      If there is a chance that technological advances will develop in the design for the equipment, the company might want to take advantage of the new design.
    - Ability to obtain market advantage by providing better quality service at same or lower price.
      -Good-do not delay.
      -Poor/neutral-delay.
      Better service means more customers or justifies higher rates.
    - Competitors' plans for obtaining similar equipment and achieving market advantage.
      -High probability-do not delay.
      -Low probability-delay.
      Company wants to maintain competitive advantage or meet competition.

■   Ability to predict timing and increased demand from new
      or increased customers.
      -Good-better quality of decision could defer switch
      longer.
      -Low-less reliable criteria for decision.
      The better a company is able to predict new business, the
      more certain it can be of its decision and, possibly, the
      longer it can wait to make a change.

(CMA)

49. a.   It is expected that students will have diverse views on
          governmental programs of the kind described in the
          article. Students should recognize that both society and
          specific individuals benefit from public job training
          programs. It is obvious how individuals in the programs
          benefit. Society benefits through lower welfare payments
          to those who successfully complete the programs and
          through the tax payments subsequently made by these
          individuals.
              The part that is likely to cause debate among
          students is the question of who bears the cost of these
          programs. Certainly, in the short-term society, or more
          specifically, taxpayers, bear the costs of the program.
          However, it may be argued that over the long-term the
          individuals in the programs bear some of the costs.
          Those that successfully complete the programs become
          taxpayers and stop being welfare recipients.

     b.   Students should have strong opinions on this issue. Some
          will note how the expenditure by society of $10,000 to
          educate a single welfare recipient provides incorrect
          incentives, i.e., government is willing to spend $10,000
          to educate the "least successful" of its citizens but it
          won't spend $10,000 to educate "average" citizens.
          Accordingly, no incentive is provided by government to be
          successful. Students may relate the $10,000 to the cost
          that they are bearing to finance their own education.
              Other students will argue that $10,000 (in a NPV
          sense) is rather inconsequential compared to the
          potential benefits to be derived by society from
          educating and training its citizens. Quantitatively,
          students may support this argument by relating the
          savings in welfare benefits and future tax payments to
          the $10,000 initial cost of the training.

218

Chapter 14
Capital Asset Selection and Capital Budgeting

Problems

51. a.   net annual cash flow:
             $260,000 -$50,000 -$22,000 -$14,000 -$14,000 =$160,000

Cash flow Description	time	Amount	Discount Factor	Present Value
Purchase machine	t0	($1,200,000)	1.00	$(1,200,000)
Net annual cash flow	t1-t10	160,000	5.6502	904,032
Salvage value	t10	50,000	.3220	16,100
NPV				$ (279,868)

    b.   Based on the NPV, the company should not buy the machine.
          The NPV < 0.

    c.   Primarily, the company should be careful to consider
          whether it has accounted for all effects of the new
          technology: product quality, production capacity, worker
          impact, and ability to adopt other new technologies in
          the future.

    d.   For an investment that might require the dismissal or
          reassignment of workers, the personnel director should be
          involved. The personnel director must be responsible for
          handling the behavioral aspects of displacing workers and
          assuring that the company is legal and ethical in dealing
          with the workers.

53. a.

State of economy	Resulting NPV	Probability	Expected value
Great	$15,000,000	.5	$7,500,000
Normal	7,500,000	.4	3,000,000
Poor	(60,000,000)	.1	(6,000,000)
		Expected NPV	$4,500,000

    b.   Yes. Holding all other things constant, a firm would
          prefer a less risky project. This project has a 10%
          probability of generating a huge negative return. If
          another project could be obtained for the same investment
          that would generate a $4.5 million NPV, the company would
          prefer the alternative.

    c.   Another method of analyzing this project would be to use
          probability distributions for each cash flow associated
          with the project. Then, a computerized package using
          fuzzy logic could be used to estimate the project's NPV.

218

55. a.   The minimum acceptable increase in revenues would
          generate a net present value of $0:
          Let R represent the net annual cash flow:
          R X 8.0607 = $800,000
          R = $800,000 ÷ 8.0607
          R = $99,246.96
          Annual gross cash receipts = R + $72,000
                                     = $171,246.96

          $171,246.96 ÷ $12 = 14,271 patrons

     b.   The payback = $800,000÷$99,246.96 = 8.06 years (rounded)

     c.   Veterinarians or other experts who could have determined
          the physical quantities of inputs required to maintain
          the snakes would have been consulted. Vendors would have
          been consulted regarding prices of inputs, and
          accountants would have helped determine the costs of
          facilities and any relevant overhead costs.

57. a. | Project | Investment | PI | Rank |
          |---------|-----------|------|------|
          | A | $110,000 | 1.11 | 9 |
          | B | 50,000 | 1.48 | 4 |
          | C | 220,000 | 1.55 | 2 |
          | D | 200,000 | 1.56 | 1 |
          | E | 20,000 | 1.50 | 3 |
          | F | 80,000 | 1.20 | 8 |
          | G | 30,000 | 1.26 | 7 |
          | H | 100,000 | 1.28 | 6 |
          | I | 400,000 | 1.43 | 5 |

          Allocation of $400,000
             Project D $200,000
             Project E   20,000
             Project B   50,000
             Project H   100,000
             Project G   30,000
                Total $400,000

     b.   The answer to part (a) may be modified as additional
          information comes to light. For example, it may be the
          case that some of the projects are mutually exclusive--
          the acceptance of one project requires the rejection of
          the others. Also, some of the projects may be mutually
          inclusive--acceptance of any project requires acceptance
          of all related projects. It may further be determined
          that new laws or regulations mandate that the company
          invest in certain of these projects.

59. a.   First, calculate the annual cash flow after tax (CFAT):
          Gross cost savings $38,000
          Less depreciation ($104,000 ÷ 8)   13,000
          Increase in taxable income $25,000
          Increase in taxes   8,000
          Increase in net income $17,000
          Add back depreciation   13,000
          Increase in CFAT $30,000

Cash flow Description	time	Amount	Discount Factor	Present Value
Purchase asset	t0	$(104,000)	1.00	$(104,000)
Annual cash flow	t1-t8	30,000	5.7466	172,398
NPV				$ 68,398

b.   **Depreciation amount**
          Year 1: $104,000 X 8/36 = $23,111
          Year 2: $104,000 X 7/36 = 20,222
          Year 3: $104,000 X 6/36 = 17,333
          Year 4: $104,000 X 5/36 = 14,444
          Year 5: $104,000 X 4/36 = 11,556
          Year 6: $104,000 X 3/36 =   8,667
          Year 7: $104,000 X 2/36 =   5,778
          Year 8: $104,000 X 1/36 =   2,889

Computation of CFAT

Year	Gross savings	Depreciation	NIBT*	Taxes	CFAT
1	$38,000	$23,111	$14,889	$4,763	$33,237
2	38,000	20,222	17,778	5,689	32,311
3	38,000	17,333	20,667	6,613	31,387
4.	38,000	14,444	23,556	7,538	30,462
5.	38,000	11,556	26,444	8,462	29,538
6.	38,000	8,667	29,333	9,387	28,613
7.	38,000	5,778	32,222	10,311	27,689
8.	38,000	2,889	35,111	11,236	26,764

*NIBT = Net income before taxes

Cash flow Description	time	Amount	Discount Factor	Present Value
Purchase asset	t0	$(104,000)	1.0000	$(104,000)
Net cash flow	t1	$33,237	.9259	30,774
Net cash flow	t2	32,311	.8573	27,700
Net cash flow	t3	31,387	.7938	24,915
Net cash flow	t4	30,462	.7350	22,390
Net cash flow	t5	29,538	.6806	20,104
Net cash flow	t6	28,613	.6302	18,032
Net cash flow	t7	27,689	.5835	16,157
Net cash flow	t8	26,764	.5403	14,461
NPV				$ 70,533

c.   The NPV is higher using the accelerated depreciation method, SYD. The reason is simple. Since all other factors are staying constant, the NPV of a project will go up if either revenues can be received earlier or cash outflows can be delayed. Here, the accelerated depreciation method delays the payment of some of the income taxes (even though the total amount of income taxes paid over the 8 year life is the same for the two methods).

d.   The discount rate that causes NPV = 0 is called the internal rate of return, IRR.
Find the IRR:
$104,000 ÷ $30,000 = 3.4667   (discount factor of IRR)
Irr > 20%.

61. a.

	Year 1	Year 2	Year 3	Year 4	Year 5	Years 6+
Receipts	$ 120,000	$240,000	$300,000	$360,000	$450,000	$540,000
Cash exp.	150,000	150,000	155,000	205,000	200,000	245,000
Depr.	75,000	75,000	75,000	75,000	75,000	75,000
Income	$(105,000)	$ 15,000	$ 70,000	$ 80,000	$175,000	$220,000
Taxes	(36,750)	5,250	24,500	28,000	61,250	77,000
CFAT	$ 6,750	$ 84,750	$120,500	$127,000	$188,750	$218,000

Cash flow Description	time	Amount	Discount Factor	Present Value
Buy equipment	t0	$(600,000)	1.0000	$(600,000.00)
Working capital	t0	(300,000)	1.0000	(300,000.00)
Displays	t0	(150,000)	1.0000	(150,000.00)
Annual cash flow	t1	6,750	.9346	6,308.55
Annual cash flow	t2	84,750	.8734	74,020.65
Annual cash flow	t3	120,500	.8163	98,364.15
Annual cash flow	t4	127,000	.7629	96,888.30
Annual cash flow	t5	188,750	.7130	134,578.75
Annual cash flow	t6-t10	218,000	2.9234	637,301.20
Salvage (after tax)	t10	16,250	.5084	8,261.50
Working capital	t10	300,000	.5084	152,520.00
NPV				$158,243.10

PI = $1,208,243.10 ÷ $1,050,000 = 1.15

b.

	Amount	Cumulative
Year 1	$ 6,750	$ 6,750
Year 2	84,750	91,500
Year 3	120,500	212,000
Year 4	127,000	339,000
Year 5	188,750	527,750
Year 6	218,000	745,750
Year 7	218,000	963,750
Year 8	218,000	1,181,750

Payback = 7 years + (($1,050,000 - $963,750) ÷ $218,000)
        = 7.40 years

c.   Yes, it meets the criterion: NPV > 0; PI > 1.

d.   As an expert in income taxation, you would be able to recommend alternative treatments of depreciation, and project changes in tax rates or the tax law.

63. a.   change in net income = $32,000 - $28,000 = $4,000
ARR = $4,000 ÷ ($140,000 ÷ 2) = 5.71%

b.   No. Sally should consider the possible change in maintenance costs; change in quality of services rendered and the marketing impact of such changes; any training costs required to operate the new machinery; installation costs of the equipment; any cost of modifying the building's electrical system or wiring; and the possibility that future technological innovations will render the equipment obsolete before its useful life is consumed.

65. a.

Time:	t0	t1-t9	t10
Amount:	($560,000)	$100,000	$160,000

b.

Cash flow Description	time	Amount	Discount Factor	Present Value
Trade machines	t0	$(560,000)	1.00	$(560,000)
Operating savings	t1-t10	100,000	5.8892	588,920
Salvage	t10	60,000	.3522	21,132
		Net present value		$ 50,052

c.   PI = $610,052 ÷ $560,000 = 1.09 (rounded)

d.   through trial and error, the IRR is found to be about 13%

e. $560,000 ÷ $100,000 = 5.6 years

f. $61,400 ÷ ($560,000 ÷2) = 21.93%

g.   IRR > 11%
ARR > 16%
Payback period > 5.5 years
The project meets all criteria except the payback.

Cases

67.

Receipts	$780,000	$780,000	$390,000	$390,000	$390,000
Salary	60,000	65,000	70,000	75,000	80,000
Uniform		1,000		1,000	
Insurance	25,000	25,000	25,000	25,000	
License plates	500	500	500	500	
Gas/oil	184,250	202,675	222,943	245,237	269,760
Repairs/Maint.	50,000	55,000	60,500	66,550	73,205
Major repairs			10,000		
Tires		2,000		2,000	
Annual cash flow	$460,250	$428,825	$ 1,057	$(25,287)	$(32,965)

b.

Cash flow Description	time	Amount	Discount Factor	Present Value
Purchase limos	t0	$(375,000)	1.0000	$(375,000)
Purchase uniforms	t0	(1,000)	1.0000	(1,000)
First yr. insurance	t0	(25,000)	1.0000	(25,000)
Personalized plates	t0	(500)	1.0000	(500)
Annual cash flow	t1	460,250	.8772	403,731
Annual cash flow	t2	428,825	.7695	329,981
Annual cash flow	t3	1,057	.6750	713
Annual cash flow	t4	(25,287)	.5921	(14,972)
Annual cash flow	t5	(32,965)	.5194	(17,122)
Sale of limos	t5	75,000	.5194	38,955
NPV				$ 339,786

Based on the NPV, the project is acceptable.

c.

Cash flow Description	time	Amount	Discount Factor	Present Value
Purchase limos	t0	$(375,000)	1.0000	$(375,000)
Purchase uniforms	t0	(1,000)	1.0000	(1,000)
First yr. insurance	t0	(25,000)	1.0000	(25,000)
Personalized plates	t0	(500)	1.0000	(500)
Annual cash flow	t1	460,250	.8621	396,782
Annual cash flow	t2	428,825	.7432	318,703
Annual cash flow	t3	1,057	.6407	677
Annual cash flow	t4	(25,287)	.5523	(13,966)
Annual cash flow	t5	(32,965)	.4761	(15,695)
Sale of limos	t5	75,000	.4761	35,707
NPV				$ 320,708

Based on the NPV, the project is acceptable.

d. One of the factors that should be considered by the company is the negative cash flow that is occurring in the last three years of the lives of the limousines. The company should consider trading cars at the end of the second or third year. Other things the company might want to consider would include: probability of a change in the prices of inputs (repairs, gas, oil, etc.); probability that demand for limousine services will change; actions that may be taken by competitors in response to the new cars; impact of the new limousines on the demand for the company's existing limousines; how the new cars will impact the quality of the service and the company's reputation.

69. Note: Students may have slightly different answers. The CMA solution uses only two-digit present value factors.

a. Present Value Analysis (using 6%)

	Initial Outlay	1998	1999	2000	2001	2002
Internal Financing						
Outlay	($1,000,000)					
Depr. tax shield		$160,000	$ 96,000	$ 57,600	$ 43,200	$ 43,200
Net CF	($1,000,000)	$160,000	$ 96,000	$ 57,600	$ 43,200	$ 43,200
PV factors	1.00	0.94	0.89	0.84	0.79	0.75
NPV	($1,000,000)	$150,400	$ 85,440	$ 48,384	$ 34,128	$ 32,400
Bank Loan						
Outlay	($100,000)					
Loan payment		($237,420)	($237,420)	($237,420)	($237,420)	($237,420)
Interest tax shield		36,000	30,103	23,617	16,482	8,638
Depr. tax shield		$160,000	$ 96,000	$ 57,600	$ 43,200	$ 43,200
Net CF	($100,000)	($ 41,420)	($111,317)	($156,203)	($177,738)	($185,582)
PV factors	1.00	0.94	0.89	0.84	0.79	0.75
NPV	($100,000)	($ 38,935)	($ 99,072)	($131,211)	($140,413)	($139,187)
Lease						
Outlay	($ 50,000)					
Tax shield on outlay		$ 20,000				
Payments net of tax ($220,000 X 60%)		($132,000)	($132,000)	($132,000)	($132,000)	($132,000)
NCF	($ 50,000)	($112,000)	($132,000)	($132,000)	($132,000)	($132,000)
PV factors	1.00	0.94	0.89	0.84	0.79	0.75
NPV	($ 50,000)	($105,280)	($117,480)	($110,880)	($104,280)	($ 99,000)

NPV for internal financing = $649,248
NPV for bank loan = $648,818
NPV for lease = $586,920

Supporting calculations

Depreciation tax shield

Year		Depreciation	Rate		Tax shield
1	$1,000,000 X .40 =	$400,000	X .40 =	$160,000
2	($1,000,000-$400,000) X .40 =	240,000	X .40 =	96,000
3	($1,000,000-$640,000) X .40 =	144,000	X .40 =	57,600
4	($1,000,000-$784,000) X .50 =	108,000	X .40 =	43,200
5	($1,000,000-$784,000) X .50 =	108,000	X .40 =	43,200

Interest tax shield

Year	Interest	Rate	Tax shield
1	$90,000	.40	$36,000
2	75,258	.40	30,103
3	59,042	.40	23,617
4	41,204	.40	16,482
5	21,596	.40	8,638

1. Metrohealth should employ the cost of debt of six percent (which represents the after-tax effect of the ten percent incremental borrowing rate) as a discount rate in calculating the net present value for all three financing alternatives.

   Investment decisions (accept versus reject) and financing decisions should be separated. Cost of capital or hurdle rates apply to investment decisions but not to financing decisions. This application is a financing decision. Incremental cost of debt is the basic rate used for discounting in financing decisions because the assumption made is that the firm would have no idle cash available for funding and would have to borrow from an outside lending institution at the incremental borrowing rate (10 percent in this case).

2. The financing alternative most advantageous to Metrohealth is leasing. This alternative has the lowest net present value ($586,920) when compared to the other two alternatives.

b.   Some qualitative factors Paul Monden should include for
      management consideration before deciding on the financing
      alternatives are:

      ■   The differential impact from one financing method
          versus another for equipment acquisitions due to
          various health care, third-party payor, reimbursement
          scenarios (the federal government with DRG
          reimbursement or insurance company reimbursement).

      ■   The technology of the equipment along with the risk of
          technological obsolescence. If major technological
          advances are expected, the preferred qualitative
          choice would be leasing from a lessor who would absorb
          any loss due to equipment obsolescence.

      ■   The maintenance agreement included in the operating
          lease.

(CMA)

Ethics and Quality Discussion

71 a. The cost side of the equation is much more easily captured than the benefit side. Costs would include the initial construction costs, and the annual operating costs (utilities, maintenance, supervision, repairs, insurance).

The benefits would include: reduction in absenteeism; more productivity per labor hour; lower health costs; lower worker's compensation premiums; greater job satisfaction; lower employee turnover and hence lower employee training costs; lower levels of sick pay; higher morale; greater employee loyalty, and lower unemployment insurance contributions.

b. The quality of the production could be directly affected through lower employee turnover, lower absenteeism, and through more mentally alert and aware workers.

c. Unless employers could firmly document the benefit of the private exercise requirement to required job performance, such a policy would be ethically suspect. For example, such a policy would likely lead to discrimination against physically-disabled individuals, older individuals, and others who are unable to exercise at a private health club because of financial or medical reasons.

However, with the current medical crisis in the U.S., it is very likely that firms will take greater efforts to screen potential employees based on their health and health consciousness. Already there exists much discrimination against smokers, and screening for illicit drug use is becoming a common practice.

73. a.   Rachel Arnett's revision of her first proposal can be
          considered a violation of the Standards of Ethical
          Conduct. She discarded her reasonable projections and
          estimates after she was questioned by William Earle.
          She used figures that had a remote chance of occurring.
          By doing this, she violated the Standard of Objectivity
          - "Communicate information fairly and objectively" and
          "disclose fully relevant information that could
          reasonably be expected to influence an intended user's
          understanding of the reports, comments, and
          recommendations presented." By altering her analysis,
          she also violated the Standard of Integrity. She
          engaged in an activity that would prejudice her ability
          to carry out her duties ethically, and she failed to
          communicate unfavorable as well as favorable information
          and professional judgments or opinions. In addition,
          she violated the Standard of Competence - "prepare
          complete and clear reports and recommendations after
          appropriate analysis for relevant and reliable
          information."

     b.   Earle was clearly in violation of the Standards of
          Ethical Conduct for Management Accountants because he
          tried to persuade a subordinate to prepare a proposal
          with data that were false and misleading. Earle has
          violated the Standards of Competence (failure to perform
          professional duties in accordance with technical
          standards; prepare complete and clear reports and
          recommendations after appropriate analyses of relevant
          and reliable information), Integrity (engaged in an
          activity that would prejudice his ability to carry out
          his duties ethically, actively or passively subvert the
          attainment of the organization's legitimate and ethical
          objectives, failure to communicate unfavorable as well
          as favorable information and professional judgments or
          opinions, and supported activity that would discredit
          the profession), and Objectivity (failed to communicate
          information fairly and objectively and did not disclose
          fully all relevant information that could reasonably be
          expected to influence an intended user's understanding
          of the reports, comments, and recommendations
          presented).

     c.   The elements of the projection and estimation process
          that are compromised because of a predetermined,
          misleading outcome include:
          ▪ The quality of the base data.
          ▪ The quality of the assumptions used.
          ▪ The probability of the projection occurring.
          ▪ The credibility of the people submitting the
             projection.

d. The internal controls Fore Corporation could implement
    to prevent unethical behavior include:
    ■   Approval of all formal capital expenditure
        proposals by the Controller and/or the Board of
        Directors.
    ■   Designating a non-accounting/finance manager to
        coordinate capital expenditure requests and/or
        segregating duties during the preparation and
        approval of capital expenditure requests.
    ■   Requiring all capital expenditure proposals be
        reviewed by senior operating management, which
        includes the Controller, before the proposals are
        submitted for approval.
    ■   Requiring the internal audit staff to review all
        capital expenditure proposals or contracting
        external auditors to review the proposal if the
        corporation lacks manpower.

(CMA)

Responsibility Accounting and Transfer Pricing in Decentralized Operations

Questions

1. In centrally organized firms, decision making is concentrated among a few individuals--those at the top of the organizational hierarchy. In decentralized firms, the authority and responsibility for making decisions is pushed down to lower level managers. The rationale is that lower level managers have more information about their areas of the business and are in the best position to make decisions for those areas.

3. While many skills are common to managers in centralized and decentralized firms, the decentralized manager must be willing to accept greater risk. The greater risk is associated with a performance evaluation that is based on the results that are achieved rather than the managerial actions taken. The managers must accept the authority to make decisions, execute the decisions, and live with the outcome. This requires the decentralized manager to be creative, goal-oriented, assertive and decisive.

5. The costs may include the costs of poor decisions by inexperienced managers; the costs associated with a divergence between organizational, organizational segment, and individual goals (these are sometimes called agency costs or costs of suboptimization); the costs of duplicating activities across subunits; the costs of a more sophisticated planning and communication network; the costs of a more sophisticated accounting system; and the costs of training new managers.

7. A segment manager should be evaluated only on factors (costs & revenues) that are directly traceable to his/her segment and under his/her control. Alternatively, the segment should be evaluated on all factors that are directly traceable to the segment and necessary for the segment's operation. These two sets of factors are not completely overlapping. For example, the salary of the segment manager can be traced to the segment (and is therefore used to evaluate the segment), but it is not controllable by the segment manager (and therefore is not used to evaluate the segment manager).

9.   In the broadest sense, a variance is a deviation between a
      planned outcome and an actual outcome. By focusing
      managerial attention on variances, the factors that generate
      a difference between the desired result and actual result
      can be identified. Once the causal factors are recognized,
      managers can take actions to exploit favorable factors and
      overcome unfavorable factors. Such actions should bring a
      closer alignment between planned and actual results.

11.   Suboptimization occurs when the goals of the individual
      manager, his/her subunit, and the organization are not in
      harmony. Generally, suboptimization occurs because subunit
      managers are too focussed on maximizing the performance of
      their subunits rather than maximizing the performance of the
      overall organization. In turn, this result is often caused
      by imperfect incentive contracting systems (performance
      based pay systems).

13.   Transfer prices are internally set (agreed upon) prices with
      which a "selling" division transfers goods or services to a
      "buying" division. The role of the transfer price is to
      provide goal congruence while retaining subunit autonomy,
      and provide motivation for managers to be effective and
      efficient in their operations.

15.   Standard costs have the advantage of being known or agreed
      upon in advance and of being a measure of efficient
      production. Actual costs may vary widely from month to
      month because of large changes in production volume,
      seasonal variations, and efficiencies.

17.   Dual pricing is the permitting of the selling division to
      record one transfer price (higher) and the buying division
      to record another (lower). This practice is intended to
      minimize suboptimization and create goal-congruent
      incentives for both divisions.

19.   Because transfer prices between multinational units of a
      company can affect profits and inventory values reported in
      two different countries, managers are cognizant of setting
      prices, within legal and ethical limits, to minimize income
      taxes and tariffs.

Exercises

21. a.   10
     b.   5
     c.   4
     d.   6
     e.   9
     f.   1
     g.   3
     h.   2
     i.   7
     j.   8

23. a.   D
     b.   A
     c.   A
     d.   D
     e.   D
     f.   A
     g.   A
     h.   A
     i.   A
     j.   N

25. a.   Price variance = ($22.00 - $19.50) X 425,000
                         = $1,062,500 U

          Volume variance = $22 X (400,000 - 425,000)
                          = $550,000 F

     b.   A sales mix variance can be computed only in firms that
          sell more than one product; this is a single product
          company.

     c.   No, a determination cannot be made as to whether profits
          were above or below estimated levels. Information on
          costs would be required to make that determination.

27. a., b., c., d.

Actual sales	SP X AM X AV	SP X SM* X AV	Budgeted sales
	$40 X 30,000	$40 X 17,500	$1,800,000
	$30 X 40,000	$30 X 52,500	800,000
$2,700,000	$2,400,000	$2,275,000	$2,600,000

	$300,000 F	$125,000 F	$325,000 U
	Price variance	Mix variance	Volume variance

Total variance = $2,700,000 - $2,600,000 = $100,000 F
*SM = 25% purses, 75% Baseball Gloves

29.   a.   The upper limit for the transfer is the lowest outside price at which the buying division can purchase a comparable water pump: $55. The lower limit is the relevant cost to produce and sell the unit: $18.40 + $4.20 + $12.60 = $35.20.

     b.   <u>$46</u>

     c. $46 - $10.80 = <u>$35.20</u>

     d.   This would be a breakeven price for the Cast Products Division. It would have incentive to make the transfer only if its profits could be increased by doing so.

31.   a.   Units sold internally = $75,000 ÷ $1.25 = 60,000
         Total production = 60,000 ÷ .4 = 150,000
         External sales = 150,000 - 60,000 = 90,000
         Internal variable costs = $30,000 ÷ 60,000 = $.50
         External variable costs = $45,000 ÷ 90,000 = $.50
         External sales price = $135,000 ÷ 90,000 = $1.50
         Change in gross profit = ($1.40 - $1.25) X 60,000
                                = <u>$9,000</u>

     b.   ($1.25 - $1.70) X 60,000 = <u>$(27,000)</u>

     c.   Transfer price = $1.25 + ($.15 ÷ 2)
                      = <u>$1.325</u>

     d.   A dual transfer price would allow the Home Products Division to record the internal sales at the external price of $1.40, and allow the Tool Division to record the transfer at the existing internal price, $1.25. The dual transfer pricing arrangement would provide incentive to both the buying and selling divisions to make the internal transfer.

33.   a.   A
     b.   D
     c.   A
     d.   D
     e.   D
     f.   A
     g.   D
     h.   A
     i.   A
     j.   D

Communication Activities

35. a.   Mr. Wallace believes that his obligation is to meet the overall level of budgeted cost; this means he has authority to overspend in some areas as long as there is offsetting underspending in other areas.

Mr. Driver believes that Mr. Wallace has an obligation to stay within the budget established for each item of expense. The substitution of overspending in one category for underspending in another is not permissible.

   b.   The budget should be subdivided into discretionary and nondiscretionary amounts. The nondiscretionary amounts would be those which Mr. Wallace would have no authority to change; the discretionary amounts would be expended subject to the judgment of Mr. Wallace. Discretionary and nondiscretionary amounts could be established for each expense item or entire expense items could be classified as discretionary or nondiscretionary. The nondiscretionary costs would represent the activities that the management wants conducted at a specified level. The nondiscretionary amounts would represent those costs that could be shifted between expense items subject to changing conditions such as temperature, rainfall, and level of use.

   c.   Depreciation is a cost that is certainly not controllable by Mr. Wallace. This suggests that in addition to separating budgetary amounts into discretionary and nondiscretionary components, they should also be separated into controllable and noncontrollable components.   Mr. Wallace should not be held accountable for noncontrollable expenses.

   d.   The board of directors should be responsible for evaluating the performance of Mr. Wallace. The board of directors would be the committee that has responsibility for oversight of employees and hiring and firing employees. The greens committee's authority and responsibility should be constrained to maintaining the physical condition of the golf course.

37.   a.   ■   Current external selling price $5,232
                 Selling Division--fair value since most are produced
                    and sold at this price externally.
                 Buying Division--price is higher than what could be
                    purchased elsewhere so this would make its
                    performance report appear worse than by buying
                    externally.
            ■   Total variable production cost ($2,100)+ 20% = $2,520
                 Selling Division-- contributes minimally to covering
                    fixed costs and therefore no profit is shown from
                    these "sales" as opposed to external sales. There
                    is little incentive to sell internally if the
                    selling division can sell all its output
                    externally.
                 Buying Division--less than external purchase price;
                    therefore, it is more beneficial to the bottomline
                    of International Tractor Company.
            ■   Total product ($3,000) cost + 20% = $3,600
                 Selling Division--covers some but not all costs for
                    this division; therefore, incentive to sell
                    internally isn't there if Engine Division can sell
                    its output externally.
                 Buying Division--purchase price below external so
                    better for margin in this division.
            ■   Bid price from external supplier ($4,640)
                 Selling Division--allows for some profit which is an
                    incentive to sell internally unless it can sell all
                    its output externally.
                 Buying Division--no incentive to buy internally
                    since it costs the same to buy from an external
                    supplier.

      b.   Upper limit = $4,640
            Lower limit = costs of $2,400 + contribution margin of
               $2,832 = $5,232
            Since the lower limit exceeds the upper limit, the
            company would be better off **not** making the internal
            transfers.

39.   Allocation of computer service costs should be made on some
      kind of an "hours used" basis to permit a more efficient use
      of company resources. The changing basis should encourage
      users to take advantage of the Computer Systems Department's
      services but not permit the Computer Systems Department to
      pass on its inefficiencies. For instance, a standard hourly
      usage rate should be developed on past experience, adjusted
      for efficiency considerations. Divisions would be charged the
      standard rate for the hours of recorded usage.
(CMA adapted)

Problems

41. a.

	Flexible Budget	Actual	Variance
Lbs. of canned fish	1,500,000	1,500,000	
Direct labor	$ 750,000	$ 600,000	$150,000 F
Repairs	150,000	160,000	10,000 U
Maintenance	900,000	650,000	250,000 F
Indirect labor	150,000	155,000	5,000 U
Power	300,000	315,000	15,000 U
Totals	$2,250,000	$1,880,000	$370,000 F

b. Actual costs for 1997 were 16.4% below the total
flexible budget. However, much of the total favorable
variance is from maintenance cost. Maintenance cost is
one category where top management would not like to see
a huge savings relative to the budget. Such savings may
indicate a failure to perform routine maintenance and
may reduce the life expectancy of the plant and
equipment, or generate very expensive repairs in future
years. The other favorable variance is for direct labor
costs. The factors driving the savings in this cost
category should be identified. Such factors may have
favorable or unfavorable implications for the firm. For
example, the favorable variance could be driven by a
policy (instituted by Mr. Bluegill) of only processing
the least labor intensive portion of each fish and
discarding the portions of the fish that could be
salvaged for canning but involve more labor-intense
processing.

c. Based on the preliminary results, it would appear that
Mr. Bluegill has cut corners to generate large favorable
cost variances. Such variances, particularly the
savings on maintenance costs, will likely reappear in
future years as large unfavorable variances.
Additionally, Mr. Bluegill may be yielding an
unacceptable level of output (1,500,000 lbs. of fish)
relative to the input (2,500,000 lbs. of fish).

d.   Additional performance measures should be instituted.
     The most fundamental change would involve the addition
     of a direct material efficiency variance to determine
     whether the yield on the raw fish is at acceptable
     levels. If there is concern about the level of
     maintenance activity, additional performance measures
     could be added to track down time due to machine
     breakdowns, scrap and waste generated by machine
     malfunctions, spoilage, etc. Additionally, measures
     should be in place to gauge the level of quality of the
     finished product, i.e.; on-time delivery measures,
     number of defective units shipped to customers (fish
     bones found in the can, spoiled meat, foreign material
     found in the can, etc.) and sales returns. Other
     measures based on the throughput concept could also be
     used to gauge the quality and efficiency of the
     production process.

43. a., b., c.

Actual sales	SP X AM X AV	SP X SM* X AV	Budgeted sales
$ 93,150	$107 X 810	$107 X 1,080	$102,720
207,000	55 X 4,140	55 X 3,150	154,000
315,900	75 X 4,050	75 X 4,770	318,000
$616,050	$618,120	$646,560	$574,720

                $2,070 U $28,440 U $71,840 F
             Price variance   Mix variance   Volume variance

Total variance = $616,050 - $574,720 = $41,330 F
 *SM = 12% Floor Lamps, 35% Hanging Lamps, 53% Ceiling
  Fixtures

d.   Overall, Ms. Subwitz performed well. Although she
     failed to achieve the budgeted price for all units sold
     and sold a less profitable mix than the budgeted mix,
     she was successful in selling 1,000 units more than
     budgeted. The additional volume more than compensated
     for the unfavorable price and mix variances.

e.   If Ms. Subwitz had the authority to set the salary and
     commission structure of her employees, she would have
     additional tools to effect changes in sales. She could
     use these tools to provide salespeople with incentives
     to sell particular products so she could achieve the
     desired price, mix and volume of sales.

45. a. The upper limit is the lowest external price $136
        The lower limit is the incremental costs plus
        opportunity costs:
             Direct materials $ 56
             Direct labor   44
             Variable overhead   18   118
             Savings to International Marine $ 18

    b. $118 + (.5 X $18) = $127

    c. Maximum price = lowest outside price = $136
        Minimum price = variable costs of North Division = $118

47. a.   Bottle   Perfume   Common Scents
    Revenue (6,000,000) $ 19,980,000 $ 127,800,000 $ 127,800,000
    Cost   (14,400,000) (116,760,000) (111,180,000)
    Margin $ 5,580,000 $ 11,040,000 $ 16,620,000
    Return on sales   28%   8.6%   13%

    b. This level of operation is most profitable for the
        Bottle Division relative to sales. The Bottle
        Division's return on sales is more than three times the
        return on sales realized in the Perfume Division.

    c. The Bottle Division once existed as a separate company.
        As such it was purchased with a management control
        system intact. It may be assumed that it was left as a
        separate division for managerial control purposes--to be
        able to separately evaluate the performance of bottling
        from perfume production. However, the big question is
        whether any purpose is served in leaving the Bottle
        Division as a profit center. It would seem that many of
        the conflicts between the Bottle and Perfume Divisions
        could be eliminated if the Bottle Division was made a
        cost center. This would be appropriate since the Bottle
        Division has no outside sales; and hence, is accountable
        for none of the company's revenues.

49. a. One of the purposes of this problem is to demonstrate that the price that generates a 20% return on sales is sensitive to assumptions made about sales volume. At the existing volume (70% of capacity) fixed costs amount to $100 per unit. If this is the assumed level of operations for the coming year, the per unit sales price that generates net income before taxes equal to 20% of sales would be:
Let S = Sales price per unit
S - $290 = .2S
.8S = $290
S = $362.50

    However, students may come up with alternative answers depending on the assumptions made with regard to volume. As volume rises, fixed costs per unit decline and the sales price required to generate a 20% return declines.

    b. As a practical matter, the highest possible price would be $260 per unit. This is the outside price and represents the cost that Conveyor Systems Division could acquire the pumps from an alternative supply source. Even though this price fails to meet the net income objectives of the Hydraulic Division, any higher price will cause the division to loose the internal business.

    c. The division should charge any price that will cause the Conveyor Systems Division to purchase internally. The company's variable cost to produce the pump is $120 + $40 + $30 = $190. Since the market price is $260, the company is $70 per unit better off if the pump is made rather than purchased. The actual transfer price is irrelevant to the determination of overall corporate profits; however, the transfer price will affect the relative profits of the buying and selling divisions. From the company perspective, any transfer price that causes the Conveyor Systems Division to purchase internally is optimal. Thus, the likely range of prices is $190 to $260.

Cases

51. a.   1.   Responsibility accounting is a system of accounting
               that recognizes various responsibility or decision
               centers throughout an organization, and reflects
               the plans and actions of these centers by assigning
               particular revenues and costs to the one having the
               pertinent responsibility for making decisions about
               these revenues and costs.

     2.   The benefits that accrue to a company using
          responsibility accounting include:
          ▪   The development of responsibility budgets and
              plans which encourages managers to plan ahead
              and promotes goal congruence.
          ▪   Participation in the planning process, causes
              company guidelines to be more readily accepted
              as achievable.
          ▪   The development of responsibility accounting
              plans which provide managers with clear
              guidelines for day-to-day decisions and free
              management from daily operations.
          ▪   Responsibility accounting which affords
              management performance evaluation criteria.

     3.   The advantages of responsibility accounting to the
          managers of a firm include:
          ▪   Under the guidelines of responsibility
              accounting, managers are responsible only for
              those items over which they have control.
          ▪   Because responsibility accounting facilitates
              the delegation of decision-making, managers
              are afforded greater freedom of action without
              daily supervision.
          ▪   Managers know what is expected of them and on
              what basis their performance will be
              evaluated.
          ▪   The ability to participate in decision making
              and to exercise control helps managers develop
              leadership skills.

b.   1.   The managers of Family Resorts are likely to
          support the budget preparation process because they
          are active participants in the process. The
          managers have been allowed to prepare and submit
          budgets on an autonomous basis. If major changes
          are needed to the budgets submitted, the managers
          are consulted before changes are implemented.
          The features of the budget presentation that would
          make it attractive to the managers include the
          following:
          ■   The managers are only responsible for costs
              that are directly under their control;
              arbitrary allocations have been avoided.
          ■   The budget presentation shows the managers
              exactly how their segment fits into the entire
              company and how their units contribute to the
              overall well being of the firm.
          ■   The presentation clearly depicts those areas
              each manager is responsible for and
              establishes the criteria on which his/her
              performance will be evaluated.

     2.   Recommendations to improve the budget process might
          include the following:
          ■   The budget could be presented using the
              contribution approach and segregating variable
              and fixed costs.
          ■   There could be a comparison to prior year
              actuals so that managers know if their
              contributions have increased or decreased.
          ■   The expense items could be presented as a
              percentage of sales.

(CMA)

Ethics and Quality Discussion

53. a. Establishing individual responsibility also requires
establishing personal accountability. This means that
not only will tasks be the responsibility of specific
individuals, but that those individuals will be held
accountable for the outcomes. Personal accountability
may overcome the lack of individual initiative and
shirking that occurs in groups. Because a given
individual will not have to share credit for success
with a group, nor be able to share blame with the group
for failures, it is likely that the attention of each
individual will be highly focussed on his/her product
lines and their performance.

    b. Establishing individual responsibility for
organizational success may inhibit creativity and risk
taking. Because an individual will be accountable for
specific organizational processes, the individual will
be less likely than a group to recommend creative and
risky solutions to problems. Also, there will be less
input to decision making with fewer individuals involved
in specific processes. Likewise, there may be less
cooperation among individuals because of the competition
that individual responsibility may foster.

    c. Yes, changes must be made. As mentioned in part a., to
successfully establish individual responsibility for
product lines, a system of accountability must also be
established. It is likely that one of the main systems
for accountability will be a responsibility accounting
system.

55.   a.   Corporate management has established an environment in
           which there is an incompatibility (lack of goal
           congruence) between the achievement of corporate
           objectives and personal ethics. Under the current
           situation, severe penalties have been imposed by top
           management whenever subordinates do not achieve the high
           levels of performance established by the predetermined
           objectives. This has caused lower level management to
           take unethical courses of action.

      b.   A company program to reduce the pressures on lower level
           management who violate ethical standards and acceptable
           business practices might include the following:
           ■   Adopt a particular style of management. Encourage
               each lower level manager to contribute to the
               establishment of the goals by which (s)he is to be
               judged.
           ■   Expand the feedback system to recognize and reward
               good performances, allow for investigation and
               explanation for substandard performances, and
               adjust for changing conditions.
           ■   Adopt a corporate code of ethics or code for
               acceptable business practices.
           ■   Show top management support for the code evidenced
               by words and actions.

(CMA)

57.   a.   In accounting applications, there are so many
           alternative definitions of the term "cost," that a
           clarifying explanation is mandatory. To omit a
           definition of cost, intentionally or unintentionally,
           can be misleading. Accounting information should not be
           distorted by definitions of terminology.

      b.   Yes, Quigley is clearly being unethical in the
           distribution of profits. Quigley is aware of the
           differences in the transfer pricing bases, and hence, he
           is aware that his bonus is largely attributable to the
           difference in the two transfer prices. This is
           equivalent to stealing from Wigley.

      c.   It is difficult to tell whether Quigley's actions are
           illegal. They certainly may be illegal to the extent
           Wigley believes, and Quigley had reinforced the idea
           that the transfer prices of each are based on the same
           definition of cost.

      d.   The simplest recommendation would be to base the
           transfer price on market prices. This would allow the
           transfer price to be established by unbiased, impersonal
           market forces. This would preclude the manipulation of
           the price by either party. Using market price for the
           transfer of services would seem to be feasible given the
           large number of firms that provide these types of
           services; market prices should be readily available.
           Additionally, the use of market price would allow
           Quigley and Wigley to make better decisions regarding
           insourcing or outsourcing services. The use of market
           price should reduce Quigley's bonus and increase
           Wigley's bonus.

Chapter 16

Measuring and Rewarding Performance

Questions

1. The measurement system should
   - assess progress toward achievement of organizational goals and objectives,
   - be based on the input of those being evaluated,
   - consider the skills, information and authority of those being evaluated, and
   - provide necessary feedback in a timely and useful manner to managers.

3. Because managerial pay is linked to their performance, managers will take actions to maximize their **measured** performance. This is why selection of performance measures is so important; if the wrong measures are selected, managers will attempt to maximize less important dimensions of performance. The selected measures should be the ones that are most highly correlated with the organization's goals and objectives.

5. Manipulation is an important concern because performance measures should be designed to capture only **real** performance not manipulation of the performance measure. If a performance measure can be manipulated by managers, then they can achieve a high level of measured performance by either performing very well or by manipulating the measure. External measures are far superior to interior measures in this respect; they are not susceptible to internal manipulation.

7. The major difference between a profit and an investment center is that the investment center has control over costs, revenues and **the level of assets** that is employed. Accordingly, investment centers need to be evaluated based on their profitability **relative** to the value of assets used. Profit centers have no responsibility for assets and can be evaluated based on profit alone.

9.· The DuPont model is a formulation of the ROI ratio. In the
    DuPont model, ROI is the product of profit margin multiplied
    by asset turnover. Each component ratio provides
    information on a distinct dimension of performance. The
    profit margin measures how much of each sales dollar was
    turned into profit; the asset turnover ratio is a measure of
    asset utilization and captures how many dollars of asset
    investment were required to generate each dollar of sales.

11. Suboptimization may be created in using ROI because the
    divisional ROIs differ from the overall organization's ROI.
    In such a circumstance, a division may invest (fail to
    invest) in new assets when, from the perspective of the
    overall organization's ROI, it would have been better not to
    invest (to invest). ROI is most likely to create a
    suboptimization problem in firms where the target and
    achieved levels of ROI vary substantially from one division
    to another. This problem is likely to be minimized when
    there is little variance among all the divisions' ROIs.

13. Some of the performance measures the company might adopt
    include the following: first pass rejection rate, number of
    customer returns, number of units scrapped or rejected,
    number of units reworked, and input waste and shrinkage.

15. Throughput is the number of good units produced and sold
    during a given period of time. Throughput is based on
    number of units sold rather than units produced because no
    revenue or profit is generated by producing units that are
    not currently in demand by customers. Thus, goods only
    create value for the firm when they are sold, not when they
    are produced.

17. Activity-based costing provides managers with a tool for
    looking at activities through the eyes of their customers.
    Customers only want to pay for activities that add value for
    them. ABC helps managers identify non-value-adding
    activities and provides a natural mechanism for relating
    activities to cost control. Thus, ABC provides a natural
    link between customer value and organizational activities
    and, further, it provides the measures necessary to evaluate
    progress in reducing costs and increasing customer value.

19. Linking the compensation system to the performance
    evaluation system provides the incentive for managers to be
    concerned about the performance measures. The linkage makes
    the maximization of the performance measures the objective
    of the manager. If correct measures are identified,
    maximization of the performance measures should result in
    the achievement of the organization's goals and objectives.

21.   By owning stock in the corporation, managers have incentive
      to "think" like stockholders. Providing stock to managers
      is a widely-used method to maintain compatibility between
      the incentives and motivations of managers and owners.

23.   For global operations maintaining a fair and equitable
      compensation system is more difficult. Some of the
      additional variables that must be considered are: the cost
      of living, safety considerations or other personal risk
      factors, differing tax laws across countries, fluctuations
      in foreign exchange rates, compensation paid by competitors,
      and cultural differences between countries.

Chapter 16
Measuring and Rewarding Performance

Exercises

25. Division 1: $25,000 \div 100,000 = \underline{25\%}$
    Division 2: $150,000 \div 1,000,000 = \underline{15\%}$
    Division 3: $200,000 \div 2,000,000 = \underline{10\%}$

27. a.   Segment income = segment assets X ROI
           = $1,700,000 X .125 = $\underline{212,500}$

    b.   Revenues = Segment income + total expenses
           = $212,500 + $637,500 = $\underline{850,000}$

    c.   Asset turnover = $850,000 \div $1,700,000 = $\underline{.50}$

    d.   Profit margin = $212,500 \div $850,000 = $\underline{.25}$ or 25%

    e.   ROI = asset turnover X profit margin
           = .50 X .25 = $\underline{12.5\%}$

29. a.   East Division: $20,000 - ($100,000 X .12) = $\underline{8,000}$
         West Division: $34,000 - ($200,000 X .12) = $\underline{10,000}$

    b.   Based on the residual income criterion, the West
         Division is more successful.

31. a.   Residual income = Segment income - target return
         $520,000 = $1,800,000 - target return
         $1,280,000 = target return

         target return = average assets X target rate of return
         $1,280,000 = average assets X .16
         $\underline{8,000,000}$ = average assets

    b.   ROI = net income $\div$ average assets
           = $1,800,000 \div $8,000,000 = $\underline{22.50\%}$

33. a.   RI = Segment income - target return,

         Segment income = ROI X asset cost
         target return = target rate X asset cost
         RI = (ROI X asset cost) - (target rate X asset cost)
         $20,000 = (.25 X asset cost) - (.25 X asset cost)
         $20,000 = .05 X asset cost
         $\underline{400,000}$ = asset cost

    b.   Segment income = ROI X asset acquisition cost
           = .25 X $400,000
           = $\underline{100,000}$

35. a. Manufacturing cycle efficiency = Processing time ÷ Total time

   = 180,000 ÷ 240,000

   = <u>75%</u>

b. Process Productivity = Total units ÷ Processing time

   = 360,000 units ÷ 180,000 hours

   = <u>2.0</u> units per hour

c. Process quality yield = Good units ÷ Total units

   = 270,000 ÷ 360,000

   = <u>75%</u>

d. Throughput = .75 X 2 X .75 = <u>1.125</u> units per hour

37. a.
   Year 1: $200,000 - ($2,000,000 ÷ 5) = $(200,000)
   Year 2: $300,000 - ($2,000,000 ÷ 5) = $(100,000)
   Year 3: $380,000 - ($2,000,000 ÷ 5) = $ (20,000)
   Year 4: $1,600,000 - ($2,000,000 ÷ 5) = $1,200,000
   Year 5: $1,600,000 - ($2,000,000 ÷ 5) = $1,200,000

b.
   Year 1: $(200,000) X .06 = $(12,000)
   Year 2: $(100,000) X .06 = $(6,000)
   Year 3: $ (20,000) X .06 = $ (1,200)
   Year 4: $1,200,000 X .06 = $ 72,000
   Year 5: $1,200,000 X .06 = $ 72,000

c. Whether Stella will be hesitant to invest or not depends largely on her personal time horizon. While investing in the project would reduce her compensation during the first three years, this reduction would be more than offset in the last two years. If Stella's time horizon is three years or less, she is unlikely to invest, If her time horizon is four years or more, she is likely to invest. Also, Stella must deal with the possibility that she would be dismissed from her position in one of the first three years due to poor performance if she invests in the project.

d. Yes. Upper management would likely view the project favorably. Using any reasonable discount rate, the project has a positive NPV.

e. The incentive system doesn't provide encouragement to invest in projects that are not immediately profitable. The incentive compensation system could be changed so that bonuses are based on actual NPV of projects versus projected NPV; the ROI measure is based on a long-term average rather than an annual measure; and could include some common stock rather than cash payments so that Stella would have more incentive to be long term oriented.

Chapter 16
Measuring and Rewarding Performance

39. a. The ROI for Atlantic Division has managed to climb two consecutive years despite the fact that segment income is declining over the same time period. The only reasonable conclusion is that the amount of average assets has been declining at a faster rate than the decline in sales; thus the ROI climbs. Such a result might arouse suspicions that the rise in ROI is attributable to the definition that is used to compute ROI. The fact that the division is high-tech would indicate that it has a large annual charge for depreciation. Perhaps the ROI is rising because it is computed on net book assets rather than gross book assets.

    b. If in fact the rise in ROI is attributable to a decline in average assets that is driven by depreciation (rather than a real reduction in the level of investment), a change in the definition of assets to gross book value rather than net book value would probably solve the problem.

41. a. It may be that there is a difference in incentives between stock and stock options. In particular, the stock options are more valuable when the risk of the underlying asset rises. To illustrate, if the current market price for two different companies is $45 for a share of stock, and the strike price for a stock option of each company is $50, the company that has the higher variance in its stock prices would have the higher-valued stock option. High variance equates to higher probability that the strike price of the stock will be hit.
        Understanding the relationship between stock options and stock prices, managers who held a large amount of stock options might take actions to make the stock more risky to improve the odds of hitting the strike price.

    b. Stock options only create value for the manager if the share price rises to some specified level. Thus, the manager benefits only if shareholders benefit from increased stock prices. Alternatively, if managers were given stock rather than options, even in a declining market, the managers would still benefit from receipt of new shares.

    c. The treasury and finance group would have experts on these topics.

43. a. The executives would command a higher salary in exchange for what they perceive as enduring hardships. To work in China they would have to live in a foreign culture, forego existing social relationships, relocate their families, possibly learn a new language, live and work in a less developed market, forego certain luxuries that are easily obtained in the U.S. including certain food items and sources of entertainment.

b. In hiring chinese managers, companies need to be aware of cultural differences between the U.S. and China. More incentives will need to be developed to encourage long-term employment for the Chinese managers. This may involve deferred compensation, more stock-based compensation, and more compensation contingent on the tenure of employment.

c. Some characteristics of the ideal manager for Chinese operations: write and speak effectively in Chinese; understand and enjoy the culture of China as well as the western culture; have knowledge of Chinese laws, the Chinese government and its politics; know how to obtain the principal materials and resources required for production; and be long-term oriented.

Problems

45. a.

	Omana	Eastside	RiverRun
Profit	$ 420,000	$ 324,000	$ 660,000
Revenues	$4,200,000	$5,400,000	$4,800,000
Profit Margin	10%	6%	13.75%
Revenues	$4,200,000	$5,400,000	$4,800,000
Average assets	$2,100,000	$1,800,000	$2,400,000
Asset turnover	2	3	2
ROI	20%	18%	27.5%

b. According to the ROI calculations, RiverRun appears to be the strongest company and Eastside appears to be the weakest.

c. While Eastside has the lowest ROI, it has the highest asset turnover ratio. Unfortunately, its low profit margin appears to be dominating its high asset turnover and the consequence is a low ROI. This suggests Eastside could improve its ROI by either lowering expenses or raising prices. In either case, profitability per dollar of sales would improve. Even if the asset turnover ratio declines slightly, the ROI would likely improve. Note that the two companies with the higher ROIs have an asset turnover ratio of only 2.

47. a.
1. $400,000 ÷ $2,000,000 = 20%
2. $1,000,000 ÷ $2,000,000 = .5
3. $400,000 ÷ .10 = $4,000,000
4. $16,000,000 X .15 = $2,400,000
5. $16,000,000 ÷ 1.4 = $11,428,571 (rounded)
6. 1.4 X 15% = 21%
7. $1,000,000 ÷ $8,000,000 = 12.5%
8. $8,000,000 ÷ $4,000,000 = 2
9. $1,000,000 ÷ $4,000,000 = 25%

b. Overall, the Storage Division posted the strongest performance as measured by ROI. While it had the lowest profit margin, it had the highest asset turnover ratio. The Transport Division placed in the middle on all three performance measures. The Package Division managed to generate the highest profit margin, but its investment in assets was too high for the achieved level of sales. This resulted in a very poor asset turnover ratio and the lowest ROI of the three divisions.

49.

	Asset turnover	Profit margin	ROI	RI
a.	IN	D	D	D*
b.	IN	D	IN	IN
c.	IN	IN	IN	IN
d.	N	IN	IN	IN
e.	N	N	N	D
f.	D	IN	I	I
g.	IN	I	I	I
h.	D	IN	I	I

*As long as the return < 100% of average assets.

51. a. Pleasure ROI = ($12,000,000 - $10,800,000)÷$10,000,000
            = <u>12%</u>
        Commercial ROI =($48,000,000 - $42,000,000)÷$30,000,000
            = <u>20%</u>

    b. The manager of Pleasure Division is the most likely to
        invest in a new project. Such an investment would
        increase the overall ROI of the division. The manager
        of Commercial Division would not invest because the
        projected ROI on the new project is lower than the
        projected divisional ROI.

    c. Such an outcome is inconsistent with overall corporate
        goals. Company wide, the projected ROI is:
        ($60,000,000-$52,800,000)÷$40,000,000 = 18%. Thus the
        company would probably want the manager of Division 2
        to make the investment and would prefer that the
        manager of Division 1 reject the investment.

    d. If the division managers were evaluated on the basis of
        residual income, they would analyze how a new
        investment would affect the projected overall RI level
        in their divisions. The projected overall changes
        could be found as follows:

	Pleasure	Commercial
Projected ROI on new project	14%	18%
Required target return	17%	17%
Residual return	−3%	1%

        Thus, according to the projections, the project under
        evaluation by the manager of Pleasure Division would
        cause his/her overall residual income to decline by an
        amount equal to 3% of the cost of the investment. On
        the other hand, the project under consideration by the
        manager of Commercial Division would generate an
        overall increase in RI equal to 1% of the cost of the
        new investment.

53. a.   Manufacturing cycle
          efficiency   = Processing time ÷ Total time
                       = 80,000 ÷ 120,000
                       = <u>67</u>% (rounded)

     b.   Process productivity = Total units ÷ Processing time
                               = 200,000 ÷ 80,000
                               = <u>2.5</u>

     c.   Process quality yield = Good units ÷ Total units
                                = 130,000 ÷ 200,000
                                = <u>65</u>%

     d.   2.5 X .67 X .65 = <u>1.09</u> units per hour (rounded)

     e.   The existence of a bottleneck would most likely be
          reflected in b., process productivity.

     f.   Defective units would be reflected in the ratio of Good
          units to Total units, Process quality yield - item c..

Cases

55. a. For 1997, NOC generated an ROI of 25%, as calculated below:

ROI = Operating income ÷ Total assets
   = $2,000,000 ÷ $8,000,000
   = <u>25%</u>

For 1994, assuming NOC paid $3.2 million for RLI, it would have generated an ROI of less than 20.%, as calculated below:

ROI = Operating income ÷ Total assets
   = $600,000 ÷ $3,200,000
   = <u>18.75%</u>

Mr. Grieco would have expected that his bonus would be lost or reduced if he had invested in RLI. The investment would have caused the ROI of NOC to drop as indicated below:

Combined ROI = Operating income ÷ Total assets
           = $2,600,000 ÷ $11,200,000
           = <u>23.21%</u>

b. To determine the effect of the acquisition, one only needs to determine the amount of residual income generated by RLI:

Operating income	$600,000
Target return ($3,200,000 X .15)	480,000
Residual income generated by RLI	<u>$120,000</u>

Because the Residual Income is positive, the acquisition of RLI would have had a positive effect on Mr. Grieco's bonus expectations.

c. No, it is the duty of top management to provide incentives to Mr. Grieco such that if it is in the best interest of Allston Automotive to invest, it is also in the best interest of Mr. Grieco to invest. Such is not the case with the ROI performance measure.

d. No, the present system heavily biases against new investment in anything. The best way managers can protect their current ROI levels is to not invest.

Ethics and Quality Discussion
57.   a.   The continual search for ways to speed up operations
            exposes weaknesses and shortcomings in business and
            production processes. Speed is the key to increasing
            throughput and getting greater efficiency from existing
            investment. Searching for ways to increase speed is
            both an approach to cost and volume control and a way
            to identify non-value-adding activities that can be
            eliminated.

      b.   Some measures that might be used to measure progress in
            speeding-up processes are:
            ■   throughput
            ■   cycle time or lead time
            ■   average length of time from receipt of customer
                 order to shipment of product
            ■   average setup time
            ■   average length of development time for new
                 products
            ■   average time spent by product in distribution
                 channel
            ■   product volume per period per employee

59.   a.   Students will have a variety of answers to this part.
            Most will probably disagree. Note that J. P. Morgan,
            in the early 1900s, stated that the differential should
            be no more than twenty times. Herman Miller, the CEO
            at Herman Miller Inc., has his pay limited to twenty
            times the average paycheck of the factory employees.
            And the CEO at Ben & Jerry's Homemade can only receive
            seven times the average for company workers. In 1991,
            Newsweek indicated that CEOs' salaries in the U.S. are
            about 100 times the average factory worker's. In
            Japan, this ratio is about seven-to-ten times.

b. Students will have a variety of answers to this part. Most will probably say that some relationship should exist. In June 1992, the SEC proposed a variety of disclosures about executive pay that address this issue. Some of the major provisions were:

- Specific disclosure of CEO compensation regardless of the amount or nature of such compensation.

- Setting the disclosure threshold for executives other than the CEO at $100,000 (rather than the current $60,000) and basing that amount on total compensation.

- Preparation of a Summary Table of the aggregate compensation of all named executives for the last three fiscal years. The salary figure would reflect the fixed amount accorded to the executive simply based on organizational position. The bonus amount would include all cash and noncash payments that are given in recognition of performance achievements. The individual disclosures for salary and bonus amounts are designed to indicate to readers the amount of annual pay that is performance-sensitive. The "Other Compensation" column would account for items such as retirement plan accruals, cash value of material perquisites, and premiums by the corporation for deferred compensation arrangements.

  The market value of any restricted stock awards would be disclosed in the year of the grant; any dividends accrued on such stock would also need to be reported each year. The total amount paid out (in cash and/or stock) under any long-term incentive plan would need to be communicated in financial, rather than simply narrative, terms. Values for SARs (stock appreciation rights), using assumed rates of stock price appreciation, would need to be presented. Any compensation not reported under one of the prior columns should be disclosed in the final "Other" column. For example, the amount of any severance - including a golden parachute - paid to a named executive during the three year covered period must be reported (even if the executive is no longer in the employ of the corporation).

- Preparation of a "Compensation Committee (or Board of Directors) Report" that specifically details the underlying rationale for the amounts of compensation paid to each of the named executives and how that amount of compensation relates to company performance. "Generalized discussions" and "boilerplate disclosures" would be considered unacceptable.

Chapter 16
Measuring and Rewarding Performance

- Preparation of a graph comparing cumulative shareholder returns for at least five years with the overall stock market performance, the S&P 500 Stock Index, and either a recognized industry index or a registrant-constructed peer group index.

- If necessary, preparation of a report that indicates the reasoning behind any lowering (or "repricing") of the exercise price that executives would have to pay for previously-granted options or SARs. Such reductions often occur after the stock price has fallen from previous levels. This report would require details on any repricing that took place in the prior ten years.

All of these proposals address the issue of what an executive is being paid for -- longevity in office, good board of director relationships, or corporate performance. It seems the SEC is of the opinion that, if other individuals employed by an organization must perform in a specified manner in conformity with their abilities to work toward the accomplishment of the corporation's critical success factors, shouldn't executives be held to the same standard?

c. Students will have a variety of answers to this part. A good example to discuss is "The salary package of Citicorp Chairman John Reed rose slightly to $1.22 million [in 1991], when the company laid off 9,000 workers and suffered a $457 million loss," (Wall Street Journal, March 4, 1992; p. E-3). Ask the students to discuss this issue from these standpoints: an employee who was laid off, John Reed, a Citicorp stockholder, and a Citicorp creditor.

d.   An executive would want a golden parachute to help compensate him/her for the loss of a position. The reasonableness to the stockholders would probably depend on the financial health of the company prior to the takeover. If the company had been profitable and the executive paid in a "reasonable" manner, the parachute could be viewed as a type of retirement bonus rewarding good performance - a case in which the stockholders would probably approve of the payment. On the other hand, if the takeover took place because the company was losing money and managerial performance had been viewed as poor, a golden parachute will probably incense the stockholders - especially if the executive had already been compensated within reason or, even more so, beyond reason.

Suggested reading on this topic:

Byrne, John, et al. "Executive Pay." Business Week (March 30, 1992), pp. 52-57.

Mitchell, Jacqueline. "Herman Miller Links Worker-CEO Pay." Wall Street Journal (May 7, 1992), pp. B1, B8.

Tully, Shawn. "What CEOs Really Make." FORTUNE (June 15, 1992), pp. 94-99.

Chapter 16
Measuring and Rewarding Performance

61. a.   Yes, performance measures should capture only **real** performance. If managers can manipulate the performance measures, they can achieve their target levels of compensation without achieving the overall goals of the organization.

b.   If manipulation is ethically inappropriate, then a consideration of the amount of a manipulation can neither make the manipulation more nor less ethical. It is always unethical. However, there are many indications in America that suggest people do think the amount matters. Such evidence is found in the survey that is cited and in the behavior of American taxpayers self-reporting their income tax liabilities.

c.   In the view of the authors, from an ethical perspective, manipulation of performance measures is never justifiable.

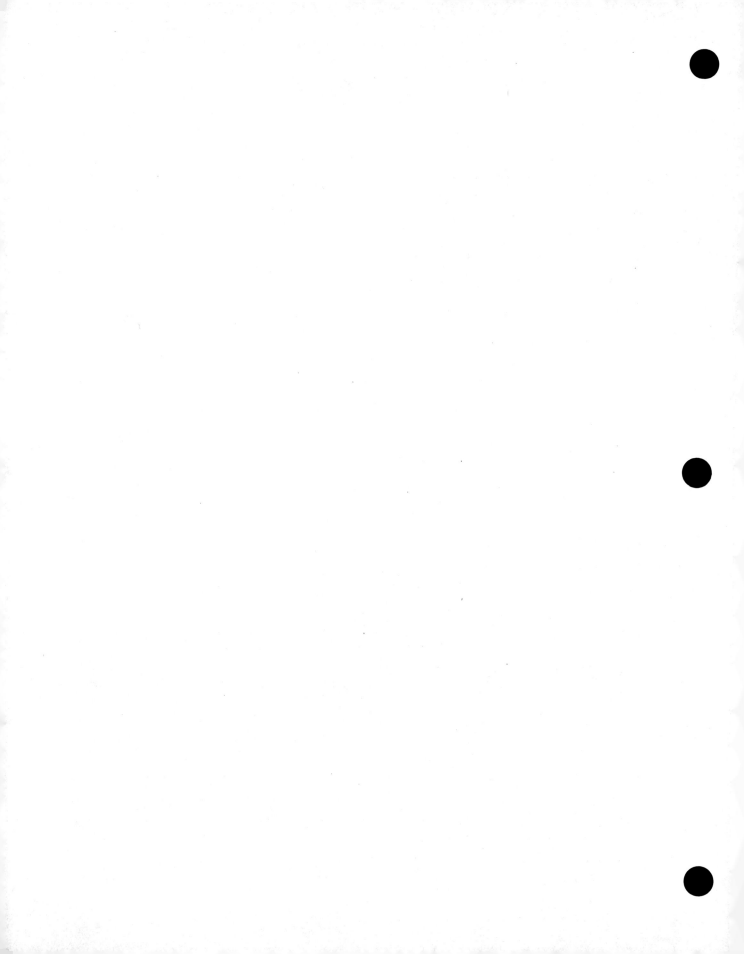